ON FRIENDS
&
LOVE

A Reader

Edward Carpenter

AZAFRAN BOOKS

Published by Azafran Books –
http://www.azafranbooks.com/

ISBN-13: 978-0-9956557-9-9 (paperback)
First published in this edition: January 2017
Edited, formatted & design concept by Solomon James
Cover design & design concept by B.S.

CONTENTS

INTRODUCTION

Edward Carpenter: Radical Mystic & Lover

Edward Carpenter was a radical before his times, and many of his ideas and behavior anticipated later trends. He was an advocate of free love, recycling, nudism, women's suffrage, and prison reform. His work and vision anticipated the sexual revolution of the 1960s. He was a friend to Rabindranath Tagore, Walt Whitman, Annie Besant, Mahatma Gandhi, amongst many others of his day. He was also an influence on both D. H. Lawrence and Sri Aurobindo. Edward Carpenter was quite simply an inspiration for his time.

Edward Carpenter was born on 29th August 1844 in Hove, a town on the south coast of England; and he died on 28th June 1929. Although born into an upper-middle class family, and educated at Trinity Hall, Cambridge, he later rejected his privileged upbringing and adopted outlooks and ways of life that whilst considered unusual for his time would in fact later become the benchmarks of an alternative culture. Carpenter was a person 'of the people' and spent the majority of his adult life around working class people, teaching in an adult education movement, and sympathizing with the 'everyman.'

In the early 1880s Carpenter, who came into inheritance money, purchased a country property at Millthorpe, outside of Sheffield, where he advocated growing one's own food and living the 'simple life' long before it became fashionable with the bohemian intelligentsia. Then in the early 1890s Carpenter spent time visiting and sitting with a holy man in what is now Sri Lanka, long before Eastern mysticism became fashionable in the twentieth century. At heart, and in his soul, Carpenter was a mystic – quiet, humble, caring, and prescient in his vision and thinking. And, more importantly, he was a mystic with his feet firmly on the ground. As he relates in one of his articles, written in 1910: 'The spiritual must have the material to give it body; the material has no meaning without the spiritual.'

As a man 'of the people,' Carpenter was also radical in his social activism; notably in joining the Social Democratic Federation (SDF), a socialist organization, and working on various projects aimed at alleviating the suffering of poor people, and the poor living conditions of industrial workers.

Most notably today Carpenter is remembered as being a campaigner for gay rights. He also campaigned for the emancipation of women and for mutuality in loving. In other words, he championed new forms of relations and intimacy; focusing on loving bonds as well as open sexuality. He was as radical in loving as he was in social causes. Other social causes that Carpenter involved himself with included capitalism and economic reforms. Carpenter was one of the early voices to openly challenge capitalism as a dominant social system.

Edward Carpenter did not resemble the cliché radical. He was often seen wearing his sandals, dressing smart yet casual, and was empathic in manner. His socialist concerns covered environmental as well as animal and human rights. His approach was literally a breath of fresh air against the conservative nature of Victorian bourgeois respectability. He showed no fear or guilt over the subject of sexuality – contrary to much of Victorian society – and often liked to bathe nude, as some of his visitors soon found out!

Carpenter was also comfortable looking backward as he was looking forward. His knowledge and interest in ancient pagan traditions and cultures, as well as a sound knowledge of the classics, was strengthened by his own personal interest in Eastern mysticism. From these insights Carpenter critiqued and criticized what he felt were the ills of western civilization.

****

This Edward Carpenter Reader *On Friendship & Love* contains the texts 'Love's Coming-Of-Age,' 'Iolaus – An Anthology of Friendship,' and Sex = Love, and its Place in a Free Society.' These principal works show his attitude and understanding toward sexual and loving relations. Carpenter's life was marked by close, and often long, relations with working-class men. Some of these relations were intimate, but certainly not all of them. His meeting with George Merrill, an uneducated working-class man from Sheffield, started a thirty-year relationship that only ended in Merrill's death in 1928. Carpenter died the following year.

As will be seen from the texts in this collection, Carpenter was not solely concerned with relations of a sexual nature. On the contrary, he was principally drawn to relations of bonding: comradeship, friendship, trust, and mutual understanding. Carpenter, through his writings and selected extracts, refers to various ancient warriors, artists, and visionaries, which suggest and show a masculine love, and a form of recognized intimacy. For Carpenter, sexual intimacy is the allegory of love in the physical world. In 'Love's Coming-Of-Age' he says, 'The aim of Love is non-differentiation--absolute union of being; but absolute union can only be found at the centre of existence - Similarly the aim of sex is union and non-differentiation.' Carpenter saw the prime object of sex as being union, rather than pleasure or desire. And this physical union was for him the allegory and expression of the real Union, and that any other pleasures derived from this union were but secondary. Carpenter goes on to say that, 'the very highest expression of Sex is in the sentiment of Love.'

Carpenter expressed in his work 'Love's Coming-Of-Age' that men's passions were stronger than that of women, but that men were lesser able to understand or master such passions. The advantage of women, he noted, was that 'her powers are more co-ordinated, are in harmony with each other, where his are disjointed or in conflict.'

'Iolaus – An Anthology of Friendship' is Edward Carpenter's study of (primarily male) friendship, which is another way of saying gay intimacy. He shows that in many earlier cultures, particularly classical antiquity, but also up to and including Elizabethan times, intense, even romantic emotional relationships between men were accepted by society. These relationships between men were often seen in the context of cultures that accepted strong male bonds. Many of these bonds were sincere and genuine life-long same-sex unions. Well-known and respected figures in the world of literature, the arts, and political leaders turn up in this anthology:--the biblical David, Alexander the Great, Michelangelo, Shakespeare, Wagner and 'Mad' King Ludwig, and many others.

The final text in this collection – 'Sex = Love, and its Place in a Free Society' – was originally published as a four penny pamphlet as part of Carpenter's drive to offer educational material. It is a short and succinct text that outlines Carpenter's views on sex as representing an 'affectional union' between consenting adults. As are all of his writings, it is a measured and heart-felt speech to a society and culture that was only just beginning to open up to new and alternative thinking and lifestyles.

Edward Carpenter may not yet be the most well-known of creative and visionary thinkers, yet his legacy lives on. It lives on in the attitudes, understanding, and visions that many of our cultures now embrace. Rather than being remembered by name, Carpenter preferred to be remembered in spirit – as his tombstone epitaph shows:

"Do not think too much of the dead husk of your friend, or mourn too much over it, but send your thoughts out towards the real soul or self which has escaped-to reach it. For so, surely you will cast a light of gladness upon his onward journey, and contribute your part towards the building of that kingdom of love which links our earth to heaven."

The enduring spirit of Edward Carpenter lives on in this new edited Reader given to us by Azafran Books. My hope is that you, the reader, will read on with an open, affectionate heart. Edward Carpenter would have asked of no more from the reader than this.

Solomon James
January 2017

LOVE'S COMING-OF-AGE

***

A SERIES OF PAPERS

ON

THE RELATIONS OF THE SEXES

CONTENTS

THE SEX-PASSION

THE subject of Sex is difficult to deal with. There is no doubt a natural reticence connected with it. There is also a great deal of prudery. The passion occupies, without being spoken of, a large part of human thought; and words on the subject being so few and inadequate, everything that is said is liable to be misunderstood. Violent inferences are made and equivocations surmised, from the simplest remarks; qualified admissions of liberty are interpreted into recommendations of unbridled license; and generally the perspective of literary expression is turned upside down.

There is in fact a vast deal of fetishism in the current treatment of the question. Nor can one altogether be surprised at this when one sees how important Sex is in the scheme of things, and how deeply it has been associated since the earliest times not only with man's personal impulses but even with his religious sentiments and ceremonials.

Next to hunger it is doubtless the most primitive and imperative of our needs. But in modern civilized life Sex enters probably even more into *consciousness* than hunger. For the hunger-needs of the human race are in the later societies fairly well satisfied, but the sex-desires are strongly restrained, both by law and custom, from satisfaction--and so assert themselves all the more in thought.

To find the place of these desires, their utterance, their control, their personal import, their social import, is a tremendous problem to every youth and girl, man and woman.

There are a few of both sexes, doubtless, who hardly feel the passion-who have never been "in love," and who experience no strong sexual appetite--but these are rare. Practically the passion is a matter of universal experience; and speaking broadly and generally we may say it is a matter on which it is quite desirable that every adult at some time or other should have actual experience. There may be exceptions; but, as said, the instinct lies so deep and is so universal, that for the understanding of life--of one's own life, of that of others, and of human nature in general--as well as for the proper development of one's own capacities, such experience is as a rule needed.

And here in passing I would say that in the social life of the future this need will surely be recognized, and that (while there will be no stigma attaching to voluntary celibacy) the state of enforced celibacy in which vast numbers of women live to-day will be looked upon as a national wrong, almost as grievous as that of prostitution--of which latter evil indeed it is in some degree the counterpart or necessary accompaniment.

Of course Nature (personifying under this term the more unconscious, even though human, instincts and forces) takes pretty good care in her own way that sex shall not be neglected. She has her own purposes to work out, which in a sense have nothing to do with the individual-her racial purposes. But she acts in the rough, with tremendous sweep and power, and with little adjustment to or consideration for the later developed and more conscious and intelligent ideals of humanity. The youth, deeply infected with the sex-passion, suddenly finds himself in the presence of Titanic forces--the Titanic but sub-conscious forces of his own nature. "In love" he feels a superhuman impulse--and naturally so, for he identifies himself with cosmic energies and entities, powers that are preparing the future of the race, and whose operations extend over vast regions of space and millennial lapses of time. He sees into the abysmal deeps of his own being, and trembles with a kind of awe at the disclosure. And what he feels concerning himself he feels similarly concerning the one who has inspired his passion. The glances of the two lovers penetrate far beyond the surface, ages down into each other, waking a myriad antenatal dreams.

For the moment he lets himself go, rejoicing in the sense of limitless power beneath him--borne onwards like a man down rapids, too intoxicated with the glory of motion to think of whither he is going; then the next moment he discovers that he is being hurried into impossible situations--situations which his own moral conscience, as well as the moral conscience of Society, embodied in law and custom, will not admit. He finds perhaps that the satisfaction of his imperious impulse is, to all appearances, inconsistent with the welfare of her he loves. His own passion arises before him as a kind of rude giant which he or the race to which he belongs may, Frankenstein-like, have created ages back, but which he now has to dominate or be dominated by; and there declares itself in him the fiercest conflict--that between his far-back Titanic instinctive and sub-conscious nature, and his later developed, more especially human and moral self.

While the glory of Sex pervades and suffuses all Nature; while the flowers are rayed and starred out towards the sun in the very ecstasy of generation; while the nostrils of the animals dilate, and their forms become instinct, under the passion, with a proud and fiery beauty; while even the human lover is transformed, and in the great splendors of the mountains and the sky perceives something to which had not the key before--yet it is curious that just here, in Man, we find the magic wand of Nature suddenly broken, and doubt and conflict and division, entering in, where a kind of unconscious harmony had erst prevailed.

And the reason of this is not far to seek. For in comparing, as we did a page or two back, the sex-needs and the hunger-needs of the human race we left out of account one great difference, namely, that while food (the object of hunger) has no moral rights of its own, and can be appropriated without misgiving on that score, the object of sex is a person, and cannot be used for private advantage without the most dire infringement of the law of equality. The moment Man rises into any sort of consciousness of the equal rights of others with himself his love-needs open up this terrible problem. His needs are no less--perhaps they are greater--than they were before, but they are stricken with a deadly wound at the thought that there is something even greater than them.

Heine I think says somewhere that the man who loves unsuccessfully knows himself to be a god. It is not perhaps till the great current of sexual love is checked and brought into conflict with the other parts of his being that the whole nature of the man, sexual and moral, under the tremendous stress rises into consciousness and reveals in fire its god-like quality. This is the work of the artificer who makes immortal souls-who out of the natural love evolves even a more perfect love. "In tutti gli amanti," says Giordano Bruno, "è questo fabro vulcano" ("in all lovers is this Olympian blacksmith present").

It is the subject of this conflict, or at least differentiation, between the sexual and the more purely moral and social instincts in man which interests us here. It is clear, I think, that if sex is to be treated rationally, that is, neither superstitiously on the one hand nor licentiously on the other, we must be willing to admit that both the satisfaction of the passion and the non-satisfaction of it are desirable and beautiful. They both have their results, and man has to reap the fruits which belong to both experiences. May we not say that there is probably some sort of Transmutation of essences continually effected and effectible in the human frame? Lust and Love--the *Aphrodite Pandemos* and the *Aphrodite Ouranios*--are subtly interchangeable. Perhaps the corporeal amatory instinct and the ethereal human yearning for personal union are really and in essence one thing with diverse forms of manifestation. However that may be, it is pretty evident that there is some deep relationship between them. It is a matter of common experience that the unrestrained outlet of merely physical desire leaves the nature drained of its higher love-forces; while on the other hand if the physical satisfaction be denied, the body becomes surcharged with waves of emotion--sometimes to an unhealthy and dangerous degree. Yet at times this emotional love may, by reason of its expression being checked or restricted, transform itself into the all-penetrating subtle influence of spiritual love.

Marcus Aurelius quotes a saying of Heraclitus to the effect that the death of earth is to become water (liquefaction), and the death of water is to become air (evaporation), and the death of air is to become fire (combustion). So in the human body are there sensual, emotional, spiritual, and other elements of which it may be said that their death on one plane means their transformation and new birth on other planes.

It will readily be seen that I am not arguing that the lower or more physical manifestations of love should be killed out in order to force the growth of the more spiritual and enduring forms--because Nature in her slow evolutions does not generally countenance such high and mighty methods; but am merely trying to indicate that there are grounds for believing in the transmutability of the various forms of the passion, and grounds for thinking that the sacrifice of a lower phase may sometimes be the only condition on which a higher and more durable phase can be attained; and that therefore Restraint (which is absolutely necessary at times) *has* its compensation.

Any one who has once realized how glorious a thing Love is in its essence, and how indestructible, will hardly need to call anything that leads to it a sacrifice; and he is indeed a master of life who, accepting the grosser desires as they come to his body, and not refusing them, knows how to transform them at will into the most rare and fragrant flowers of human emotion.

Until these subjects are openly put before children and young people with some degree of intelligent and sympathetic handling, it can scarcely be expected that anything but the utmost confusion, in mind and in morals, should reign in matters of Sex. That we should leave our children to pick up their information about the most sacred, the most profound and vital, of all human functions, from the mere gutter, and learn to know it first from the lips of ignorance and vice, seems almost incredible, and certainly indicates the deeply-rooted unbelief and uncleanness of our own thoughts. Yet a child at the age of puberty, with the unfolding of its emotional and sexual nature, is eminently capable of the most sensitive, affectional, and serene appreciation of what Sex means (generally more so, as things are to-day, than its worldling parent or guardian); and can absorb the teaching, if sympathetically given, without any shock or disturbance to its sense of shame--that sense which is so natural and valuable a safeguard of early youth. To teach the child first, quite openly, its physical relation to its own mother, its long indwelling in her body, and the deep and sacred bond of tenderness between mother and child in consequence; then, after a time, to explain the relation of fatherhood, and how the love of the parents for each other was the cause of its own (the child's) existence: these things are easy and natural--at least they are so to the young mind--and excite in it no surprise, or sense of unfitness, but only gratitude and a kind of tender wonderment. Then, later on, as the special sexual needs and desires develop, to instruct the girl or boy in the further details of the matter, and the care and right conduct of her or his own sexual nature; on the meaning and the dangers of solitary indulgence--if this habit has been contracted; on the need of self-control and the presence of affection in all relations with others, and (without undue asceticism) on the possibility of deflecting physical desire to some degree into affectional and emotional channels, and the great gain so resulting; all these are things which an ordinary youth of either sex will easily understand and appreciate, and which may be of priceless value, saving such an one from years of struggle in foul morasses, and waste of precious life-strength. Finally, with the maturity of the moral nature, the supremacy of the pure human relation should be taught--not the extinguishment of desire, but the attainment of the real kernel of it, its dedication to the well-being of another--the evolution of the *human* element in love, balancing the natural--till at last the snatching of an unglad pleasure, regardless of the other from whom it is snatched, or the surrender of one's body to another, for any reason except that of love, become things impossible.

Between lovers then a kind of hardy temperance is much to be recommended--for all reasons, but especially because it lifts their satisfaction and delight in each other out of the region of ephemeralities (which too soon turn to dull indifference and satiety) into the region of more lasting things--one step nearer at any rate to the Eternal Kingdom. How intoxicating indeed, how penetrating--like a most precious wine--is that love which is the sexual transformed by the magic of the will into the emotional and spiritual! And what a loss on the merest grounds of prudence and the economy of pleasure is its unbridled waste along physical channels! So nothing is so much to be dreaded between lovers as just this--the vulgarisation of love --and this is the rock upon which marriage so often splits.

There is a kind of illusion about physical desire similar to that which a child suffers from when, seeing a beautiful flower, it instantly snatches the .same, and destroys in a few moments the form and fragrance which attracted it. He only gets the full glory who holds himself back a little, and truly possesses who is willing if need be not to possess.

On the other hand it must not be pretended that the physical passions are by their nature unclean, or otherwise than admirable and desirable in their place. Any attempt to absolutely disown or despite them, carried out over long periods either by individuals or bodies of people, only ends in the *thinning out* of the human nature--by the very consequent stinting of the supply of its growth-material, and is liable to stultify itself in time by leading to reactionary excesses. It must never be forgotten that the physical basis throughout life is of the first importance, and supplies the nutrition and food-stuff without which the higher powers cannot exist or at least manifest themselves. Intimacies founded on intellectual and moral affinities alone are seldom very deep and lasting; if the physical basis in any form is quite absent, the acquaintanceship is liable to die away again like an ill-rooted plant. In many cases (especially of women) the nature is never really understood or disclosed till the sex feeling is touched--however lightly. Besides it must be remembered that in order for a perfect intimacy between two people their bodies must by the nature of the case be free to each other. The bodily intimacy or endearment may not be the object for which they come together; but if it is denied, its denial will bar any real sense of repose and affiance, and make the relation restless, vague, tentative and unsatisfied.

In these lights it will be seen that what we call asceticism and what we call libertinism are two sides practically of the same shield. So long as the tendency towards mere pleasure-indulgence is strong and uncontrolled, so long will the instinct towards asceticism assert itself--and rightly, else we might speedily find ourselves in headlong Phaethonian career. Asceticism is in its place (as the word would indicate) as an *exercise*; but let it not be looked upon as an end in itself, for that is a mistake of the same kind as going to the opposite extreme. Certainly if the welfare and happiness of the beloved one were always really the main purpose in our minds we should have plenty of occasion for self-control, and an artificial asceticism would not be needed. We look for a time doubtless when the hostility between these two parts of man's unperfected nature will be merged in the perfect love; but at present and until this happens their conflict is certainly one of the most pregnant things in all our experience; and must not by any means be blinked or evaded, but boldly faced. It is in itself almost a sexual act. The mortal nature through it is, so to speak, torn asunder; and through the rent so made in his mortality does it sometimes happen that a new and immortal man is born.

Sex-pleasures afford a kind of type of all pleasure. The dissatisfaction which at times follows on them is the same as follows on all pleasure which is sought, and which does not come unsought. The dissatisfaction is not in the nature of pleasure itself but in the nature of *seeking*. In going off in pursuit of things external, the "I" (since it really has everything and needs nothing) deceives itself, goes out from its true home, tears itself asunder, and admits a gap or rent in its own being. This, it must be supposed, is what is meant by sin--the separation or sundering of one's being-and all the pain that goes therewith. It all consists in seeking those external things and pleasures; not (a thousand times be it said) in the external things or pleasures themselves. They are all fair and gracious enough; their place is to stand round the throne and offer their homage-rank behind rank in their multitudes-if so be we will accept it. But for us to go out of ourselves to run after *them*, to allow ourselves to be divided and rent in twain by their attraction, that is an inversion of the order of heaven.

To this desertion of one's true self sex tempts most strongly, and stands as the type of Maya and the world-illusion; yet the beauty of the loved one and the delight of corporeal union all turn to dust and ashes if bought at the price of disunion and disloyalty in the higher spheres--disloyalty even to the person whose mortal love is sought. The higher and more durable part of man, whirled along in the rapids and whirlpools of desire, experiences tortures the moment it comes to recognize that It is something other than physical. Then comes the struggle to regain its lost Paradise, and the frightful effort of co-ordination between the two natures, by which the centre of consciousness is gradually transferred from the fugitive to the more permanent part, and the mortal and changeable is assigned its due place in the outer chambers and forecourts of the temple.

Pleasure should come as the natural (and indeed inevitable) accompaniment of life, believed in with a kind of free faith, but never sought as the object of life. It is in the inversion of this order that the uncleanness of the senses arises. Sex to-day throughout the domains of civilization is thoroughly unclean. Everywhere it is slimed over with the thought of pleasure. Not for joy, not for mere delight in and excess of life, not for pride in the generation of children, not for a symbol and expression of 'deepest soul-union,' does it exist-but for our own gratification. Hence we disown it in our thoughts, and cover it up with false shame and unbelief-knowing well that to seek a social act for a private end is a falsehood. The body itself is kept religiously covered, smothered away from the rush of the great purifying life of Nature, infected with dirt and disease, and a subject for prurient thought and exaggerated lust such as in its naked state it would never provoke. The skin becomes sickly and corrupt, and of a dead leaden white hue, which strangely enough is supposed to be more beautiful than the rich rose-brown, delicately shaded into lighter tints in the less exposed parts, which it would wear if tanned by daily welcome of sun and wind. Sexual embraces themselves seldom receive the benison of Dame Nature, in whose presence alone, under the burning sun or the high canopy of the stars and surrounded by the fragrant atmosphere, their meaning can be fully understood: but take place in stuffy dens of dirty upholstery and are associated with all unbeautiful things.

Even literature, which might have been expected to preserve some decent expression on this topic, reflects all too clearly by its silence or by its pruriency the prevailing spirit of unbelief; and in order to find any sane faithful strong and calm words on the subject, one has to wade right back through the marshes and bogs of civilized scribbledom, and toil eastward across its and wastes to the very dawn-hymns of the Aryan races.

In one of the Upanishads of the Vedic sacred books (the Brihadaranyaka Upanishad) there is a fine passage in which instruction is given to the man who desires a noble son as to the prayers which he shall offer to the gods on the occasion of congress with his wife. In primitive simple and serene language it directs him how, at such times, he should pray to the various forms of deity who preside over the operations of Nature: to Vishnu to prepare the womb of the future mother, to Prajápati to watch over the influx of the semen, and to the other gods to nourish the fœtus, etc. Nothing could be (I am judging from the only translation I have met with, a Latin one) more composed, serene, simple, and religious in feeling, and well might it be if such instructions were preserved and followed, even to-day; yet such is the pass we have come to that actually Max Müller in his translations of the Sacred Books of the East appears to have been unable to persuade himself to render these and a few other quite similar passages into English, but gives them in the original Sanskrit! One might have thought that as Professor in the University of Oxford, presumably *sans peur et sans reproche*, and professedly engaged in making a translation of these books for students, it was his duty and it might have been his delight to make intelligible just such passages as these, which give the pure and pious sentiment of the early world in so perfect a form; unless indeed he thought the sentiment impure and impious-in which case we have indeed a measure of the degradation of the public opinion which must have swayed his mind.

As to the only German translation of the Upanishad which I can find, it baulks at the same passages in the same feeble way--repeating *nicht wiederzugeben, nicht wiederzugeben*, over and over again, till at last one can but conclude that the translator is right, and that the simplicity and sacredness of the feeling is in this our time indeed "not to be reproduced."

Our public opinion, our literature, our customs, our laws, are saturated with the notion of the uncleanness of Sex, and are so making the conditions of its cleanness more and more difficult. Our children, as said, have to pick up their intelligence on the subject in the gutter. Little boys bathing on the outskirts of our towns are hunted down by idiotic policemen, apparently infuriated by the sight of the naked body, even of childhood. Lately in one of our northern towns, the boys and men bathing in a public pool set apart by the corporation for the purpose, were-though forced to wear some kind of covering--kept till nine o'clock at night before they were allowed to go into the water--lest in the full daylight Mrs. Grundy should behold any portion of their bodies! and as for women and girls their disabilities in the matter are most serious.

Till this dirty and dismal sentiment with regard to the human body is removed there can be little hope of anything like a free and gracious public life. With the regeneration of our social ideas the whole conception of Sex as a thing covert and to be ashamed of, marketable and unclean, will have to be regenerated. That inestimable freedom and pride which is the basis of all true manhood and womanhood will have to enter into this most intimate relation to preserve it frank and pure--pure from the damnable commercialism which buys and sells all human things, and from the religious hypocrisy which covers and conceals; and a healthy delight in and cultivation of the body and all its natural functions, and a determination to keep them pure and beautiful, open and sane and free, will have to become a recognized part of national life.

Possibly, and indeed probably, as the sentiment of common life and common interest grows, and the capacity for true companionship increases with the decrease of self-regarding anxiety, the importance of the mere sex-act will dwindle till it comes to be regarded as only one very specialized factor in the full total of human love. There is no doubt that with the full realization of affectional union the need of actual bodily congress loses some of its urgency; and it is not difficult to see in our present-day social life that the want of the former is (according to the law of transmutation) one marked cause of the violence and extravagance of the lower passions. But however things may change with the further evolution of man, there is no doubt that first of all the sex-relation must be divested of the sentiment of uncleanness which surrounds it, and rehabilitated again with a sense almost of religious consecration; and this means, as I have said, a free people, proud in the mastery and the divinity of their own lives, and in the beauty and openness of their own bodies.

Sex is the allegory of Love in the physical world. It is from this fad that it derives its immense power. The aim of Love is non-differentiation--absolute union of being; but absolute union can only be found at the centre of existence. Therefore whoever has truly found another has found not only that other, and with that other himself, but has found also a third--who dwells at the centre and holds the plastic material of the universe in the palm of his hand, and is a creator of sensible forms.

Similarly the aim of sex is union and non-differentiation--but on the physical plane,--and in the moment when this union is accomplished creation takes place, and the generation (in the plastic material of the sex-elements) of sensible forms.

In the animal and lower human world--and wherever the creature is incapable of realizing the perfect love (which is indeed able to transform it into a god)--Nature in the purely physical instincts does the next best thing, that is, she effects a corporeal union and so generates another creature who by the very process of his generation shall be one step nearer to the universal soul and the realization of the desired end. Nevertheless the moment the other love and all that goes with it is realized the natural sexual love has to fall into a secondary place--the lover must stand on his feet and not on his head--or else the most dire confusions ensue, and torments æonian.

Taking all together I think it may fairly be said that the prime object of Sex is union, the physical union as the allegory and expression of the real union, and that generation is a secondary object or result of this union. If we go to the lowest material expressions of Sex--as among the protozoic cells--we find that they, the cells, unite together, two into one; and that, as a result of the nutrition that ensues, this joint cell after a time (but not always) breaks up by fission into a number of progeny cells; or if on the other hand we go to the very highest expression of Sex, in the sentiment of Love, we find the latter takes the form chiefly and before all else of a desire for union, and only in lesser degree of a desire for race-propagation.

I mention this because it probably makes a good deal of difference in our estimate of Sex whether the one function or the other is considered primary. There is perhaps a slight tendency among medical and other authorities to overlook the question of the important physical actions and reactions, and even corporeal modifications, which may ensue upon sexual intercourse between two people, and to fix their attention too exclusively upon their childbearing function; but in truth it is probable, I think, from various considerations, that the spermatozoa pass through the tissues and affect the general body of the female, as well as that the male absorbs minutest cells *from* the female; and that generally, even without the actual Sex-act, there is an interchange of vital and ethereal elements--so that it might be said there is a kind of generation taking place *within* each of the persons concerned, through their mutual influence on each other, as well as that more specialized generation which consists in the propagation of the race.

At the last and taking it as a whole one has the same difficulty in dealing with the subject of Love which meets one at every turn in modern life-the monstrous separation of one part of our nature from another-the way in which, no doubt in the necessary course of evolution, we have cut ourselves in twain as it were, and assigned "right" and "wrong," heaven and hell, spiritual and material, and other violent distinctions, to the separate portions. We have eaten of the Tree of Knowledge of good and evil with a vengeance! The Lord has indeed driven us out of Paradise into the domain of that "fabro vulcano" who with tremendous hammer-strokes must *hammer the knowledge of good and evil out of us again.* I feel that I owe an apology to the beautiful god for daring even for a moment to think of dissecting him soul from body, and for speaking as if these artificial distinctions were in any wise eternal. Will the man or woman, or race of men and women, never come, to whom love in its various manifestations shall be from the beginning a perfect whole, pure and natural, free and standing sanely on its feet?

MAN

THE UNGROWN

MAN, the ordinary human male, is a curious animal. While mastering the world with his pluck, skill, enterprise, he is in matters of Love for the most part a child. The passion plays havoc with him; nor does he ride the Lion, as Ariadne is fabled to have done.

In this he differs from the other sex; and the difference can be seen in earliest years. When the boy is on his rocking horse, the girl is caressing her doll. When the adolescent youth, burning to master a real quadruped, is still somewhat contemptuous of Love's power, "sweet seventeen" has already lost and regained her heart several times, and is accomplished in all the finesse of feeling.

To the grown man love remains little more than a plaything. Affairs, politics, fighting, moneymaking, creative art, constructive industry, are his serious business; the affections are his relaxation; passion is the little fire with which he toys, and which every now and then flares out and burns him up. His affections, his passions, are probably as a rule stronger than woman's; but he never attains to understand them or be master of their craft. With woman all this is reversed.

A man pelts along on his hobby--his business, his career, his latest invention, or what not--forgetful that there is such a thing in the world as the human heart; then all of a sudden he 'falls in love,' tumbles headlong in the most ludicrous way, fills the air with his cries, struggles frantically like a fly in treacle: and all the time hasn't the faintest idea whether he has been inveigled into the situation, or whether he got there of his own accord, or what he wants now he is there. Suicides, broken hearts, lamentations, and certainly a whole panorama, marvelous in beauty, of lyrical poetry and art, mark the experience of love's distress in Man. Woman in the same plight neither howls nor cries, she does not commit suicide or do anything extravagant, she creates not a single poem or work of art of any account; but she simply goes her way and suffers in silence, shaping her life to the new conditions. Never for a moment does she forget that her one serious object is Love; but never for a moment does she 'give herself away' or lose her head, in the pursuit of that object.

It is perhaps in a kind of revenge for this that man for so many centuries has made woman his serf. Feeling that she really somehow mastered him on the affectional plane, he in revenge on the physical plane has made the most of his superior strength, and of his power over her; or, more probably, not thinking about it at all, he has simply allowed all along the sex-passion (so strong in him) to prompt him to this mastery.

For the sex-passion in man is undoubtedly a force--huge and fateful--which has to be reckoned with. Perhaps (speaking broadly) *all* the passions and powers, the intellect and affections and emotions and all, are really profounder and vaster in Man than in Woman-are more varied, root deeper, and have wider scope; but then the woman has this advantage, that her powers are more co-ordinated, are in harmony with each other, where his are disjointed or in conflict. A girl comes of age sooner than a boy. And the coming-of-age of Love (which harmonizes all the faculties in the human being) may take place early in the woman, while in the man it is delayed long and long, perhaps never completely effected. The problem is so much bigger, so much more complex, with him; it takes longer for its solution. Women are sometimes impatient with men on this score; but then they do not see, judging from their own little flock, what a big herd of cattle the man has to bring home.

Anyhow, the point is that Man with his great uncoordinated nature *has* during these later centuries dominated the other sex, and made himself the ruler of society. In consequence of which we naturally have a society made after his pattern--a society advanced in mechanical and intellectual invention, with huge passional and emotional elements, but all involved in whirling confusion and strife--a society ungrown, which on its material side may approve itself a great success, but on its more human and affectional side seems at times an utter failure.

This ungrown, half-baked sort of character is conspicuous in the class of men who organize the modern world--the men of the English-speaking well-to-do class. The boy of this class begins life at a public school. He does not learn much from the masters; but he knocks about among his fellows in cricket and football and athletics, and turns out with an excellent organizing capacity and a tolerably firm and reliable grip on the practical and material side of life--qualities which are of first-rate importance, and which give the English ruling classes a similar mission in the world to the Romans of the early Empire. A certain standard too (for what it is worth) of schoolboy honor and fairness is thumped into him. It is very narrow and conventional, but at its best rises as high as a conception of self-sacrifice and duty, though never to the conception of love. At the same time a strong and lavish diet and an easy life stimulate his functional energies and his animal passions to a high degree.

Here certainly is some splendid material, and if well pounded into shape, kneaded and baked, might result in a useful upper crust for society. But alas! it remains, or actually degenerates into, a most fatuous dough. The boy never learns anything after he leaves school. He gets no more thumps. He glides easily into the higher walks of the world--backed by his parents' money--into Law or Army or Church or Civil Service or Commerce. He has really no serious fights to fight, or efforts to make, sees next to nothing of actual life; has an easy time, can marry pretty well whom he chooses, or console himself with unmarried joys; and ultimately settles down into the routine and convention of his particular profession--a picture of beefy self-satisfaction. Affection and tenderness of feeling, though latent in him, have never, owing to the unfortunate conditions of his life, been developed; but their place begins to be taken by a rather dreary cynicism. Sex, always strong, still even now in its waning days, retains the first place; and the mature man, having no adequate counterpoise to it in the growth of his sympathetic nature, is fain to find his highest restraints or sanctions in the unripe code of his school-days or the otiose conventions and prejudices of the professional clique to which he belongs.

So it comes about that the men who have the sway of the world to-day are in the most important matters quite ungrown; they really have never come of age in any adequate sense. Like Ephraim they are "a cake not turned." Wherever they turn up: in Lords or Commons, Civil or Military, Law or Church or Medicine, the judge on the bench, the Bishop, the ruler of India, the exploiter of South Africa, the man who booms a company in the city, or who builds up a great commercial trust and gets a title for supporting a Government: it is much the same. Remove the distinctive insignia of their clique and office, and you find underneath--no more than a public school-boy. Perhaps, indeed, rather less; for while the school-boy mind is there, and the school-boy code of life and honor, the enthusiasm and the promise of youth are gone.

It is certainly very maddening at times to think that the Destinies of the world, the organization of society, the wonderful scope of possible statesmanship, the mighty issues of trade and industry, the loves of Women, the lives of criminals, the fate of savage nations, should be in the hands of such a set of general nincompoops; men so fatuous that it actually does not hurt them to see the streets crammed with prostitutes by night, or the parks by day with the semi-lifeless bodies of tramps; men, to whom it seems quite natural that our marriage and social institutions should lumber along over the bodies of women, as our commercial institutions grind over the bodies of the poor, and our "imperial" enterprise over the bodies of barbarian races, destroyed by drink and devilry. But then no doubt the world is made like that. Assuredly it is no wonder that the more go-ahead Women (who have come round to the light by their own way, and through much darkness and suffering) should rise in revolt; or that the Workmen (finding their lives in the hands of those who do not know what life is) should do the same.

Leaving now the Middle-class man of to-day, the great representative of modern civilization, and the triumphant outcome of so many centuries of human progress, to enjoy his distinctions--we may turn for a moment to the only other great body of men who are of any importance: the more capable and energetic manual workers.

In the man of this class we have a type superior in many ways to the other. In the first place he knows something of what Life is; from an early age probably he has had to do something towards his own living. Anyhow he has been called upon in a thousand ways to help his parents, or his brothers and sisters, and has developed a fair capacity of sympathy and affection--a thing which can hardly be said of the public school boy; while his work, narrow though it may be, has given him a certain definite ability and grasp of actual fact. If, as is now happening in hundreds of thousands of cases, there is superadded to all this some of the general culture which arises from active reading and study, it is clear that the result is going to be considerable. It may not count much to-day, but it will to-morrow.

On the other hand this class is lamentably wanting in the very point where the other man excels--the organizing faculty. Take a workman from the bench, where he has never so to speak had to look beyond his nose, and place him in a position of responsibility and command, and he is completely at sea. He turns out hopelessly slattern and ineffectual, or a martinet or a bully; he has no sense of perspective and stickles absurdly over little points while he lets the great ones go; and it is almost impossible for him to look before and after as he should do, or bring to a proper focus a whole field of considerations. In all this he is a mere child: and evidently by himself unfit to rule the world.

In many respects the newer Women and the Workmen resemble each other. Both have been bullied and sat upon from time immemorial, and are beginning to revolt; both are good at detailed and set or customary work, both are bad at organization; both are stronger on the emotional than on the intellectual side; and both have an ideal of better things, but do not quite see their way to carry it out. Their best hope perhaps lies in their both getting hold of the Middle-class Man and thumping him on each side till they get him to organize the world for them. The latter has no ideal, no object, no enthusiasm, of his own. He cannot set himself to work; and consequently he is just made use of by the commercial spirit of the day. It is really lamentable to think how his great organizing capacity--which might create a holy Human empire of the world--is simply at present the tool of the Jew and the Speculator. In Parliamentary, Military, Indian, Home or Colonial politics, the quondam public school-boy is just led by the nose by the money-grubbing interest, to serve its purposes; and half the time has not the sense to see that he is being so led.

It might seem that it would be the greatest blessing and benefit to the man of this class to find him an ideal to work to. Certainly it is his only real and conceivable function to form an alliance with the two other great classes of the modern nations-the women and the workmen-and organize for them. Whether he will see it so, we know not; but if this might come about great things would happen in the world.

WOMAN

THE SERF

A HALF-GROWN man is of course a tyrant. And so it has come about that the rule of Man in the world has for many ages meant the serfdom of Woman.

Far back in History, at a time when in the early societies the thought of inequality had hardly arisen, it would appear that the female in her own way--as sole authenticator of birth and parentage, as guardian of the household, as inventress of agriculture and the peaceful arts, as priestess or prophetess or sharer in the councils of the tribe--was as powerful as man in his, and sometimes even more so. But from thence, down to to-day, what centuries of repression, of slavehood, of dumbness and obscurity have been her lot!

There is much to show that the greed of Private Property was the old Serpent which brought about the fall of our first parents; for as this sentiment--the chief incentive to modern Civilization--rose and spread with a kind of contagion over the advancing races of mankind, the human Male, bitten by it, not only claimed possession of everything he could lay hands upon, but ended by enslaving and appropriating his own mate, his second self--reducing her also to a mere chattel, a slave and a plaything.

Certainly it is curious that, with whatever occasional exceptions, the periods of man's ascendancy have been the periods of so much sadness and degradation of women. He, all through, more and more calmly assuming that it must be her province to live and work for him; shutting her more and more into the seclusion of the boudoir and the harem, or down to the drudgery of the hearth; confining her body, her mind; playing always upon her sex-nature, accentuating always that--as though she were indeed nought else but sex; yet furious if her feelings were not always obedient to his desire; arrogating to himself a masculine license, yet revenging the least unfaithfulness on her part by casting her out into the scorned life of the prostitute; and granting her more and more but one choice in life--to be a free woman, and to die, unsexed, in the gutter; or for creature-comforts and a good name to sell herself, soul and body, into life-long bondage. While she, more and more, has accepted as inevitable the situation; and moved, sad-eyed, to her patient and uncomplaining work, to the narrow sphere and petty details of household labor and life, of patience and self-effacement, of tenderness and love, little noticed and less understood; or twisted herself into a ridiculous mime of fashion and frivolity, if so she might find a use for her empty head, and some favor with her lord; her own real impulses and character, her own talents and genius, all the while smothered away and blighted, her brain dwarfed, and her outlook on the world marred by falsity and ignorance.

Such, or something like it, has been the fate of woman through the centuries. And if, like man, she had been light-armed for her own defense, it might have been possible to say it was her own fault that she allowed all this to take place; but when we remember that she all the while has had to bear the great and speechless burden of Sex--to be herself the ark and cradle of the Race down the ages--then we may perhaps understand what a tragedy it has all been. For the fulfillment of sex is a relief and a condensation to the Man. He goes his way, and, so to speak, thinks no more about it. But to the Woman it is the culmination of her life, her profound and secret mission to humanity, of incomparable import and delicacy.

It is difficult, of course, for men to understand the depth and sacredness of the mother-feeling in woman--its joys and hopes, its leaden weight of cares and anxieties. The burden of pregnancy and gestation, the deep inner solicitude and despondency, the fears that all may not be well, the indrawing and absorption of her life into the life of the child, the increasing effort to attend to anything else, to care for anything else; her willingness even to die if only the child may be born safe: these are things which man--except it be occasionally in his rôle as artist or inventor--does but faintly imagine. Then, later on, the dedication to the young life or lives, the years of daylong and nightlong labor and forethought, in which the very thought of self is effaced, of tender service for which there is no recognition, nor ever will or can be--except in the far future; the sacrifice of personal interests and expansions in the ever-narrowing round of domestic duty; and in the end the sad wonderment and grievous unfulfilled yearning as one by one the growing boy and girl push their way into the world and disavow their home-ties and dependence; the sundering of heartstrings even as the navel-cord had to be sundered before: for these things, too, Woman can hope but little sympathy and understanding from the other sex.

But this fact, of man's non-perception of it, does not make the tragedy less. Far back out of the brows of Greek goddess, and Sibyll, and Norse and German seeress and prophetess, over all this petty civilization look the grand untamed eyes of a primal woman the equal and the mate of man; and in sad plight should we be if we might not already, lighting up the horizon from East and West and South and North, discern the answering looks of those new comers who, as the period of women's enslavement is passing away, send glances of recognition across the ages to their elder sisters.

After all, and underneath all the falsities of this period, may we not say that there is a deep and permanent relation between the sexes, which must inevitably assert itself again?

To this relation the physiological differences perhaps afford the key. In woman--modern science has shown--the more fundamental and primitive nervous centers, and the great sympathetic and vaso-motor system of nerves generally, are developed to a greater extent than in man; in woman the whole structure and life rallies more closely arid obviously round the sexual function than in man; and, as a general rule, in the evolution of the human race, as well as of the lower races, the female is less subject to variation and is more constant to and conservative of the type of the race than the male. With these physiological differences are naturally allied the facts that, of the two, Woman is the more primitive, the more intuitive, the more emotional. If not so large and cosmic in her scope, the great unconscious processes of Nature lie somehow nearer to her; to her, sex is a deep and sacred instinct, carrying with it a sense of natural purity; nor does she often experience that divorce between the sentiment of Love and the physical passion which is so common with men, and which causes them to be aware of a grossness and a conflict in their own natures; she is, or should be, the interpreter of Love to man, and in some degree his guide in sexual matters. More, since she keeps to the great lines of evolution and is less biased and influenced by the momentary currents of the day; since her life is bound up with the life of the child; since in a way she is nearer the child herself, and nearer to the savage; it is to her that Man, after his excursions and wanderings, mental and physical, continually tends to return as to his primitive home and resting-place, to restore his balance, to find his centre of life, and to draw stores of energy and inspiration for fresh conquests of the outer world. "In women men find beings who have not wandered so far as they have from the typical life of earth's creatures; women are for men the human embodiments of the restful responsiveness of Nature. To every man, as Michelet has put it, the woman whom he loves is as the Earth was to her legendary son; he has but to fall down and kiss her breast and he is strong again."

If it be true that by natural and physiological right Woman stands in some such primitive relationship to Man, then we may expect this relationship to emerge again into clear and reasonable light in course of time; though it does not of course follow that a relationship founded on physiological distinctions is *absolutely* permanent--since these latter may themselves vary to some degree. That a more natural and sensible relation of some kind between the sexes is actually coming to birth, few who care to read the signs of the times can well doubt. For the moment, however, and by way of parenthesis before looking to the future, we have to consider a little more in detail the present position of women under civilization. Not that the consideration will be altogether gracious and satisfactory, but that it may--we are fain to hope--afford us some hints for the future.

It was perhaps not altogether unnatural that Man's craze for property and individual ownership should have culminated in the enslavement of woman--his most precious and beloved object. But the consequence of this absurdity was a whole series of other absurdities. What between insincere flattery and rose-water adorations on the one hand, and serfdom and neglect on the other, woman was, as Havelock Ellis says, treated as "a cross between an angel and an idiot." And after a time, adapting herself to the treatment, she really became something between an angel and an idiot--a bundle of weak and flabby sentiments, combined with a wholly undeveloped brain. Moreover by being continually specialized and specialized in the sexual and domestic direction, she lost touch with the actual world, and grew, one may say, into a separate species from man--so that in the later civilizations the males and females, except when the sex-attraction has compelled them as it were to come together, have been wont to congregate in separate herds, and talk languages each unintelligible to the other. Says the author of the *Woman's Question*: "I admit there is no room for pharisaical self-laudation here. The bawling mass of mankind on a race-course or the stock-exchange is degrading enough in all conscience. Yet this even is hardly so painful as the sight which meets our eyes between three and four in the afternoon in any fashionable London street. Hundreds of women--mere dolls--gazing intently into shop-windows at various bits of colored ribbon. . . . Perhaps nothing is more disheartening than this, except the mob of women in these very same streets between twelve and one at night."

The 'lady,' the household drudge, and the prostitute, are the three main types of woman resulting in our modern civilization from the process of the past-and it is hard to know which is the most wretched, which is the most wronged, and which is the most unlike that which in her own heart every true woman would desire to be.

In some sense the 'lady' of the period which is just beginning to pass away is the most characteristic product of Commercialism. The sense of Private

Property, arising and joining with the "angel and idiot" theory, turned Woman more and more--especially of course among the possessing classes--into an emblem of possession--a mere doll, an empty idol, a brag of the man's exclusive right in the sex--till at last, as her vain splendors increased and her real usefulness diminished, she ultimated into the 'perfect lady.' But let every woman who piques and preens herself to the fulfillment of this ideal in her own person, remember what is the cost and what is the meaning of her quest: the covert enslavement to, and the covert contempt of Man.

The instinct of helpful personal service is so strong in women, and such a deep-rooted part of their natures, that to be treated as a mere target for other people's worship and service--especially when this is tainted with insincerity--must be most obnoxious to them. To think that women still exist by hundreds and hundreds of thousands, women with hearts and hands formed for love and helpfulness, who are brought up as 'ladies' and have to spend their lives listening to the idiotic platitudes of the Middle-class Man, and "waited upon" by wage-bought domestics, is enough to make one shudder. The modern 'gentleman' is bad enough, but the 'lady' of bourgeois-dom, literally "crucified twixt a smile and whimper," prostituted to a life which in her heart she hates--with its petty ideals, its narrow horizon, and its empty honors--is indeed a pitiful spectacle.

In Baronial times the household centered round the Hall, where the baron sat supreme; to-day it centers round the room where the lady reigns. The "with" is withdrawn from the withdrawing-room, and that apartment has become the most important of all. Yet there is an effect of mockery in the homage paid to the new sovereign; and, as far as her rule is actual, a doubt whether she is really qualified yet for the position. The contrast between the two societies, the Feudal and the Commercial, is not inaptly represented by this domestic change. The former society was rude and rough, but generous and straightforward; the latter is polished and nice, but full of littleness and *finesse*. The Drawing-room, with its feeble manners and effects of curtains and embroidery, gives its tone to our lives now-a-days. But we look forward to a time when this room also will cease to be the centre of the house, and another--perhaps the Common-room--will take its place.

Below a certain level in society--the distinctively commercial--there are no drawing-rooms. Among the working masses, where the woman is of indispensable importance in daily life, and is not sequestered as an idol, there is no room specially set apart for her worship-a curious change takes place in her nominal position, and whereas in the supernal sphere she sits in state and has her tea and bread and butter brought to her by obsequious males, in the cottage the men take their ease and are served by the women. The customs of the cottage, however, are rooted in a natural division of labor by which the man undertakes the outdoor, and the woman the indoor work; and there is, I think, quite as much real respect shown to her here as in the drawing-room.

In the cottage, nevertheless, the unfortunate one falls into the second pit that is prepared for her--that of the household drudge; and here she leads a life which, if it has more honesty and reality in it than that of the lady,' is one of abject slavery. Few men again realize, or trouble themselves to realize, what a life this of the working house-wife is. They are accustomed to look upon their own employment, whatever it may be, as 'work' (perhaps because it brings with it 'wages'); the woman's they regard as a kind of pastime. They forget what monotonous drudgery it really means, and yet what incessant forethought and care; they forget that the woman has no eight hours day, that her work is always staring her in the face, and waiting for her, even on into the night; that the body is wearied, and the mind narrowed down, "scratched to death by rats and mice" in a perpetual round of petty cares. For not only does civilization and multifarious invention (including smoke) make the burden of domestic life immensely complex, but the point is that each housewife has to sustain this burden to herself in lonely effort. What a sight, in any of our great towns, to enter into the cottages or tenements which form the endless rows of suburban streets, and to find in each one a working wife struggling alone in semi-darkness and seclusion with the toils of an entire separate household--with meals to be planned and provided, with bread to be baked, clothes to be washed and mended, children to be kept in order, a husband to be humored, and a house to be swept and dusted; herself wearied and worried, debilitated with confinement and want of fresh air, and low-spirited for want of change and society! How futile! and how dreary!

There remains the third alternative for women; nor can it be wondered at that some deliberately choose a life of prostitution as their only escape from the existence of the lady or the drudge. Yet what a choice it is! On the one hand is the caged Woman, and on the other hand is the free: and which to choose? "How can there be a doubt," says one, "surely freedom is always best." Then there falls a hush. "Ah!" says society, pointing with its finger, "but a free *Woman*!"

And yet is it possible for Woman ever to be worthy her name, unless she is free?

To-day, or up to to-day, just as the wage-worker has had no means of livelihood except by the sale of his bodily labor, so woman has had no means of livelihood except by the surrender of her bodily sex.

She could dispose of it to one man for life, and have in return the respect of society and the caged existence of the lady or the drudge, or she could sell it night by night and be a "free woman," scorned of the world and portioned to die in the gutter. In either case (if she really thinks about the matter at all) she must lose her self-respect, What a choice, what a frightful choice!--and this has been the fate of Woman for how long?

If, as a consequence of all this, woman has gone down hill, there is no doubt that man has gravitated too. (Or was it really that Jack fell down first, and "Jill came tumbling after"?) Anyhow I think that nothing can be more clear--and this I believe should be taken as the basis of any discussion on the relation of the sexes--than that whatever injures the one sex injures the other; and that whatever defects or partialities may be found in the one must from the nature of the case be tallied by corresponding defects and partialities in the other. The two halves of the human race are complementary, and it is useless for one to attempt to glorify itself at the expense of the other. As in Olive Schreiner's allegory of Woman ("Three Dreams in a Desert"), man and woman are bound together by a vital band, and the one cannot move a step in advance of the other.

If we were called upon to characterize these mutual defects (inbred partly by the false property relation) we should be inclined to say they were brutality and conceit on the one hand, and finesse and subtlety on the other. Man, as owner, has tended to become arrogant and callous and egotistic; woman, as the owned, slavish and crafty and unreal.

As a matter of fact, and allowing that sweeping generalizations of this kind are open to a good many exceptions, we do find (at any rate in the British Isles) a most wonderful and celestial indifference to anything but their own affairs amongst the 'lords of creation,' an indifference so ingrained and constitutional that it is rarely conscious of itself, and which assumes quite easily and naturally that the weaker sex exists for the purpose of playing the foil, so to speak, to the chief actor in life's drama. Nor does the fact that this indifference is tempered, from time to time, by a little gallantry afford much consolation--as may be imagined--to the woman who perceives that the gallantry is inspired by nothing more than a passing sex-desire.

On the other hand Jill has come tumbling after pretty quickly, and has tumbled to the conclusion that though she cannot sway her lord by force, she may easily make use of him by craft. *Finesse*, developed through scores of generations, combined with the skilful use of the glamour belonging to her sex, have given her an extraordinary faculty of carrying out her own purposes, often through the most difficult passes, without ever exposing her hand. Possibly the knowledge of this forms one reason why women distrust each other so much more than men distrust each other. Certainly one of the rarest of God's creatures is a truly undesigning female, but--when dowered with intellect such as might seem to justify it in being designing--one of the most admirable and beautiful!

Looking a little deeper, and below the superficial contrast which an unsatisfactory relation between the sexes has doubtless created, one seems to discern some of those more vital and deep-rooted differentiations spoken of on an earlier page. It is a commonly received opinion that woman tends more to intuition and man to logic; and certainly the male mind seems better able to deal with abstractions and generalizations, and the female mind with the personal and the detailed and the concrete. And while this difference may be in part attributable to the artificial confinement of women to the domestic sphere, there is probably something more organic in it than that. At any rate it gives to Woman some of her best qualities--a quick and immediate perception, appreciation of character, tact, and a kind of artistic sense in the ordering of her own life, so that you do not see the tags and unraveled ends which appear in man's conduct. While the man is blundering about, fighting with himself, hesitating, doubting, weighing, trying vainly to co-ordinate all the elements of his nature, the woman (often no doubt in a smaller sphere) moves serene and prompt to her ends. Her actions are characterized by grace and finality; she is more at unity with herself; and she has the inestimable advantage of living in the world of persons--which may well seem so much more important and full of interest than that of things.

On the other hand, this want of the power of generalization has made it difficult for woman (at any rate up to to-day) to emerge from a small circle of interests, and to look at things from the point of view of public advantage and good. While her, sympathies for individuals are keen and quick, abstract and general ideas such as those of justice, Truth, and the like have been difficult of appreciation to her; and her deficiency in logic has made it almost impossible to act upon her through the brain. A man, if he is on the wrong tack, can be argued with; but with a woman of this type, if her motives are nefarious, there is no means of changing them by appeal to her reason, or to the general sense of justice and Right--and unless controlled by the stronger sway of a determined personal will (of a man) her career is liable to be pretty bad.

Generally it will be admitted, as we are dealing with points of mental and moral difference between the sexes, Man has developed the more active, and Woman the more passive qualities; and it is pretty obvious, here too, that this difference is not only due to centuries of social inequality and of property-marriage, but roots back in some degree to the very nature of their respective sexual functions. That there are permanent complementary distinctions between the male and female, dating first perhaps from sex, and thence spreading over the whole natures, physical, mental and moral, of each, no one can reasonably doubt. These distinctions have however, we contend, been strangely accentuated and exaggerated during the historic period--till at last a point of maximum divergence and absolute misunderstanding has been reached. But that point is behind us now.

WOMAN

IN FREEDOM

IT is clear enough, from what has been said, that what Woman most needs to-day, and is mostly seeking for, is a basis of independence for her life. Nor is her position likely to be improved until she is able to face man on an equality; to find, self-balanced, her natural relation to him; and to dispose of herself and of her sex perfectly freely, and not as a thrall must do.

Doubtless if man were an ideal creature his mate might be secure of equal and considerate treatment from him without having to insist upon an absolute economic independence but as that is only too obviously not the case there is nothing left for her to-day but to unfold the war-flag of her "rights," and (dull and tiresome as it may be) to go through a whole weary round of battles till peace is concluded again upon a better understanding.

Yet it must never be forgotten that nothing short of large social changes, stretching beyond the sphere of women only, can bring about the complete emancipation of the latter. Not till our whole commercial system, with its barter and sale of human labor and human love for gain, is done away, and not till a whole new code of ideals and customs of life has come in, will women really be free. They must remember that their cause is also the cause of the oppressed laborer over the whole earth, and the laborer has to remember that his cause is theirs.

And since Motherhood is, after all, woman's great and incomparable work, people will come to see that a sane maternity is one of the very first things to be considered--and that really, though not the only consideration, it is a work which if properly fulfilled does involve the broadest and largest culture. Perhaps this might seem to some only too obvious; yet when for a moment we glance around at the current ideals, when we see what Whitman calls "the incredible holds and webs of silliness, millinery and every kind of dyspeptic depletion" in which women themselves live, when we see the absolute want of training for motherhood and the increasing physical incapacity for it, and even the feminine censure of those who pass through the ordeal too easily, we begin to realize how little the present notion of what woman should be is associated with the healthy fulfillment of her most perfect work. A woman capable at all points to bear children, to guard them, to teach them, to turn them out strong and healthy citizens of the great world, stands at the farthest remove from the finnikin doll or the meek drudge whom man by a kind of false sexual selection has through many centuries evolved as his ideal.

The nervous and sexual systems of women to-day, ruined among the rich by a life and occupations which stimulate the emotional sensibilities without ever giving the strength and hardiness which flow from healthy and regular industry, and often ruined among the poor by excessive labor carried on under most unhealthy conditions, make real wife-hood and motherhood things almost unknown. "Injudicious training", says Bebel, "miserable social conditions (food, dwelling, occupation) produce weak, bloodless, nervous beings, incapable of fulfilling the duties of matrimony. The consequences are menstrual troubles and disturbances in the various organs connected with sexual functions, rendering maternity dangerous or impossible. Instead of a healthy, cheerful companion, a capable mother, a helpmate equal to the calls made upon her activity, the husband has a nervous excitable wife, permanently under the doctor's hands, and too fragile to bear the slightest draught or noise."

The Modern Woman sees plainly enough that no decent advance for her sex is possible until this whole question is fairly faced--involving, as of course it will do, a life very different from her present one, far more in the open air, with real bodily exercise and development, some amount of regular manual work, a knowledge of the laws of health and physiology, an altogether wider mental outlook, and greater self-reliance and nature-hardihood. But when once these things are granted, she sees that she will no longer be the serf, but the equal, the mate, and the comrade of Man.

Before any such new conception it is obvious enough that the poor little pinched ideal of the 'lady,' which has ruled society so long, will fade away into distance and obscurity. People may rail at the new developments, but what, it may be asked, can any decently sensible woman think of her present position--of the mock salutations and heroic politenesses of the conventional male--with their suggestion of an empty homage to weakness and incapacity; of the unwritten law which condemns her, if occupying any place in society, to bridle in her chin and use an affected speech in order that it may be patent to everybody that she is not free; which forbids natural and spontaneous gesture as unbecoming and suspicious-and indeed in any public place as liable to the attention of the policeman; what can she think of the perpetual lies under which she has to live--too numerous to be recorded; except that all these things are intolerable? Rather than remain in such a coil the modern woman is sensible enough to see that she must face the stigma of doing things 'unlady-like;' and that only by facing it can she win her true place in the world, and a real comradeship with the only class of man who is capable of such a thing--namely, the man who is willing not to be 'a gentleman.'

That a new code of manners between the sexes, founded not on covert lust but on open and mutual helpfulness, has got to come in, is obvious enough. The cry of equality need not like a red rag infuriate the Philistine bull. That woman is in general muscularly weaker than man, and that there are certain kinds of effort, even mental, for which she is less fitted--as there are other kinds of effort for which she is more fitted--may easily be granted; but this only means, in the language of all good manners, that there are special ways in which men can assist women, as there are special ways in which women can assist men. Anything which goes beyond this, and the friendly exchange of equal services, and which assumes, in the conventionalities of the private household or the public place, that the female claims a general indulgence (because of her general incapacity) is an offence--against the encouragement of which women themselves will no doubt be on their guard.

I say the signs of revolt on the part of the lady class--revolt long delayed but now spreading all along the line--are evident enough. When, however, we come to the second type of woman mentioned in the preceding pages, the working-wife, we-naturally enough--do not find much conscious movement. The life of the household drudge is too like that of a slave, too much consumed in mere toil, too little illuminated by any knowledge, for her to rise of herself to any other conception of existence. Nevertheless it is not difficult to see that general and social changes are working to bring about her liberation also. Improved house-construction, public bakeries and laundries, and so forth, and, what is much more important, a more rational and simple and healthful notion of food and furniture, are tending very largely to reduce the labors of Housework and Cookery; and conservative though women are in their habits, when these changes are brought to their doors they cannot but see the advantage of them. Public institutions too are more and more taking over the responsibilities and the cost of educating and rearing children; and even here and there we may discern a drift towards the amalgamation of households, which by introducing a common life and division of labor among the women-folk will probably do much to cheer and lighten their lot. None of these changes, however, will be of great use unless or until they wake the overworked woman herself to see and insist on her rights to a better life, and until they force from the man a frank acknowledgment of her claim. And surely here and there the man himself will do something to educate his mate to this point. We see no reason indeed why he should not assist in some part of the domestic work, and thus contribute his share of labor and intelligence to the conduct of the house; nor why the woman--being thus relieved--should not occasionally, and when desirable, find salaried work outside, and so contribute to the maintenance of the family, and to her own security and sense of independence. The over-differentiation of the labors of the sexes to-day is at once a perpetuation of the servitude of women and a cause of misunderstanding between her and man, and of lack of interest in each other's doings.

The third type of woman, the prostitute, provides us with that question which--according to Bebel--is the sphinx-riddle that modern society cannot solve, and yet which unsolved threatens society's destruction. The commercial prostitution of love is the last outcome of our whole social system, and its most clear condemnation. It flaunts in our streets, it hides itself in the garment of respectability under the name of matrimony, it eats in actual physical disease and death right through our midst; it is fed by the oppression and the ignorance of women, by their poverty and denied means of livelihood, and by the hypocritical puritanism which forbids them by millions not only to gratify but even to speak of their natural desires; and it is encouraged by the callousness of an age which has accustomed men to buy and sell for money every most precious thing--even the life-long labor of their brothers, therefore why not also the very bodies of their sisters?

Here there is no solution *except* the freedom of woman--which means of course also the freedom of the masses of the people, men and women, and the ceasing altogether of economic slavery. There is no solution which will not include the redemption of the terms 'free woman' and 'free love' to their true and rightful significance. Let every woman whose heart bleeds for the sufferings of her sex, hasten to declare herself and to constitute herself, as far as she possibly can, a free woman. Let her accept the term with all the odium that belongs to it; let her insist on her right to speak, dress, think, act, and above all to use her sex, as she deems best; let her face the scorn and the ridicule; let her "lose her own life" if she likes; assured that only so can come deliverance, and that only when the free woman is honored will the prostitute cease to exist. And let every man who really would respect his counterpart, entreat her also to act so; let him never by word or deed tempt her to grant as a bargain what can only be precious as a gift; let him see her with pleasure stand a little aloof; let him help her to gain her feet; so at last, by what slight sacrifices on his part such a course may involve, will it dawn upon him that he has gained a real companion and helpmate on life's journey.

The whole evil of commercial prostitution arises out of the domination of Man in matters of sex.

Better indeed were a Saturnalia of *free* men and women than the spectacle which as it is our great cities present at night. Here in Sex, the women's instincts are, as a rule, so clean, so direct, so well-rooted in the needs of the race, that except for man's domination they would scarcely have suffered this perversion. Sex in man is an unorganized passion, an individual need or impetus; but in woman it may more properly be termed a constructive instinct, with the larger signification that that involves. Even more than man should woman be 'free' to work out the problem of her sex-relations as may commend itself best to her--hampered as little as possible by legal, conventional, or economic considerations, and relying chiefly on her own native sense and tact in the matter. Once thus free--free from the mere cash-nexus to a husband, from the money-slavery of the streets, from the nameless terrors of social opinion, and from the threats of the choice of perpetual virginity or perpetual bondage--would she not indeed choose her career (whether that of wife and mother, or that of free companion, or one of single blessedness) far better for herself than it is chosen *for* her to-day--regarding really in some degree the needs of society, and the welfare of children, and the sincerity and durability of her relations to her lovers, and less the petty motives of profit and fear?

The point is that the whole conception of a nobler Womanhood for the future has to proceed candidly from this basis of her complete freedom as to the disposal of her sex, and from the healthy conviction that, with whatever individual aberrations, she will on the whole use that freedom rationally and well. And surely this--in view too of some decent education of the young on sexual matters--is not too great a demand to make on our faith in women. If it is, then indeed we are undone--for short of this we can only retain them in servitude, and society in its form of the hell on earth which it largely is to-day.

Refreshing therefore in its way is the spirit of revolt which is spreading on all sides. Let us hope such revolt will continue. If it lead here and there to strained or false situations, or to temporary misunderstandings--still, declared enmity is better than unreal acquiescence. Too long have women acted the part of mere appendages to the male, suppressing their own individuality and fostering his self-conceit. In order to have souls of their own they must free themselves, and greatly by their own efforts. They must learn to fight. Whitman in his poem "A woman waits for me," draws a picture of a woman who stands in the sharpest possible contrast with the feeble bourgeois ideal--a woman who can "swim, row, ride, wrestle, shoot, run, strike, retreat, defend herself," etc.; and Bebel, in his book on Woman, while pointing out that in Sparta, "where the greatest attention was paid to the physical development of both sexes, boys and girls went about naked till they had reached the age of puberty, and were trained together in bodily exercises, games and wrestling," complains that nowadays "the notion that women require strength, courage and resolution is regarded as very heterodox." But the truth is that qualities of courage and independence are not agreeable in a slave, and that is why man during all these centuries has consistently discountenanced them--till at last the female herself has come to consider them 'unwomanly.' Yet this last epithet is absurd for if tenderness is the crown and glory of woman, nothing can be more certain than that true tenderness is only found in strong and courageous natures; the tenderness of a servile person is no tenderness at all.

It has not escaped the attention of thinkers on these subjects that the rise of Women into freedom and larger social life here alluded to--and already indeed indicated by the march of events--is likely to have a profound influence on the future of our race. It is pointed out that among most of the higher animals, and indeed among many of the early races of mankind, the males have been selected by the females on account of their prowess or superior strength or beauty, and this has led to the evolution in the males and in the race at large of a type which (in a dim and unconscious manner) was the ideal of the female. But as soon as in the history of mankind the property-love set in, and woman became the chattel of man, this action ceased. She, being no longer free, could not possibly choose man, but rather the opposite took place, and man began to select woman for the characteristics pleasing to him. The latter now adorned herself to gratify his taste, and the female type and consequently the type of the whole race have been correspondingly affected. With the return of woman to freedom the ideal of the female may again resume its sway. It is possible indeed that the more dignified and serious attitude of women towards sex may give to sexual selection when exercised by them a nobler influence than when exercised by the males. Anyhow it is not difficult to see that women really free would never countenance for their mates the many mean and unclean types of men who to-day seem to have things all their own way, nor consent to have children by such men; nor is it difficult to imagine that the feminine influence might thus sway to the evolution of a more manly and dignified race than has been disclosed in these last days of commercial civilization!

The Modern Woman with her clubs, her debates, her politics, her freedom of action and costume, is forming a public opinion of her own at an amazing rate; and seems to be preparing to "spank" and even thump the Middle-class Man in real earnest! What exactly evolution may be preparing for us, we do not know, but apparently some lively sparring matches between the sexes. Of course all will not be smooth sailing. The women of the new movement are naturally largely drawn from those in whom the maternal instinct is not especially strong; also from those in whom the sexual instinct is not preponderant. Such women do not altogether represent their sex; some are rather mannish in temperament; some are 'homogenic,' that is, inclined to attachments to their own, rather than to the opposite, sex; some are ultra-rationalizing and brain-cultured; to many, children are more or less a bore; to others, man's sex-passion is a mere impertinence, which they do not understand, and whose place they consequently misjudge. It would not do to say that the majority of the new movement are thus out of line, but there is no doubt that a large number are; and the course of their progress will be correspondingly curvilinear.

Perhaps the deficiency in maternal instinct would seem the most serious imputation. But then, who knows (as we have said) what evolution is preparing? Sometimes it seems possible that a new sex is on the make--like the feminine neuters of Ants and Bees--not adapted for child-bearing, but with a marvelous and perfect instinct of social service, indispensable for the maintenance of the common life. Certainly most of those who are freeing themselves--often with serious struggles--from the 'lady' chrysalis are fired with an ardent social enthusiasm; and if they may personally differ in some respects from the average of their sex, it is certain that their efforts will result in a tremendous improvement in the general position of their more commonplace sisters.

If it should turn out that a certain fraction of the feminine sex should for one reason or another not devote itself to the work of maternity, still the influence of this section would react on the others to render their notion of motherhood far more dignified than before. There is not much doubt that in the future this most important of human labors will be carried on with a degree of conscious intelligence hitherto unknown, and which will raise it from the fulfillment of a mere instinct to the completion of a splendid social purpose. To save the souls of children as well as their bodies, to raise heroic as well as prosperous citizens, will surely be the desire and the work of the mothers of our race.

It will perhaps be said that after going about to show (as in the previous chapter) the deficiency of women hitherto in the matter of the generalizing faculty, it is somewhat inconsistent to express any great hope that they will ever take much active interest in the general social life to which they belong; but indeed the answer to this is that they are already beginning to do so. The social enthusiasm and activity shown by women in Britain, Russia, and the United States is so great and well-rooted that it is impossible to believe it a mere ephemeral event; and though in the older of these countries it is at present confined to the more wealthy classes, we can augur from that--according to a well-known principle--that it will in time spread downwards to the women of the nation.

Important as is the tendency of women in the countries mentioned to higher education and brain development, I think it is evident that the widening and socialization of their interests is not taking place so much through mere study of books and the passing of examinations in political economy and other sciences, as through the extended actual experience which the life of the day is bringing to them. Certainly the book-studies are important and must not be neglected; but above all is it imperative (and men, if they are to have any direct sway in the future destinies of the other sex, must look to it) that women, so long confined to the narrowest mere routine and limited circle of domestic life, should see and get experience, all they can, of the actual world. The theory, happily now exploding, of keeping them I innocent' through sheer ignorance partakes too much of the 'angel and idiot' view. To see the life of slum and palace and workshop, to enter into the trades and professions, to become doctors, nurses, and so forth, to have to look after themselves and to hold their own as against men, to travel, to meet with sexual experience, to work together in trade-unions, to join in social and political uprisings and rebellions, etc., is what women want just now. And it is evident enough that at any rate among the more prosperous sections in this country such a movement is going on apace. If the existence of the enormous hordes of unattached females that we find living on interest and dividends to-day is a blemish from a Socialistic point of view; if we find them on the prowl all over the country, filling the theatres and concert-rooms and public entertainments in the proportion of three to one male, besetting the trains, swarming onto the tops of the 'buses, dodging on bicycles under the horses' heads, making speeches at street corners, blocking the very pavements in the front of fashionable shops, we must not forget that for the objects we have just sketched, even this class is going the most direct way to work, and laying in stores of experience, which will make it impossible for it ever to return to the petty life of times gone by.

At the last, and after centuries of misunderstanding and association of triviality and superficiality with the female sex, it will perhaps dawn upon the world that the truth really lies in an opposite direction--that, in a sense, there is something more deep-lying fundamental and primitive in the woman nature than in that of the man; that instead of being the over-sensitive hysterical creature that civilization has too often made her, she is essentially of calm large and acceptive even though emotional temperament. "Her shape arises," says Walt Whitman,

> "She less guarded than ever, yet more guarded than ever,
> The gross and soil'd she moves among do not make her gross and soil'd,
> She knows the thoughts as she passes, nothing is concealed from her.
> She is none the less considerate or friendly therefor,
> She is the best belov'd, it is, without exception; she has no reason to fear, and she does not fear."

The Greek goddesses look down and across the ages to the very outposts beyond civilization; and already from far America, Australasia, Africa, Norway, Russia, as even in our midst from those who have crossed the border-line of all class and caste, glance forth the features of a grander type --fearless and untamed--the primal merging into the future Woman; who, combining broad sense with sensibility, the passion for Nature with the love of Man, and commanding indeed the details of life, yet risen out of localism and convention, will help us to undo the bands of death which encircle the present society, and open the doors to a new and a wider life.

MARRIAGE

A RETROSPECT

OF the great mystery of human Love, and that most intimate personal relation of two souls to each other--perhaps the firmest, most basic and indissoluble fact (after our own existence) that we know; of that strange sense--often, perhaps generally, instantaneous--of long precedent familiarity and kinship, that deep reliance on and acceptation of another in his or her entirety; of the tremendous strength of the chain which thus at times will bind two hearts in lifelong dedication and devotion, persuading and indeed not seldom compelling the persons concerned to the sacrifice of some of the other elements of their lives and characters; and, withal, of a certain inscrutable veiledness from each other which so frequently accompanies the relation of the opposite sexes, and which forms at once the abiding charm, and the pain, sometimes the tragedy, of their union; of this palpitating winged living thing, which one may perhaps call the real Marriage--I would say but little; for indeed it is only fitting or possible to speak of it by indirect language and suggestion, nor may one venture to rudely drag it from its sanctuary into the light of the common gaze.

Compared with this, the actual marriage, in its squalid perversity as we too often have occasion of knowing it, is as the wretched idol of the savage to the reality which it is supposed to represent; and one seems to hear the Aristophanic laughter of the gods as they contemplate man's little clay image of the Heavenly Love--which, cracked in the fire of daily life, he is fain to bind together with rusty hoops of law, and parchment bonds, lest it should crumble and fall to pieces altogether.

The whole subject, wide as life itself--as Heaven and Hell--eludes anything like adequate treatment, and we need make no apology for narrowing down our considerations here to just a few practical points; and if we cannot navigate upward into the very heart of the matter-namely, into the causes which make some people love each other with a true and perfect love, and others unite in obedience to but a counterfeit passion--yet we may fairly, I imagine, study some of the conditions which give to actual marriage its present form, or which in the future are likely to provide real affection, with a more satisfactory expression than it has as a rule to-day.

As long as man is only half-grown, and woman is a serf or a parasite, it can hardly be expected that Marriage should be particularly successful. Two people come together, who know but little of each other, who have been brought up along different lines, who certainly do not understand each other's nature; whose mental interests and occupations are different, whose worldly interests and advantage are also different; to one of whom the subject of sex is probably a sealed book, to the other perhaps a book whose most dismal page has been opened first. The man needs an outlet for his passion; the girl is looking for a 'home' and a proprietor. A glamour of illusion descends upon the two, and drives them into each other's arms. It envelopes in a gracious and misty halo all their differences and misapprehensions. They marry without misgiving; and their hearts overflow with gratitude to the white-surpliced old gentleman who reads the service over them.

But at a later hour, and with calmer thought, they begin to realize that it is a life-sentence which he has so suavely passed upon them--not reducible (as in the case of ordinary convicts) even to a term of 20 years. The brief burst of their first satisfaction has been followed by satiety on the physical plane, then by mere vacuity of affection, then by boredom, and even nausea. The girl, full perhaps of a tender emotion, and missing the sympathy and consolation she expected in the man's love, only to find its more materialistic side--"This, this then is what I am wanted for;" the man, who looked for a companion, finding he can rouse no mortal interest in his wife's mind save in the most exasperating trivialities;--whatever the cause may be, a veil has fallen from before their faces, and there they sit, held together now by the least honorable interests, the interests which they themselves can least respect, but to which Law and Religion lend all their weight. The monetary dependence of the woman, the mere sex-needs of the man, the fear of public opinion, all form motives, and motives of the meanest kind, for maintaining the seeming tie; and the relation of the two hardens down into a dull neutrality, in which lives and characters are narrowed and blunted, and deceit becomes the common weapon which guards divided interests.

A sad picture! And of course in this case a portrayal deliberately of the seamy side of the matter. But who shall say what agonies are often gone through in those first few years of married life? Anyhow, this is the sort of problem which we have to face to-day, and which shows its actuality by the amazing rate at which it is breaking out in literature on all sides.

It may be said--and often of course is said--that such cases as these only prove that marriage was entered into under the influence of a passing glamour and delusion, and that there was not much real devotion to begin with. And no doubt there is truth enough in such remarks. But--we may say in reply--because two people make a mistake in youth, to condemn them, for that reason, to lifelong suffering and mutual degradation, or to see them so condemned, without proposing any hope or way of deliverance, but with the one word "serves you right" on the lips, is a course which can commend itself only to the grimmest and dullest Calvinist. Whatever safe-guards against a too frivolous view of the relationship may be proposed by the good sense of society in the future, it is certain that the time has gone past when Marriage can continue to be regarded as a supernatural institution to whose maintenance human bodies and souls must be indiscriminately sacrificed; a humaner, wiser, and less panic-stricken treatment of the subject must set in; and if there are difficulties in the way they must be met by patient and calm consideration of human welfare--superior to any law, however ancient and respectable.

I take it then that, without disguising the fact that the question is a complex one, and that our conclusions may be only very tentative, we have to consider as rationally as we conveniently can, first, some of the drawbacks or defects of the present marriage customs, and secondly such improvements in these as may seem feasible.

And with regard to the former, one of the most important points--which we have already touched on--is the extraordinary absence of any allusion to these subjects in the teaching of young folk. In a day when every possible study seems to be crammed into the school curriculum, it is curious that the one matter which is of supreme importance to the individual and the community is most carefully ignored. That one ought to be able to distinguish a passing sex-spell from a true comradeship and devotion is no doubt a very sapient remark; but since it is a thing which mature folk often fail to do, how young things with no experience of their own or hint from others should be expected to do it is not easy to understand. The search for a fitting mate [77], especially among the more sensitive and highly-organized types of mankind, is a very complex affair; and it is really monstrous that the girl or youth should have to, set out--as they mostly have to do to-day--on this difficult quest without a word of help as to the choice of the way or the very real doubts and perplexities that beset it.

If the pair whom we have supposed as about to be married had been brought up in almost any tribe of savages, they would a few years previously have gone through regular offices of initiation into manhood and womanhood, during which time ceremonies (possibly indecent in our eyes) would at any rate have made many misapprehensions impossible. As it is, the civilized girl is led to the 'altar' often in uttermost ignorance and misunderstanding as to the nature of the sacrificial rites about to be consummated. The youth too is ignorant in his way. Perhaps he is unaware that love in the female is, in a sense, more diffused than in the male, less specially sexual: that it dwells longer in caresses and embraces, and determines itself more slowly towards the reproductive system. Impatient, he injures and horrifies his partner, and unconsciously perhaps aggravates the very hysterical tendency which marriage might and should have allayed.

Among the middle and well-to-do classes especially, the conditions of high civilization, by inducing an overfed masculinity in the males and a nervous and hysterical tendency in the females, increase the difficulties mentioned; and it is among the 'classes' too that the special evils exist of sex-starvation and sex-ignorance on the one hand, and of mere licentiousness on the other.

Among the comparatively uncivilized mass of the people, where a good deal of familiarity between the sexes takes place before marriage, and where probably there is less ignorance on the one side and less licentiousness on the other, these ills are not so prominent. But here too the need for some sensible teaching is clear; and sheer neglect of the law of Transmutation, or sheer want of self-control, are liable to make the proletarian union brutish enough.

So far with regard to difficulties arising from personal ignorance and inexperience. But stretching beyond and around all these are those others that arise from the special property- relation between the two sexes, and from deep-lying historic and economic causes generally. The long historic serfdom of woman, creeping down into the moral and intellectual natures of the two sexes, has exaggerated the naturally complementary relation of the male and the female into an absurd caricature of strength on the one hand and dependence on the other. This is well seen in the ordinary marriage-relation of the common-prayer-book type. The frail and delicate female is supposed to cling round the sturdy husband's form, or to depend from his arm in graceful incapacity; and the spectator is called upon to admire the charming effect of the union--as of the ivy with the oak--forgetful of the terrible moral, namely, that (in the case of the trees at any rate) it is really a death-struggle which is going on, in which either the oak must perish suffocated in the embraces of its partner, or in order to free the former into anything like healthy development the ivy must be sacrificed.

Too often of course of such marriages the egoism, lordship and physical satisfaction of the man are the chief motive causes. The woman is practically sacrificed to the part of the maintenance of these male virtues. It is for her to spend her days in little forgotten details of labor and anxiety for the sake of the man's superior comfort and importance, to give up her needs to his whims, to 'humor' him in all ways she can; it is for her to wipe her mind clear of all opinions in order that she may hold it up as a kind of mirror in which he may behold reflected his lordly self; and it is for her to sacrifice even her physical health and natural instincts in deference to what is called her 'duty' to her husband.

How bitterly *alone* many such a woman feels! She has dreamed of being folded in the arms of a strong man, and surrendering herself, her life, her mind, her all, to his service. Of course it is an unhealthy dream, an illusion, a mere luxury of love; and it is destined to be dashed. She has to learn that self-surrender may be just as great a crime as self-assertion. She finds that her very willingness to be sacrificed only fosters in the man, perhaps for his own self-defense, the egotism and coldness that so cruelly wound her.

For how often does he with keen prevision see that if he gives way from his coldness the clinging dependent creature will infallibly overgrow and smother him!--that she will cut her woman-friends, will throw aside all her own interests and pursuits in order to 'devote' herself to him, and, affording no sturdy character of her own in which *he* can take any interest, will hang the festoons of her affection on every ramification of his wretched life-nor leave him a corner free--till he perishes from all manhood and social or heroic uses into a mere matrimonial clothes peg, a warning and a wonderment to passers by!

However, as an alternative, it sometimes happens that the Woman, too wise to sacrifice her own life indiscriminately to the egoism of her husband, and not caring for the 'festoon' method, adopts the middle course of *appearing* to minister to him while really pursuing her own purposes. She cultivates the gentle science of indirectness. While holding up a mirror for the Man to admire himself in, *behind that mirror* she goes her own way and carries out her own designs, separate from him; and while sacrificing her body to his wants, she does so quite deliberately and for a definite reason, namely, because she has found out that she can so get a shelter for herself and her children, and can solve the problem of that maintenance which society has hitherto denied to her in her own right. For indeed by a cruel fate women have been placed in exactly that position where the sacrifice of their self-respect for base motives has easily passed beyond a temptation into being a necessity. They have had to live, and have too often only been able to do so by selling themselves into bondage to the man. Willing or unwilling, overworked or dying, they have had to bear children to the caprice of their lords; and in this serf-life their very natures have been blunted; they have lost--what indeed should be the very glory and crown of woman's being--the perfect freedom and the purity of their love.

At this whole spectacle of woman's degradation the human male has looked on with stupid and open-mouthed indifference--as an ox might look on at a drowning ox-herd--not even dimly divining that his own fate was somehow involved. He has calmly and obliviously watched the woman drift farther and farther away from him, till at last, with the loss of an intelligent and mutual understanding between the sexes, Love with unequal wings has fallen lamed to the ground. Yet it would be idle to deny that even in such a state of affairs as that depicted, men and women have in the past and do often even now find some degree of satisfaction--simply indeed because their types of character are such as belong to, and have been evolved in accordance with, this relation.

To-day, however, there are thousands of women--and everyday more thousands--to whom such a lopsided alliance is detestable; who are determined that they will no longer endure the arrogant lordship and egoism of men, nor countenance in themselves or other women the craft and servility which are the necessary complements of the relation; who see too clearly in the oak-and-ivy marriage its parasitism on the one hand and strangulation on the other to be sensible of any picturesque-ness; who feel too that they have capacities and powers of their own which need space and liberty, and some degree of sympathy and help, for their unfolding; and who believe that they have work to do in the world, as important in its own way as any that men do in theirs. Such women have broken into open warfare--not against marriage, but against a marriage which makes true and equal love an impossibility. They feel that as long as women are economically dependent they *cannot* stand up for themselves and insist on those rights which men from stupidity and selfishness will not voluntarily grant them.

On the other hand there are thousands--and one would hope every day more thousands--of men who (whatever their forerunners may have thought) do *not* desire or think it delightful to have a glass continually held up for them to admire themselves in; who look for a partner in whose life and pursuits they can find some interest, rather than for one who has no interest but in them; who think perhaps that they would rather minister than be (like a monkey fed with nuts in a cage) the melancholy object of another person's ministrations; and who at any rate feel that love, in order to be love at all, must be absolutely open and sincere, and free from any sentiment of dependence or inequality. They see that the present cramped condition of women is not only the cause of the false relation between the sexes, but that it is the fruitful source--through its debarment of any common interests--of that fatal boredom of which we have spoken, and which is the bugbear of marriage; and they would gladly surrender all of that masterhood and authority which is supposed to be their due, if they could only get in return something like a frank and level comradeship.

Thus while we see in the present inequality of the sexes an undoubted source of marriage troubles and unsatisfactory alliances, we see also forces at work which are tending to reaction, and to bringing the two nearer again to each other--so that while differentiated they will not perhaps in the future be quite so *much* differentiated as now, but only to a degree which will enhance and adorn, instead of destroy, their sense of mutual sympathy.

There is another point which ought to be considered as contributing to the ill-success of many marriages, and which no doubt is closely connected with that just discussed--but which deserves separate treatment. I mean the harshness of the line, the kind of 'ring-fence,' which social opinion (at any rate in this country) draws round the married pair with respect to their relations to outsiders. On the one hand, and within the fence, society allows practically the utmost passional excess or indulgence, and condones it; on the other hand (I am speaking of the middling bulk of the people, not of the extreme aristocratic and slum classes) beyond that limit, the slightest familiarity, or any expression of affection which might by any possibility be interpreted as deriving from sexual feeling, is sternly anathematized. Marriage, by a kind of absurd fiction, is represented as an oasis situated in the midst of an arid desert--in which latter, it is pretended, neither of the two parties is so fortunate as to find any objects of real affectional interest. If they do they have carefully to conceal the same from the other party.

The result of this convention is obvious enough. The married pair, thus *driven* as well as drawn into closest continual contact with each other, are put through an ordeal which might well cause the stoutest affection to quail. To have to spend all your life with another person is severe; but to have all outside personal interests, except of the most abstract kind, debarred, and if there happens to be any natural jealousy in the case, to have it tenfold increased by public interference, is terrible; and yet unless the contracting parties are fortunate enough to be, both of them, of such a temperament that they are capable of strong attachments to persons of their own sex--and this does not always exclude jealousy--such must be their fate.

It is hardly necessary to say, not only how dull a place this makes the home, but also how narrowing it acts on the lives of the married pair. However appropriate the union may be in itself it cannot be good that it should degenerate--as it tends to degenerate so often, and where man and wife are most faithful to each other--into a mere *égoisme à deux*. And right enough no doubt as a great number of such unions actually are, it must be confessed that the bourgeois marriage as a rule, and just in its most successful and pious and respectable form, carries with it an odious sense of Stuffiness and narrowness, moral and intellectual; and that the type of Family which it provides is too often like that which is disclosed when on turning over a large stone we disturb an insect Home that seldom sees the light.

But in cases where the marriage does not happen to be particularly successful or unsuccessful, when perhaps a true but not overpoweringly intense affection is satiated at a needlessly early stage by the continual and unrelieved impingement of the two personalities on each other, then the boredom resulting is something frightful to contemplate--and all the more so because of the genuine affection behind it, which contemplates with horror its own suicide. The weary couples that may be seen at seaside places and pleasure resorts--the respectable working-man with his wife trailing along by his side, or the highly respectable stock-jobber arm-in-arm with his better and larger half--their blank faces, utter want of any common topic of conversation which has not been exhausted a thousand times already, and their obvious relief when the hour comes which will take them back to their several and divided occupations--these illustrate sufficiently what I mean. The curious thing is that jealousy (accentuated as it is by social opinion) sometimes increases in exact proportion to mutual boredom; and there are thousands of cases of married couples leading a cat-and-dog life, and knowing that they weary each other to distraction, who for that very reason dread all the more to lose sight of each other, and thus never get a chance of that holiday from their own society, and renewal of outside interests, which would make a real good time for them possible.

Thus the sharpness of the line which society draws around the pair, and the kind of fatal snap-of-the-lock with which marriage suddenly cuts them off from the world, not only precluding the two, as might fairly be thought advisable, from sexual, but also barring any openly affectional relations with outsiders, and corroborating the selfish sense of monopoly which each has in the other,--these things lead inevitably to the narrowing down of lives and the blunting of general human interests, to intense mutual ennui, and when (as an escape from these evils) outside relations are covertly indulged in, to prolonged and systematic deceit.

From all which the only conclusion seems to be that marriage must be either alive or dead. As a dead thing it can of course be petrified into a hard and fast formula, but if it is to be a living bond, that living bond must be trusted to, to hold the lovers together; nor be too forcibly stiffened and contracted by private jealousy and public censorship, lest the thing that it would preserve for us perish so, and cease altogether to be beautiful. It is the same with this as with everything else. If we would have a living thing, we must give that thing some degree of liberty--even though liberty bring with it risk. If we would debar all liberty and all risk, then we can have only the mummy and dead husk of the thing.

Thus far I have had the somewhat invidious task, but perhaps necessary as a preliminary one, of dwelling on the defects and drawbacks of the present marriage system. I am sensible that, with due discretion, some things might have been said, which have not been said, in its praise; its successful, instead of its unsuccessful, instances might have been cited; and taking for granted the dependence of women, and other points which have already been sufficiently discussed, it might have been possible to show that the bourgeois arrangement was on the whole as satisfactory as could be expected. But such a course would neither have been sincere nor have served any practical purpose. In view of the actually changing relations between the sexes, it is obvious that changes in the form of the marriage institution are impending, and the questions which are really pressing on folks' mind are: What are those changes going to be? And, Of what kind do we wish them to be?

MARRIAGE

A FORECAST

IN answer to the last question it is not improbable that the casual reader might suppose the writer of these pages to be in favor of a general and indiscriminate loosening of all ties--for indeed it is always easy to draw a large inference even from the simplest expression.

But such a conclusion would be rash. There is little doubt, I think, that the compulsion of the marriage-tie (whether moral, social, or merely legal) acts beneficially in a considerable number of cases--though it is obvious that the more the compelling force takes a moral or social form and the less purely legal it is, the better; and that any changes which led to a cheap and continual transfer of affections from one object to another would be disastrous both to the character and happiness of a population. While we cannot help seeing that the marriage-relation--in order to become the indwelling-place of Love--must be made far more *free* than it is at present, we may also recognize that a certain amount of external pressure is not (as things are at least) without its uses: that, for instance, it tends on the whole to concentrate affectional experience and romance on one object, and that though this may mean a loss at times in breadth it means a gain in depth and intensity; that, in many cases, if it were not for some kind of bond, the two parties, after their first passion for each other was past, and when the unavoidable period of friction had set in, might in a moment of irritation easily fly apart, whereas being forced for a while to tolerate each other's defects they learn thereby one of the best lessons of life-a tender forbearance and gentleness, which as time goes on does not unfrequently deepen again into a more pure and perfect love even than at first--a love founded indeed on the first physical intimacy, but concentrated and intensified by years of linked experience, of twined associations, of shared labors, and of mutual forgiveness; and in the third place that the existence of a distinct tie or pledge discredits the easily-current idea that mere pleasure-seeking is to be the object of the association of the sexes--a phantasmal and delusive notion, which if it once got its head, and the bit between its teeth, might soon dash the car of human advance in ruin to the ground.

But having said thus much, it is obvious that external public opinion and pressure are looked upon only as having an *educational* value; and the question arises whether there is beneath this any *reality* of marriage which will ultimately emerge and make itself felt, enabling men and women to order their relations to each other, and to walk freely, unhampered by props or pressures from without.

And it would hardly be worth while writing on this subject, if one did not believe in some such reality. Practically I do not doubt that the more people think about these matters, and the more experience they have, the more they must ever come to feel that there *is* such a thing as a permanent and life-long union--perhaps a many--life-long-union--founded on some deep elements of attachment and congruity in character; and the more they must come to prize the constancy and loyalty which rivets such unions, in comparison with the fickle passion which tends to dissipate them.

In all men who have reached a certain grade of evolution, and certainly in almost all women, the deep rousing of the sexual nature carries with it a romance and tender emotional yearning towards the object of affection, which lasts on and is not forgotten, even when the sexual attraction has ceased to be strongly felt. This, in favorable cases, forms the basis of what may almost be called an amalgamated personality. That there should exist one other person in the world towards whom all openness of interchange should establish itself, from whom there should be no concealment; whose body should be as dear to one, in every part, as one's own; with whom there should be no sense of Mine or Thine, in property or possession; into whose mind one's thoughts should naturally flow, as it were to know themselves and to receive a new illumination; and between whom and oneself there should be a spontaneous rebound of sympathy in all the joys and sorrows and experiences of life; such is perhaps one of the dearest wishes of the soul. It is obvious however that this state of affairs cannot be reached at a single leap, but must be the gradual result of years of intertwined memory and affection. For such a union Love must lay the foundation, but patience and gentle consideration and self-control must work unremittingly to perfect the structure. At length each lover comes to know the complexion of the other's mind, the wants, bodily and mental, the needs, the regrets, the satisfactions of the other, almost as his or her own--and without prejudice in favor of self rather than in favor of the other; above all, both parties come to know in course of time, and after perhaps some doubts and trials, that the great want, the great need, which holds them together, is not going to fade away into thin air; but is going to become stronger and more indefeasible as the years go on. There falls a sweet, an irresistible, trust over their relation to each other, which consecrates as it were the double life, making both feel that nothing can now divide; and robbing each of all desire to remain, when death has indeed (or at least in outer semblance) removed the other.

So perfect and gracious a union--even if not always realized--is still, I say, the *bonâ fide* desire of most of those who have ever thought about such matters. It obviously yields far more and more enduring joy and satisfaction in life than any number of frivolous relationships. It commends itself to the common sense, so to speak, of the modern mind--and does not require, for its proof, the artificial authority of Church and State. At the same time it is equally evident--and a child could understand this--that it requires some rational forbearance and self-control for its realization, and it is quite intelligible too, as already said, that there *may* be cases in which a little outside pressure, of social opinion, or even actual law, may be helpful for the supplementing or reinforcement of the weak personal self-control of those concerned.

The modern Monogamic Marriage however, certified and sanctioned by Church and State, though apparently directed to this ideal, has for the most part fallen short of it. For in constituting--as in a vast number of cases--a union resting on nothing but the outside pressure of Church and State, it constituted a thing obviously and by its nature bad and degrading; While in its more successful instances by a too great exclusiveness it has condemned itself to a fatal narrowness and stuffiness.

Looking back to the historical and physiological aspects of the question it might of course be contended--and probably with some truth--that the human male is, by his nature and needs, polygamous. Nor is it necessary to suppose that polygamy in certain countries and races is by any means so degrading or unsuccessful an institution as some folk would have it to be. But, as Letourneau in his "Evolution of Marriage" points out, the progress of society in the past has on the whole been from confusion to distinction; and we may fairly suppose that with the progress of our own race (for each race no doubt has its special genius in such matters), and as the spiritual and emotional sides of man develop in relation to the physical, there is probably a tendency for our deeper alliances to become more unitary. Though it might be said that the growing complexity of man's nature would be likely to lead him into more rather than fewer relationships, yet on the other hand it is obvious that as the depth and subtlety of any attachment that will really hold him increases, so does such attachment become more permanent and durable, and less likely to be realized in a number of persons. Woman, on the other hand, cannot be said to be by her physical nature polyandrous as man is polygynous. Though of course there are plenty of examples of women living in a state of polyandry both among savage and civilized peoples, yet her more limited sexual needs, and her long periods of gestation, render one mate physically sufficient for her; while her more clinging affectional nature perhaps accentuates her capacity of absorption in the one.

In both man and woman then we may say that we find a distinct tendency towards the formation of this double unit of wedded life (I hardly like to use the word Monogamy on account of its sad associations)--and while we do not want to stamp such natural unions with any false irrevocability or dogmatic exclusiveness, what we do want is a recognition to-day of the tendency to their formation as a natural *fact*, independent of any artificial laws, just as one might believe in the natural bias of two atoms of certain different chemical substances to form a permanent compound atom or molecule.

It might not be so very difficult to get quite young people to understand this--to understand that even though they may have to contend with some superfluity of passion in early years, yet that the most deeply-rooted desire within them will probably in the end point to a permanent union with one mate; and that towards this end they must be prepared to use self-control against the aimless straying of their passions, and patience and tenderness towards the realization of the union when its time comes. Probably most youths and girls, at the age of romance, would easily appreciate this position; and it would bring to them a much more effective and natural idea of the sacredness of Marriage than they ever get from the artificial thunder of the Church and the State on the subject.

No doubt the suggestion of the mere possibility of any added freedom of choice and experience in the relations of the sexes will be very alarming to some people--but it is so, I think, not because they are at all ignorant that men already take to themselves considerable latitude, and that a distinct part of the undoubted evils that accompany that latitude springs from the fact that it is not recognized; not because they are ignorant that a vast number of respectable women and girls suffer frightful calamities and anguish by reason of the utter *inexperience* of sex in which they are brought up and have to live; but because such good people assume that any the least loosening of the formal barriers between the sexes must mean (and must be meant to mean) an utter dissolution of all ties, and the reign of mere licentiousness. They are convinced that nothing but the most unyielding and indeed exasperating straight-jacket can save society from madness and ruin.

To those, however, who can look facts in the face, and who see that as a matter of fact the *reality* of Marriage is coming more and more to be considered in the public mind in comparison with its *formalities*, the first thought will probably be one of congratulation that after such ages of treatment as a mere formality there should be any sense of the reality of the tie left; and the second will be the question how to give this reality its natural form and expression. Having satisfied ourselves that the formation of a more or less permanent double unit is--for our race and time--on the whole the natural and ascendant law of sex-union, slowly and with whatever exceptions establishing and enforcing itself independently of any artificial enactments that exist, then we shall not feel called upon to tear our hair or rend our garments at the prospect of added freedom for the operation of this force, but shall rather be anxious to consider how it may best *be* freed and given room for its reasonable development and growth.

I shall therefore devote the rest of the chapter to this question. And it will probably seem (looking back to what has already been said) that the points which most need consideration, as means to this end, are (1) the furtherance of the freedom and self-dependence of women; (2) the provision of some rational teaching, of heart and of head, for both sexes during the period of youth; (3) the recognition in marriage itself of a freer, more companionable, and less pettily exclusive relationship; and (4) the abrogation or modification of the present odious law which binds people together for *life*, without scruple, and in the most artificial and ill-assorted unions.

It must be admitted that the first point (1) is of basic importance. As true Freedom cannot be without Love so true Love cannot be without Freedom. You cannot truly give yourself to another, unless you are master or mistress of yourself to begin with. Not only has the general *custom* of the self-dependence and self-ownership of women, in moral, social, and economic respects, to be gradually introduced, but the Law has to be altered in a variety of cases where it lags behind the public conscience in these matters--as in actual marriage, where it still leaves woman uncertain as to her rights over her own body, or in politics, where it still denies to her a voice in the framing of the statutes which are to bind her.

With regard to (2) hardly any one at this time of day would seriously doubt the desirability of giving adequate teaching to boys and girls. That is a point on which we have sufficiently touched, and which need not be farther discussed here. But beyond this it is important, and especially perhaps, as things stand now, for girls-that each youth or girl should personally see enough of the other sex at an early period to be able to form some kind of judgment of his or her relation to that sex and to sex-matters generally. It is monstrous that the first case of sex-glamour--the true nature of which would be exposed by a little experience--should, perhaps for two people, decide the destinies of a life-time. Yet the more the sexes are kept apart, the more overwhelming does this glamour become, and the more ignorance is there, on either side, as to its nature. No doubt it is one of the great advantages of co-education of the sexes, that it tends to diminish these evils. Co-education, games and sports to some extent in common, and the doing away with the absurd superstition that because Corydon and Phyllis happen to kiss each other sitting on a gate, therefore they must live together all their lives, would soon mend matters considerably. Nor would a reasonable familiarity of this kind between the sexes in youth necessarily mean an increase of casual or clandestine sex-relations. But even if casualties did occur they would not be the fatal and unpardonable sins that they now--at least for girls--are considered to be. Though the recognition of anything like common pre-matrimonial sex-intercourse would probably be foreign to the temper of a northern nation; yet it is open to question whether Society here, in its mortal and fetichistic dread of the thing, has not, by keeping the young of both sexes in ignorance and darkness and seclusion from each other, created worse ills and suffering than it has prevented, and whether, by giving sexual acts so feverish an importance, it has not intensified the particular evil that it dreaded, rather than abated it.

In the next place (3) we come to the establishment in marriage itself of a freer and broader and more healthy relationship than generally exists at the present time. Attractive in some ways as the ideal of the exclusive attachment is, it runs the fatal risk, as we have already pointed out, of lapsing into a mere stagnant double selfishness. But, after all, Love is fed not by what it takes, but by what it gives; and the love of man and wife too must he fed by the love they give to others. If they cannot come out of their secluded haven to reach a hand to others, or even to give some boon of affection to those who need it more than themselves, or if they mistrust each other in doing so, then assuredly they are not very well fitted to live together.

A marriage, so free, so spontaneous, that it would allow of wide excursions of the pair from each other, in common or even in separate objects of work and interest, and yet would hold them all the time in the bond of absolute sympathy, would by its very freedom be all the more poignantly attractive, and by its very scope and breadth all the richer and more vital--would be in a sense indestructible; like the relation of two suns which, revolving in fluent and rebounding curves, only recede from each other in order to return again with renewed swiftness into close proximity--and which together blend their rays into the glory of one double star.

It has been the inability to see or understand this very simple truth that has largely contributed to the failure of the Monogamic union. The narrow physical passion of jealousy, the petty sense of private property in another person, social opinion, and legal enactments, have all converged to choke and suffocate wedded love in egoism, lust, and meanness. But surely it is not very difficult (for those who believe in the real thing) to imagine so sincere and natural a trust between man and wife that neither would be greatly alarmed at the other's friendship with a third person, nor conclude at once that it meant mere infidelity--or difficult even to imagine that such a friendship might be hailed as a gain by both parties. And if it is quite impossible (to some people) to see in such intimacies anything but a confusion of all sex-relations and a chaos of mere animal desire, we can only reply that this view exposes with fatal precision the kind of thoughts which our present marriage-system engenders. In order to suppose a rational marriage at all one must credit the parties concerned with *some* modicum of real affection, candor, common sense and self-control.

Withal seeing the remarkable and immense *variety* of love in human nature, when the feeling is really touched--how the love-offering of one person's soul and body is entirely different from that of another person's, so much so as almost to require another name--how one passion is predominantly physical, and another predominantly emotional, and another contemplative, or spiritual, or practical, or sentimental; how in one case it is jealous and exclusive, and in another hospitable and free, and so forth-it seems rash to lay down any very hard and fast general laws for the marriage-relation, or to insist that a real and honorable affection can only exist under this or that special form. It is probably through this fact of the variety of love that it does remain possible, in some cases, for married people to have intimacies with outsiders, and yet to continue perfectly true to each other; and in rare instances, for triune and other such relations to be permanently maintained.

We now come to the last consideration, namely (4) the modification of the present law of marriage. It is pretty clear that people will not much longer consent to pledge themselves irrevocably for life as at present. And indeed there are already plentiful indications of a growing change of practice. The more people come to recognize the sacredness and naturalness of the real union, the less will they be willing to bar themselves from this by a life-long and artificial contract made in their salad days. Hitherto the great bulwark of the existing institution has been the dependence of Women, which has given each woman a direct and most material interest in keeping up the supposed sanctity of the bond--and which has prevented a man of any generosity from proposing an alteration which would have the appearance of freeing himself at the cost of the woman; but as this fact of the dependence of women gradually dissolves out, and as the great fact of the spiritual nature of the true Marriage crystallizes into more clearness--so will the formal bonds which bar the formation of the latter gradually break away and become of small import.

Love when felt at all deeply has an element of transcendentalism in it, which makes it the most natural thing in the world for the two lovers--even though drawn together by a passing sex-attraction--to swear eternal troth to each other; but there is something quite diabolic and mephistophelean in the practice of the Law, which creeping up behind, as it were, at this critical moment, and overhearing the two thus pledging themselves, claps its book together with a triumphant bang, and exclaims:

"There now you are married and done for, for the rest of your natural lives."

What actual changes in Law and Custom the collective sense of society will bring about is a matter which in its detail we cannot of course foresee or determine. But that the drift will be, and must be, towards greater freedom, is pretty clear. Ideally speaking it is plain that anything like a perfect union must have perfect freedom for its condition; and while it is quite supposable that a lover might out of the fullness of his heart *make* promises and give pledges, it is really almost inconceivable that anyone having that delicate and proud sense which marks deep feeling, could possibly *demand* a promise from his loved one. As there is undoubtedly a certain natural reticence in sex, so perhaps the most decent thing in true Marriage would be to say nothing, make no promises--either for a year or a lifetime. Promises are bad at any time, and when the heart is full silence befits it best. Practically, however, since a love of this kind is slow to be realized, since social custom is slow to change, and since the partial dependence and slavery of Woman must yet for a while continue, it is likely for such period that formal contracts of some kind will still be made; only these (it may be hoped) will lose their irrevocable and rigid character, and become in some degree adapted to the needs of the contracting parties.

Such contracts might of course, if adopted, be very various in respect to conjugal rights, conditions of termination, division of property, responsibility for and rights over children, etc. In some cases possibly they might be looked upon as preliminary to a later and more permanent alliance; in others they would provide, for disastrous marriages, a remedy free from the inordinate scandals of the present Divorce Courts. It may however be said that rather than adopt any new system of contracts, public opinion in this country would tend to a simple facilitation of Divorce, and that if the latter were made (with due provision for the children) to depend on mutual consent, it would become little more than an affair of registration, and the scandals of the proceeding would be avoided. In any case we think that marriage-contracts, if existing at all, must tend more and more to become matters of private arrangement as far as the relations of husband and wife are concerned, and that this is likely to happen in proportion as woman becomes more free, and therefore more competent to act in her own right, It would be felt intolerable, in any decently constituted society, that the old blunderbuss of the Law should interfere in the delicate relations of wedded life. As it is to-day the situation is most absurd. On the one hand, having been constituted from times back in favor of the male, the Law still gives to the husband barbarous rights over the person of his spouse; on the other hand, to compensate for this, it rushes in with the farcicalities of Breach of Promise; and in any case, having once pronounced its benediction over a pair--however hateful the alliance may turn out to be to both parties, and however obvious its failure to the whole world--the stupid old thing blinks owlishly on at its own work, and professes itself totally unable to undo the knot which once it tied!

The only point where there is a permanent ground for State-interference--and where indeed there is no doubt that the public authority should in some way make itself felt--is in the matter of the children resulting from any alliance. Here the relation of the pair ceases to be private and becomes social; and the interests of the child itself, and of the nation whose future citizen the child is, have to be safe-guarded. Any contracts, or any proposals of divorce, before they could be sanctioned by the public authority, would have to contain satisfactory provisions for the care and maintenance of the children in such casualties as might ensue; nor ought there to be maintained any legal distinction between 'natural' and 'legitimate' children, since it is clear that whatever individuals or society at large may, in the former case, think of the conduct of the parents, no disability should on that account accrue to the child, nor should the parents (if identifiable) be able to escape their full responsibility for bringing it into the world. If those good people who make such a terrific outcry against folk entering into married life without going through all the abracadabra of the Law, *on account of the children*, would try and get the law altered so as to give illegitimate children the same status and claim on their parents as legitimate children, it would show more genuinely for their anxiety about the children, and would really be doing something in the interests of positive morality.

If it be objected that private contracts, or such facilitations of Divorce as here spoken of, would simply lead to frivolous experimental relationships entered into and broken-off *ad infinitum*, it must be remembered that the responsibility for due rearing and maintenance of children must give serious pause to such a career; and that to suppose that any great mass of the people would find their good iii a kind of matrimonial game of General Post is to suppose that the mass of the people have really never acquired or been taught the rudiments of common sense in such matters--is to suppose a case for which there would hardly be a parallel in the customs of any nation or tribe that we know of.

In conclusion, it is evident that no very great change for the better in marriage-relations can take place except as the accompaniment of deep-lying changes in Society at large; and that alterations in the Law alone will effect but a limited improvement. Indeed it is not very likely, as long as the present commercial order of society lasts, that the existing Marriage-laws--founded as they are on the idea of property--*will* be very radically altered, though they may be to some extent. More likely is it that, underneath the law, the common practice will slide forward into newer customs. With the rise of the new society, which is already outlining itself within the structure of the old, many of the difficulties and bugbears, that at present seem to stand in the way of a more healthy relation between the sexes, will of themselves disappear.

It must be acknowledged, however, that though a gradual broadening out and humanizing of Law and Custom are quite necessary, it cannot fairly be charged against these ancient tyrants that they are responsible for *all* the troubles connected with sex.

There are millions of people to-day who never could marry happily--however favorable the conditions might be--simply because their natures do not contain in sufficient strength the elements of loving surrender to another; and, as long as the human heart is what it is, there will be natural tragedies arising from the willingness or unwillingness of one person to release another when the former finds that his or her love is not returned. While it is quite necessary that these natural tragedies should not be complicated and multiplied by needless legal interference--complicated into the numberless artificial tragedies which are so exasperating when represented on the stage or in romance, and so saddening when witnessed in real life--still we may acknowledge that, short of the millennium, they will always be with us, and that no institution of marriage alone, or absence of institution, will rid us of them. That entire and unswerving refusal to 'cage' another person, or to accept an affection not perfectly free and spontaneous, which will, we are fain to think, be always more and more the mark of human love, must inevitably bring its own price of mortal suffering with it; yet the Love so gained, whether in the individual or in society, will be found in the end to be worth the pang--and as far beyond the other love, as is the wild bird of Paradise that comes to feed out of our hands unbidden more lovely than the prisoner we shut with draggled wings behind the bars. Love is doubtless the last and most difficult lesson that humanity has to learn; in a sense it underlies all the others. Perhaps the time has come for the modern nations when, ceasing to be children, they may even try to learn it.

THE INTERMEDIATE SEX

IN late years (and since the arrival of the New Woman amongst us) many things in the relation of men and women to each other have altered, or et any rate become clearer. The growing sense of equality in habits and customs--university studies, art, music, politics, the bicycle, etc.--all these things have brought about a *rapprochement* between the sexes. If the modem woman is a little more masculine in some ways than her predecessor, the modern man (it is to be hoped), while by no means effeminate, is a little more sensitive in temperament and artistic in feeling than the original John Bull. It is beginning to be recognized that the sexes do not or should not normally form two groups hopelessly isolated in habit and feeling from each other, but that they rather represent the two poles of *one* group--which is the human race; so that while certainly the extreme specimens at either pole are vastly divergent, there are great numbers in the middle region who (though differing corporeally as men and women) are by emotion and temperament very near to each other. We all know women with a strong dash of the masculine temperament, and we all know men whose almost feminine sensibility and intuition seem to belie their bodily form. Nature, it might appear, in mixing the elements which go to compose each individual, does not always keep her two groups of ingredients--which represent the two sexes--properly apart, but often throws them crosswise in a somewhat baffling manner, now this way and now that; yet wisely, we must think--for if a severe distinction of elements were always maintained, the two sexes would soon drift into far latitudes and absolutely cease to understand each other. As it is, there are some remarkable and (we think) indispensable types of character, in whom there is such a union or balance of the feminine and masculine qualities that these people become to a great extent the interpreters of men and women to each other.

There is another point which has become clearer of late. For as people are beginning to see that the sexes form in a certain sense a continuous group, so they are beginning to see that Love and Friendship-- which have been so often set apart from each other as things distinct--are in reality closely related and shade imperceptibly into each other. Women are beginning to demand that Marriage shall mean Friendship as well as Passion; that a comrade-like Equality shall be included in the word Love; and it is recognized that from the one extreme of a 'Platonic' friendship (generally between persons of the same sex) up to the other extreme of passionate love (generally between persons of opposite sex) no hard and fast line can at any point be drawn effectively separating the different kinds of attachment. We know, in fact, of Friendships so romantic in sentiment that they verge into love, we know of Loves so intellectual and spiritual that they hardly dwell in the sphere of Passion.

A moment's thought will show that the general conceptions indicated above--if anywhere near the truth--point to an immense diversity of human temperament and character in matters relating to sex and love; but though such diversity has probably always existed, it has only in comparatively recent times become a subject of study.

More than thirty years ago, however, an Austrian writer, K. H. Ulrichs, drew attention in a series of pamphlets (*Memnon*, *Ara Spei*, *Inclusa*, etc.) to the existence of a class of people who strongly illustrate the above remarks, and with whom especially this paper is concerned. He pointed out that there were people born in such a position--as it were on the dividing line between the sexes--that while belonging distinctly to one sex as far as their bodies are concerned they may be said to belong *mentally* and *emotionally* to the other; that there were men, for instance, who might be described as of feminine soul enclosed in a male body (*anima muliebris in corpore virili inclusa*), or in other cases, women whose definition would be just the reverse. And he maintained that this doubleness of nature was to a great extent proved by the special direction of their love-sentiment. For in such cases, as indeed might be expected, the (apparently) masculine person instead of forming a love-union with a female tended to contract romantic friendships with one of his own sex; while the apparently feminine would, instead of marrying in the usual way, devote herself to the love of another feminine.

People of this kind (*i.e.*, having this special variation of the love-sentiment) he called Urnings; and though we are not obliged to accept his theory about the crosswise connection between 'soul' and 'body,' since at best these words are somewhat vague and indefinite; yet his work was important because it was one of the first attempts, in modern times, to recognize the existence of what might be called an Intermediate sex, and to give at any rate some explanation of it.

Since that time the subject has been widely studied and written about by scientific men and others, especially on the Continent (though in England it is still comparatively unknown), and by means of an extended observation of present-day cases, as well as the indirect testimony of the history and literature of past times, quite a body of general conclusions has been arrived at--of which I propose in the following pages to give some slight account.

Contrary to the general impression, one of the first points that emerges from this study is that 'Urnings,' or Uranians, are by no means so very rare; but that they form, beneath the surface of society, a large class. It remains difficult, however, to get an exact statement of their numbers; and this for more than one reason: partly because, owing to the want of any general understanding of their case, these folk tend to conceal their true feelings from all but their own kind, and indeed often deliberately act in such a manner as to lead the world astray--(whence it arises that a normal man living in a certain society will often refuse to believe that there is a single Urning in the circle of his acquaintance, while one of the latter, or one that understands the nature, living in the same society, can count perhaps a score or more)--and partly because it is indubitable that the numbers do vary very greatly, not only in different countries, but even in different classes in the same country. The consequence of all this being that we have estimates differing very widely from each other. Dr. Grabowsky, a well-known writer in Germany, quotes figures (which we think must be exaggerated) as high as 1 man in every 22, while Dr. Albert Moll (*Die Conträre Sexual-enphfindung*, chap. 3) gives estimates varying from 1 in every 50 to as low as 1 in every 500. These figures apply to such as are exclusively of the said nature, *i.e.*, to those whose deepest feelings of love and friendship go out only to persons of their own sex. Of course, if in addition are included those double-natured people (of whom there is a great number) who experience the normal attachment, with the homogenic tendency in less or greater degree superadded, the estimates must be greatly higher.

In the second place it emerges (also contrary to the general impression) that men and women of the exclusive Uranian type are by no means necessarily morbid in any way--unless, indeed, their peculiar temperament be pronounced in itself morbid. Formerly it was assumed, as a matter of course, that the type was merely a result of disease and degeneration; but now with the examination of the actual facts it appears that, on the contrary, many are fine, healthy specimens of their sex, muscular and well-developed in body, of powerful brain, high standard of conduct, and with nothing abnormal or morbid of any kind observable in their physical structure or constitution. This is, of course, not true of all, and there still remain a certain number of cases of weakly type to support the neuropathic view. Yet it is very noticeable that this view is much less insisted on by the later writers than by the earlier. It is also worth noticing that it is now acknowledged that even in the most healthy cases the special affectional temperament of the

'Intermediate' is, as a rule, ineradicable; so much so that when (as in not a few instances) such men and women, from social or other considerations, have forced themselves to marry, and even have children, they have still not been able to overcome their own bias, or the leaning after all of their life-attachment to some friend of their own sex.

This subject, though obviously one of considerable interest and importance, has been hitherto, as I have pointed out, but little discussed in this country, partly owing to a certain amount of doubt and distrust which has, not unnaturally perhaps, surrounded it. And certainly if the men and women born with the tendency in question were only exceedingly rare, though it would not be fair on that account to ignore them, yet it would hardly be necessary to dwell at great length on their case. But as the class is really, on any computation, numerous, it becomes a duty for society not only to understand them but to help them to understand themselves.

For there is no doubt that in many cases people of this kind suffer a good deal from their own temperament--and yet after all it is possible that they may have an important part to play in the evolution of the race. Anyone who realizes what Love is, the dedication of the heart, so profound, so absorbing, so mysterious, so imperative, and always just in the noblest natures so strong, cannot fail to see how difficult, how tragic even, must often be the fate of those whose deepest feelings are destined from the earliest days to be a riddle and a stumbling-block, unexplained to themselves, passed over in silence by others. To call people of such temperament 'morbid,' and so forth, is of no use. Such a term is, in fact, absurdly inapplicable to many, who are amongst the most active, the most amiable and accepted members of society; besides, it forms no solution of the problem in question, and only amounts to marking down for disparagement a fellow-creature who has already considerable difficulties to contend with. Says Dr. Moll, "Anyone who has seen many Urnings will probably admit that they form a by no means enervated human group; on the contrary, one finds powerful, healthy-looking folk among them"; but in the very next sentence he says that they "suffer severely" from the way they are regarded; and in the manifesto of a considerable community of such people in Germany occur these words, "The rays of sunshine in the night of our existence are so rare, that we are responsive and deeply grateful for the least movement, for every single voice that speaks in our favor in the forum of mankind."

In dealing with this class of folk, then, while I do not deny that they present a difficult problem, I think that just for that very reason their case needs discussion. It would be a great mistake to suppose that their attachments are necessarily sexual, or connected with sexual acts. On the contrary (as abundant evidence shows), they are often purely emotional in their character; and to confuse Uranians (as is so often done) with libertines having no law but curiosity m self-indulgence is to do them a great wrong. At the same time, it is evident that their special temperament may sometimes cause them difficulty in regard to their sexual relations. Into this subject we need not enter. But we may point out how hard it is, especially for the young among them, that a veil of complete silence should be drawn over the subject, leading to the most painful misunderstandings, and perversions and confusions of mind; and that there should be no hint of guidance; nor any recognition of the solitary and really serious inner struggles they may have to face! If the problem is a difficult one--as it undoubtedly is--the fate of those people is already hard who have to meet it in their own persons, without their suffering in addition from the refusal of society to give them any help. It is partly for these reasons, and to throw a little light where it may be needed, that I have thought it might be advisable in this paper simply to give a few general characteristics of the Intermediate types.

As indicated then already, in bodily structure there is, as a rule, nothing to distinguish the subjects of our discussion from ordinary men and women; but if we take the general mental characteristics it appears from almost universal testimony that the male tends to be of a rather gentle, emotional disposition--with defects, if such exist, in the direction of subtlety, evasiveness, timidity, vanity, etc.; while the female is just the opposite--fiery, active, bold and truthful, with defects running to brusqueness and coarseness. Moreover, the mind of the former is generally intuitive and instinctive in its perceptions, with more or less of artistic feeling; while the mind of the latter is more logical, scientific, and precise than usual with the normal woman. So marked indeed are these general characteristics that sometimes by means of them (though not an infallible guide) the nature of the boy or girl can be detected in childhood, before full development has taken place; and needless to say it may often be very important to be able to do this.

It was no doubt in consequence of the observation of these signs that K. H. Ulrichs proposed his theory; and though the theory, as we have said, does not by any means meet *all* the facts, still it is perhaps not without merit, and may be worth bearing in mind.

In the case, for instance, of a woman of this temperament (defined we suppose as "a male soul in a female body") the theory helps us to understand how it might be possible for her to fall *bonâ fide* in love with another woman. Krafft-Ebing, of Vienna, gives the case of a lady (A.), 28 years of age, who fell deeply in love with a younger one (B.). "I loved her divinely," she said. They lived together, and the union lasted four years, but was then broken by the marriage of B. A. suffered in consequence from frightful depression; but in the end--though without real love--got married herself. Her depression however, only increased, and deepened into illness. The doctors, when consulted, said that all would be well if she could only have a child. The husband, who loved his wife sincerely, could not understand her enigmatic behavior. She was friendly to him, suffered his caresses, but for days afterwards remained "dull, exhausted, plagued with irritation of the spine, and nervous." Presently a journey of the married pair led to another meeting with the female friend--who had now been wedded (but also unhappily) for three years. "Both ladies trembled with joy and excitement as they fell into each other's arms, and were thenceforth inseparable. The man found that this friendship relation was a singular one, and hastened the departure. When the opportunity occurred, he convinced himself from the correspondence between his wife and her 'friend' that their letters were exactly like those of two lovers."

It appears that the loves of such women are often very intense, and (as also in the case of male Urnings) life-long. Both classes feel themselves blessed when they love happily. Nevertheless, to many of them it is a painful fact that--in consequence of their peculiar temperament--they are, though fond of children, not in the position to found a family.

We have so far limited ourselves to some very general characteristics of the Intermediate race. It may help to clear and fix our ideas if we now describe more in detail, first, what may be called the extreme and exaggerated types of the race, and then the more normal and perfect types. By doing so we shall get a more definite and concrete view of our subject.

In the first place, then, the extreme specimens--as in most cases of extremes--are not particularly attractive, sometimes quite the reverse. In the male of this kind we have a distinctly effeminate type, sentimental, lackadaisical, mincing in gait and manners, something of a chatterbox, skilful at the needle and in woman's work, sometimes taking pleasure in dressing in woman's clothes; his figure not unfrequently betraying a tendency towards the feminine, large at the hips, supple, not muscular, the face wanting in hair, the voice inclining to be high-pitched, etc.; while his dwelling-room is orderly in the extreme, even natty, and choice of decoration and perfume. His affection too is often feminine in character, clinging, dependent and jealous, as of one desiring to be loved almost more than to love.

On the other hand, as the extreme type of the homogenic female, we have a rather markedly aggressive person, of strong passions, masculine manners and movements, practical in the conduct of life, sensuous rather than sentimental in love, often untidy, and *outré* in attire; her figure muscular, her voice rather low in pitch; her dwelling-room decorated with sporting-scenes, pistols, etc., and not without a suspicion of the fragrant weed in the atmosphere; while her love (generally to rather soft and feminine specimens of her own sex) is often a sort of furor, similar to the ordinary masculine love, and at times almost uncontrollable.

These are types which, on account of their salience, everyone will recognize more or less. Naturally, when they occur, they excite a good deal of attention, and it is not an uncommon impression that most persons of the homogenic nature belong to either one or other of these classes. But in reality, of course, these extreme developments are rare, and for the most part the temperament in question is embodied in men and women of quite normal and unsensational exterior. Speaking of this subject, and the connection between effeminateness and the homogenic nature in men, Dr. Moll says: "It is, however, as well to point out at the outset that effeminacy does not by any means show itself in all Urnings. Though one may find this or that indication in a great number of cases, yet it cannot be denied that a very large percentage, perhaps by far the majority of them, do not exhibit pronounced effeminacy." And it may be supposed that we may draw the same conclusion with regard to women of this class--namely, that the majority of them do not exhibit pronounced masculine habits. In fact, while these extreme cases are of the greatest value from a scientific point of view as marking tendencies and limits of development in certain directions, it would be a serious mistake to look upon them as representative cases of the whole phases of human evolution concerned.

If now we come to what may be called the more normal type of the Uranian man, we find a man who, while possessing thoroughly masculine powers of mind and body, combines with them the tenderer and more emotional soul-nature of the woman--and sometimes to a remarkable degree. Such men, as said, are often muscular and well-built, and not distinguishable in exterior structure and the carriage of body from others of their own sex; but emotionally they are extremely complex, tender, sensitive, pitiful and loving, full of storm and stress, of ferment and fluctuation of the heart; the logical faculty may or may not, in their case, be well-developed, but intuition is always strong; like women they read characters at a glance, and know, without knowing how, what is passing in the minds of others; for nursing and waiting on the needs of others they have often a peculiar gift; at the bottom lies the artist-nature, with the artist's sensibility and perception. Such an one is often a dreamer, of brooding reserved habits, often a musician, or a man of culture, courted in society, which nevertheless does not understand him--though sometimes a child of the people, without any culture, but almost always with a peculiar inborn refinement. De Joux, who speaks on the whole favorably of Uranian men and women, says of the former: "They are enthusiastic for poetry and music, are often eminently skilful in the fine arts, and are overcome with emotion and sympathy at the least sad occurrence. Their sensitiveness, their endless tenderness for children, their love of flowers, their great pity for beggars and crippled folk are truly womanly." And in another passage he indicates the artist-nature, when he says: "The nerve-system of many an Urning is the finest and the most complicated musical instrument in the service of the interior personality that can be imagined."

It would seem probable that the attachment of such an one is of a very tender and profound character; indeed, it is possible that in this class of men we have the love sentiment in one of its most perfect forms--a form in which from the necessities of the situation the sensuous element, though present, is exquisitely subordinated to the spiritual. Says one writer on this subject, a Swiss, "Happy indeed is that man who has won a real Urning for his friend--he walks on roses, without ever having to fear the thorns"; and he adds, "Can there ever be a more perfect sick-nurse than an Urning?" And though these are *ex parte* utterances, we may believe that there is an appreciable grain of truth in them. Another writer, quoted by De Joux, speaks to somewhat the same effect, and may perhaps be received in a similar spirit. "We form," he says, "a peculiar aristocracy of modest spirits, of good and refined habit, and in many masculine circles are the representatives of the higher mental and artistic element. In us dreamers and enthusiasts lies the continual counterpoise to the sheer masculine portion of society--inclining, as it always does, to mere restless greed of gain and material sensual pleasures."

That men of this kind despise women, though a not uncommon belief, is one which hardly appears to be justified. Indeed, though naturally not inclined to "fall in love" in this direction, such men are by their nature drawn rather near to women, and it would seem that they often feel a singular appreciation and understanding of the emotional needs and destinies of the other sex, leading in many cases to a genuine though what is called 'Platonic' friendship. There is little doubt that they are often instinctively sought after by women, who, without suspecting the real cause, are conscious of a sympathetic chord in the homogenic which they miss in the normal man. To quote De Joux once more: "It would be a mistake to suppose that all Urnings must be women-haters. Quite the contrary. They are not seldom the faithfulest friends, the truest allies, and most convinced defenders of women."

To come now to the more normal and perfect specimens of the homogenic *woman*, we find a type in which the body is thoroughly feminine and gracious, with the rondure and fullness of the female form, and the continence and aptness of its movements, but in which the inner nature is to a great extent masculine; a temperament active, brave, originative, somewhat decisive, not too emotional; fond of outdoor life, of games and sports, of science, politics, or even business; good at organization, and well-pleased with positions of responsibility, sometimes indeed making an excellent and generous leader. Such a woman, it is easily seen, from her special combination of qualities, is often fitted for remarkable work, in professional life, or as manageress of institutions, or even as ruler of a country. Her love goes out to younger and more feminine natures than her own; it is a powerful passion, almost of heroic type, and capable of inspiring to great deeds; and when held duly in leash may sometimes become an invaluable force in the teaching and training of girlhood, or in the creation of a school of thought or action among women. Many a Santa Clara, or abbess-founder of religious houses, has probably been a woman of this type; and in all times such women--not being bound to men by the ordinary ties--have been able to work the more freely for the interests of their sex, a cause to which their own temperament impels them to devote themselves *con amore*.

I have now sketched--very briefly and inadequately it is true--both the extreme types and the more healthy types of the 'Intermediate' man and woman: types which can be verified from history and literature, though more certainly and satisfactorily perhaps from actual life around us. And unfamiliar though the subject is, it begins to appear that it is one which modem thought and science will have to face. Of the latter and more normal types it may be said that they exist, and have always existed, in considerable abundance, and from that circumstance alone there is a strong probability that they have their place and purpose. As pointed out there is no particular indication of morbidity about them, unless the special nature of their love-sentiment be itself accounted morbid; and in the alienation of the sexes from each other, of which complaint is so often made to-day, it must be admitted that they do much to fill the gap.

The instinctive artistic nature of the male of this class, his sensitive spirit, his wavelike emotional temperament, combined with hardihood of intellect and body; and the frank, free nature of the female, her masculine independence and strength wedded to thoroughly feminine grace of form and manner; may be said to give them both, through their double nature, command of life in all its phases, and a certain freemasonry of the secrets of the two sexes which may well favor their function as reconcilers and interpreters. Certainly it is remarkable that some of the world's greatest leaders and artists have been dowered either wholly or in part with the Uranian temperament--as in the cases of Michel Angelo, Shakespeare, Marlowe, Alexander the Great, Julius Caesar, or, among women, Christine of Sweden, Sappho the poetess, and others.

THE FREE SOCIETY

TAKING, finally, a somewhat wider outlook over the whole subject of the most intimate human relations than was feasible in the foregoing chapters, we may make a few general remarks.

One of the great difficulties in the way of arriving at any general understanding on questions of sex--and one which we have already had occasion to note--is the extraordinary diversity of feeling and temperament which exists in these matters. Needless to say, this is increased by the reserve, natural or artificial, which so seldom allows people to express their sentiments quite freely. In the great ocean there are so many currents, cold and warm, fresh, and salt, and brackish; and each one thinks that the current in which he lives is the whole ocean. The man of the world hardly understands, certainly does not sympathize with, the recluse or ascetic--and the want of appreciation is generally returned; the maternal, the sexual, and the philanthropic woman, are all somewhat unintelligible to each other; the average male and the average female approach the great passion from totally different sides, and are continually at odds over it; and again both of these great sections of humanity fail entirely to understand that other and well-marked class of persons whose love-attraction is (inborn) towards their own sex, and indeed hardly recognize the existence of such a class, although as a matter of fact it is a large and important one in every community. In fad, all these differences have hitherto been so little the subject of impartial study that we are still amazingly in the dark about them.

When we look back to History, and the various customs of the world in different races and tribes and at different periods of time, we seem to see these natural divergences of human temperament reflected in the extraordinary diversity of practices that have obtained and been recognized. We see that, in some cases, the worship of sex took its place beside the worship of the gods; and--what appears equally strange--that the orgiastic rites and saturnalia of the early world were intimately connected with religious feeling; we find that, in other cases, asceticism and chastity and every denial of the flesh were glorified and looked upon as providing the only way to the heavenly kingdom; we discover that marriage has been instituted and defined and sanctioned in endless forms, each looked upon as the only moral and possible form in its own time and country; and that the position of women under these different conditions has varied in the most remarkable way--that in some of the primitive societies where group-marriages of one kind or another prevailed their dignity and influence were of the highest, that under some forms of Monogamy, as among the Nagas of Bengal, women have been abjectly degraded, while under other forms, as in Ancient Egypt and the later Roman Empire, they have been treated with respect; and so forth. We cannot fail, I say, to recognize the enormous diversity of practice which has existed over the world in this matter of the relations of the sexes; nor, I may add, can we venture--if we possess any sense of humanity--to put our finger down finally on any one custom or institution, and say, Here alone is the right way.

On the contrary, it seems to me probable that, broadly speaking, a really free Society will accept and make use of all that has gone before. If, as we have suggested, historical forms and customs are the indication of tendencies and instincts which still exist among us, then the question is, not the extinction of these tendencies, but the finding of the right place and really rational expression for them. That the various customs of past social life do subsist on beneath the surface of modern society, we know well enough; and it seems likely that society in the future will have to recognize and to a certain extent transform these. In fact, in recognizing it will inevitably transform, for it will bring them out from darkness into light, and from the old conditions and surroundings of the past societies into the new conditions of the modern. Polygamy, for instance, or some related form of union, supposing it really did spontaneously and naturally arise in a society which gave perfect freedom and independence to women in their relation to men, would be completely different in character from the old-world polygamy, and would cease to act as a degrading influence on women, since it would be the spontaneous expression of their attachment to each other and to a common husband; Monogamy, under similar circumstances, would lose its narrowness and stuffiness; and the life of the Hetaira, that is of the woman who chooses to be the companion of more than one man might not be without dignity, honor, and sincere attachment.

Again it is easy to see, if the sense of cleanness in sex ever does come in, if the physical body ever becomes clean (which it certainly is not now-a-days), clean and beautiful and accepted, within and without--and this of course it can only be through a totally changed method of life, through pure and clean food, nakedness to a large extent, and a kind of saturation with the free air and light of heaven; and if the mental and moral relation ever becomes clean, which can only be with the freedom of woman and the sincerity of man, and so forth; it is easy to see how entirely all this would alter our criticism of the various sex-relations, and our estimate of their place and fitness.

In the wild and even bacchanalian festivals of all the earlier nations, there was an element of Nature--sex-mysticism which has become lost in modern times, or quite unclean and depraved; yet we cannot but see that this element is a vital and deep-lying one in humanity, and in some form or other will probably reassert itself. On the other hand, in the Monkish and other ascetic movements of Christian or pre-Christian times, with their efforts towards a proud ascendancy over the body, there was (commonly sneered at though it may be in the modern West) an equally vital and important truth, which will have to be rehabilitated. The practices of former races and times, however anomalous they may sometimes appear to us, were after all in the main the expression of needs and desires which *had* their place in human nature, and which still for the most part have their place there, even though overlaid and suppressed beneath existing convention; and who knows, in all the stifled longings of thousands and thousands of hearts, how the great broad soul of Humanity--which reaches to and accepts all times and races--is still ever asserting herself and swelling against the petty bonds of this or that age? The nearer Society comes to its freedom and majority the more lovingly will it embrace this great soul within it, and recognizing in all the customs of the past the partial efforts of that soul to its own fulfillment will refuse to deny them, but rather seek, by acceptance and reunion, to transform and illumine them all.

Possibly, to some, these remarks will only suggest a return to general confusion and promiscuity; and of course to such people they will seem inconsistent with what has been said before on the subject of the real Marriage and the tendency of human beings, as society evolves, to seek more and more sincerely a life-long union with their chosen mate; but no one who thinks twice about the matter could well make this mistake. For the latter tendency, that namely "from confusion to distinction," is in reality the tendency of all evolution, and cannot be set aside. It is in the very nature of Love that as it realizes its own aim it should rivet always more and more towards a durable and distinct relationship, nor rest till the permanent mate and equal is found. As human beings progress their relations to each other must become much *more* definite and distinct instead of less so--and there is no likelihood of society in its onward march lapsing backward, so to speak, to formlessness again.

But it is just the advantage of this onward movement towards definiteness that it allows-as in the evolution of all organic life--of more and more *differentiation* as the life rises higher in the scale of existence. If society should at any future time recognize--as we think likely it will do--the variety of needs of the human heart and of human beings, it will not therefore confuse them, but will see that these different needs indicate different functions, all of which may have their place and purpose. If it has the good sense to tolerate a Nature-festival now and then, and a certain amount of animalism let loose, it will not be so foolish as to be unable to distinguish this from the deep delight and happiness of a permanent spiritual mating; or if it recognizes in some case, a woman's temporary alliance with a man for the sake of obtaining a much-needed child, it will not therefore be so silly as to mark her down for life as a common harlot. It will allow in fact that there are different forms and functions of the love-sentiment, and while really believing that a life-long comradeship (possibly with little of the sexual in it) is the most satisfying form, will see that a cast-iron Marriage-custom which, as to-day, expects two people either to live eternally in the same house and sit on opposite sides of the same table, or else to be strangers to each other--and which only recognizes two sorts of intimacy, orthodox and criminal, wedded and adulterous--is itself the source of perpetual confusion and misapprehension.

No doubt the Freedom of Society in this sense, and the possibility of a human life which shall be the fluid and ever-responsive embodiment of true Love in all its variety of manifestation, goes with the Freedom of Society in the economic sense. When mankind has solved the industrial problem so far that the products of our huge mechanical forces have become a common heritage, and no man or woman is the property-slave of another, then some of the causes which compel prostitution, property-marriage, and other perversions of affection, will have disappeared; and in such economically free society human unions may at last take place according to their own inner and true laws.

Hitherto we have hardly thought whether there were any inner laws or not; our thoughts have been fixed on the outer; and the Science of Love, if it may so be called, has been strangely neglected. Yet if, putting aside for a moment all convention and custom, one will look quietly within himself, he will perceive that there are most distinct and inviolable inner forces, binding him by different ties to different people, and with different and inevitable results according to the quality and the nature of the affection bestowed--that there is in fact in that world of the heart a kind of cosmical harmony and variety, and an order almost astronomical.

This is noticeably true of what may be called the planetary law of distances in the relation of people to one another. For of some of the circle of one's acquaintance it may be said that one loves them cordially at a hundred miles' distance; of others that they are dear friends at a mile; while others again are indispensable far nearer than that. If by any chance the friend whose planetary distance is a mile is forced into closer quarters, the only result is a violent development of repulsion and centrifugal force, by which probably he is carried even beyond his normal distance, till such time as he settles down into his right place; while on the other hand if we are separated for a season from one who by right is very near and who we know belongs to us, we can bids our time, knowing that the forces of return will increase with the separation. How marked and definite these personal distances are may be gathered from considering how largely the art of life consists in finding and keeping them, and how much trouble arises from their confusion, and from the way in which we often only find them out after much blundering and suffering and mutual recrimination.

So marked indeed are these and other such laws that they sometimes suggest that there really is a cosmic world of souls, to which we all belong--a world of souls whose relations are eternal and clearly-defined; and that our terrestrial relations are merely the working-out and expression of far antecedent and unmodifiable facts--an idea which for many people is corroborated by the curious way in which, often at the very first sight, they become aware of their exact relation to a new-comer. In some cases this brings with it a strange sense of previous intimacy, hard to explain; and in other cases, not so intimate, it still will seem to fix almost instantaneously the exact propinquity of the relation--so that though in succeeding years, or even decades of years, the mutual acquaintanceship may work itself out with all sorts of interesting and even unexpected developments and episodes, yet this *mean distance* does not vary during the whole time, so to speak, by a single hair's breadth.

Is it possible, we may ask (in the light of such experiences), that there really is a Free Society in another and deeper sense than that hitherto suggested--a society to which we all in our inmost selves consciously or unconsciously belong--the Rose of souls that Dante beheld in Paradise, whose every petal is an individual, and an individual only through its union with all the rest--the early Church's dream, of an eternal Fellowship in heaven and on earth--the Prototype of all the brotherhoods and communities that exist on this or any planet; and that the innumerable selves of men, united in the one Self, members of it and of one another (like the members of the body) stand in eternal and glorious relationship bound indissolubly together? We know of course that the reality of things cannot be adequately expressed by such phrases as these, or by any phrases, yet possibly some such conception comes as near the truth as any *one* conception can; and, making use of it, we may think that our earthly relations are a continual attempt--through much blindness and ineffectualness and failure--to feel after and to find these true and permanent relations to others.

Surely in some subtle way if one person sincerely love another, heart and soul, that other becomes a part of the lover, indissolubly wrought into his being Mentally the two grow and become compact together. No thought that the lover thinks, no scene that he looks on, but the impress of his loved one in some way is on it--so that as long as he exists (here or anywhere) with his most intimate self that other is threaded and twined inseparable. So clinging is the relation. Perhaps in the outer world we do not always see such relations quite clear, and we think when death or other cause removes the visible form from us that the hour of parting has come. But in the inner world it is clear enough, and we divine that we and our mate are only two little petals that grow near each other on the great Flower of Eternity; and that it is because we are near each other in that unchanging world, that in the world of change our mortal selves are drawn together, and will be drawn always, wherever and whenever they may meet.

But since the petals of the immortal Flower are by myriads and myriads, so have we endless lessons of soul-relationship to learn--some most intimate, others doubtless less so, but all fair and perfect--so soon as we have discovered what these relationships really are, and are in no confusion of mind about them. For even those that are most distant are desirable, and have the germ of love in them, so soon as they are touched by the spirit of Truth (which means the fearless statement of the life which is in us, in poise against the similar statement of life in others); since, indeed, the spirit of Truth is the life of the whole, and only the other side of that Love which binds the whole together.

Looking at things in this light it would seem to us that the ideal of terrestrial society for which we naturally strive is that which would embody best these enduring and deep-seated relations of human souls; and that every society, as far as it is human and capable of holding together, is in its degree a reflection of the celestial City. Never is the essential, real, Society quite embodied in any mundane Utopia, but ever through human history is it working unconsciously in the midst of mortal affairs and impelling towards an expression of itself.

At any rate, and however all this may be, the conclusion is that the *inner* laws in these matters--the inner laws of the sex-passion, of love, and of all human relationship--must gradually appear and take the lead, since they alone are the powers which can create and uphold a rational society; and that the outer laws--since they are dead and lifeless things--must inevitably disappear. Real love is only possible in the freedom of society; and freedom is only possible when love is a reality. The subjection of sex-relations to legal conventions is an intolerable bondage, but of course it is a bondage inescapable as long as people are slaves to a merely physical desire. The two slaveries in fact form a sort of natural counterpoise, the one to the other. When love becomes sufficient of a reality to hold the sex-passion as its powerful yet willing servant, the absurdity of Law will be at an end.

Surely it is not too much to suppose that a reasonable society will be capable of seeing these and other such things; that it will neither on the one hand submit to a cast-iron system depriving it of all grace and freedom of movement, nor on the other hand be in danger of falling into swamps of promiscuity; but that it will have the sense to recognize and establish the innumerable and delicate distinctions of relation which build up the fabric of a complex social organism. It will understand perhaps that sincere Love is, as we have said, a real fact and its own justification, and that however various or anomalous or unusual may be the circumstances and combinations under which it appears, it demands and has to be treated by society with the utmost respect and reverence--as a law unto itself, probably the deepest and most intimate law of human life, which only in the most exceptional cases, if at all, may public institutions venture to interfere with.

In all these matters it is surprising to-day what children we are--how we take the innumerable flowers and try to snip and shape all their petals and leaves to one sorry pattern, or how with a kind of grossness we snatch at and destroy in a few moments the bloom and beauty which are rightfully undying. Perhaps it will only be for a society more fully grown than ours to understand the wealth and variety of affectional possibilities which it has within itself, and the full enchantment of the many relations in which the romance of love by a tender discrimination and æsthetic continence is preserved for years and decades of years in, as it were, a state of evergrowing perfection.

REMARKS AND NOTES

SOME REMARKS

ON THE

EARLY STAR AND SEX WORSHIPS

THERE seems to be a certain propriety in the fact that two of the oldest and most universal cults have been the worship of the stars on the one hand, and of the emblems of sex on the other. The stars, the most abstract, distant and universal of phenomena, symbols of changeless law and infinitude, before which human will and passion sink into death and nothingness; and sex, the very focus of passion and desire, the burning point of the will to live. Between these two poles the human mind has swayed since the eldest time.

With these earlier worships, too, the later religions have mingled in inextricable but not meaningless entanglement. The Passover, the greatest feast of the Jews, borrowed from the Egyptians, handed down to become the supreme festival of Christianity, and finally blending in the North of Europe with the worship of the Norse goddess Eastre, is as is well known closely connected with the celebration of the Spring equinox and of the *passing over* of the sun from south to north of the equator--*i.e.*, from his winter depression to his summer dominion. The Sun, at the moment of passing the equinoctial point, stood 3000 years ago in the Zodiacal constellation of the Ram or he-lamb. The Lamb, therefore, became the symbol of the young triumphant god. The Israelites (Exodus xii. 14.) were to smear their doorways (symbol of the passage from darkness to light) with the blood of the Lamb, in remembrance of the conflict of their god with the powers of darkness (the Egyptians). At an earlier date--owing to the precession of the equinoxes--the sun at the spring passage stood in the constellation of the Bull; so, in the older worships of Egypt and of Persia and of India, it was the Bull that was sacred and the symbol of the god. Moses is said to have abolished the worship of the Calf and to have consecrated the Lamb at the passover--and this appears to be a rude record of the fact that the astronomical changes were accompanied or followed by priestly changes of ceremonial. Certainly it is curious that in later Egyptian, times the bull-headed god was deposed in favor of the ram-headed god Ammon; and that Christianity adopted the Lamb for the symbol of its Savior.

Similarly, the Virgin Mary with the holy Child in her arms can be traced by linear descent from the early Christian Church at Alexandria up through the later Egyptian times to Isis with the infant Horus, and thence to the constellation Virgo shining in the sky. In the representation of the Zodiac in the Temple of Denderah (in Egypt) the figure of Virgo is annotated by a smaller figure of Isis with Horus in her arms; and the Roman church fixed the celebration of Mary's assumption into glory at the very date (15th August) of the said constellation's disappearance from sight in the blaze of the solar rays, and her birth on the date (8th Sep.) of the same constellation's reappearance.

The history of Israel reveals a long series of avowedly sexual and solar worships carried on alongside with that of Jehovah--worships of Baal, Ashtaroth, Nehushtan, the Host of Heaven, etc.--and if we are to credit the sacred record, Moses himself introduced the notoriously sexual Tree and Serpent worship (Numbers xxi. 9, and 2 Kings xviii. 4.); while Solomon, not without dramatic propriety, borrowed from the Phoenicians the two phallic pillars surmounted by pomegranate wreaths, called Jachin and Boaz, and placed them in front of his temple (I Kings Vii. 21). The Cross itself (identical as a symbol with the *phallus* of the Greeks and the *lingam* of the East), the Fleur de Lys, which has the same signification, and the Crux Ansata, borrowed by the early Christians from Egypt and indicating the union of male and female, are woven and worked into the priestly vestments and altar-cloths of Christianity, just as the astronomical symbols are woven and worked into its Calendar, and both sets of symbols, astronomical and sexual, into the very construction of our Churches and Cathedrals. Jesus himself--so entangled is the worship of this greatest man with the earlier cults--is purported to have been born like the other sungods, Bacchus, Apollo, Osiris, on the 25th day of December, the day of the sun's re-birth (*i.e.*, the first day which obviously lengthens after the 21st December--the day of the doubting apostle Thomas!) and to have died upon an instrument which, as already hinted, was ages before and all over the world held in reverence as a sexual symbol.

I have only touched the fringe of this great subject. The more it is examined into the more remarkable is the mass of corroborative matter belonging to it. The conclusion towards which one seems to be impelled is that these two great primitive ideas,, sexual and astronomical, are likely to remain the poles of human emotion in the future, even as they have been in the past.

Some cynic has said that the two great ruling forces of mankind are Obscenity and Superstition. Put in a less paradoxical form, as that the two ruling forces are Sex and the belief in the Unseen, the saying may perhaps be accepted. To call the two Love and Faith (as Dr. Bucke does in his excellent book on *Man's Moral Nature*) is perhaps to run the risk of becoming *too* abstract and spiritual.

Roughly speaking we may say that the worship of Sex and Life characterized the Pagan races of Europe and Asia Minor anterior to Christianity, while the worship of Death and the Unseen has characterized Christianity. It remains for the modern nations to accept both Life and Death, both the Greek and the Hebrew elements, and all that these general terms denote, in a spirit of the fullest friendliness and sanity and fearlessness.

A curious part of all the old religions, Pagan or Christian--and this connects itself with the above--is Asceticism: that occasional instinct of voluntary and determined despite to the body and its senses. Even in the wildest races, rejoicing before all things in the consciousness of Life, we find festivals of fierce endurance and torments willingly undergone with a kind of savage glee; and during the Christian centuries--monks, mystics, and world-spiting puritans--this instinct was sometimes exalted into the very first place of honor. I suppose it will have to be recognized--whatever absurd aberrations the tendency may have been liable to--that it is a basic thing in human nature, and as ineradicable in its way as the other equally necessary instinct towards Pleasure. To put it in another way, perhaps the ordinary Hedonism makes a mistake in failing to recognize the joy of Ascendancy, and (if it is not a 'bull' to say so) the pleasure which lies in the denial of pleasure. In order to enjoy life one must be a master of life--for to be a slave to its inconsistencies can only mean torment; and in order to enjoy the senses one must be master of *them.* To dominate the actual world you must, like Archimedes, base your fulcrum somewhere beyond.

In such moods a man delights to feel his supremacy, not only over the beasts of the field, but over his own bodily and mental powers: no ordinary pleasure so great, but its rejection serves to throw out into relief this greater; no task so stern, but endurance is sterner; no pain so fierce but it wakes the soul to secret laughter. If there is something narrow in the creed of the ascetic on its negative side--that of denial--one cannot but feel that on its positive side, the establishment of authority and kingship, it has a real and vital meaning.

In another mood, however (equally undeniable and important), man acknowledges his delight in life, and gives the rein to his desires to chariot him to the extremest bounds of his kingdom. The kiss of the senses is beautiful beyond all and every abstraction; the touch of the sunlight, the glory of form and color, the magic of sweet sound, the joy of human embraces, the passion of sex--all so much the more perfect because they are as it were something divine made actual and realizable. In such a mood asceticism in any form seems the grossest impiety and folly, and the pursuit of the Unseen a mere abandonment of the world for its shadow.

Are not these two moods both necessary--the great rhythmical heart-beat, the *systole* and *diastole*, of the human soul? The one, a going forth and gathering of materials from all sources, the other an organizing of them under the most perfect light, or rather (it may be said) a consumption of them to feed the most perfect flame; the one centrifugal, the other centripetal; the one individual, the other universal; and so forth--each required for the purposes of the other, and making the other possible?

Do we not want a truly experiential view of what may be called Religion--derived from the largest actual acquaintance with, and acceptance of, all the facts both of mundane and extra-mundane consciousness--neither (like some secularists) denying the one, nor (like some religionists) minimizing or contemning the other? And is it not possible that in the early Star and Sex worships we have evidence of the attempt of the human mind to establish some such sane polarity?

NOTE

ON THE PRIMITIVE GROUP-MARRIAGE

ONE of the early forms of union among human beings appears to have been that of the *Group-marriage*, which was an alliance between a group of men and a group of women. It had various forms, but rested in general on the fact that the women in primitive societies did not, on marriage, leave their parental habitation but remained there and were visited by the men--by one man first, who would come with presents of game, etc., from the chase, and would afterwards bring his 'brothers' or friends. Thus in general a group of 'brothers' would come into relation with a group of 'sisters.' In such a state of society, however, it is obvious that parentage would be very uncertain, and the terms brother and sister would not always have the stricter meanings which we give them. Such a group-marriage was the, 'Punalua' or 'friend' marriage of Morgan's North American Indians; which is also supposed by Marx and Engels to have prevailed at an early time throughout Polynesia. See Lewis Morgan's *Ancient*

Society and Friedrich Engels' *Ursprung der Familie.* In later times the group-marriage became restricted in various directions, according to the genius of various races--marriage of cousins, for instance, being severely prohibited among some barbaric tribes, while among others *all* relatives (in the maternal line) were barred. Thus ultimately, in some quarters, sprang up a Pair-marriage; which however was only loosely defined; which had much of the old group-marriage lingering round it; and in which the children still belonged to the woman, and descent was traced in the maternal line only.

Under these conditions of society the woman was comparatively well off. Remaining as she did in her own *gens* or clan and among her own relations, and the husband being as it were a visitor from the outside, she was by no means subject to him; in fact, in order to gain access, he had to make himself agreeable not only to her but to her own family! She had the disposal of the, children; there was no danger of their being sequestrated to her husband; and whatever little property she had she could leave to them; to her was all the honor of ancestry, The husband on the other hand, even if he knew which his own children were, could see little of them, and could not leave his possessions to them without alienating those possessions from his clan--which the clan-customs would not permit. Thus in marriage he practically had to take the second place.

With the growth however of property and the sense of property, there came a time when the men could stand this state of affairs no longer, and insisted, violently at first, in carrying off the women and locating them in their own tents and among their own clans--a change rudely recorded probably in legends like the Rape of the Sabines, and in all the later customs of Marriage by Capture. And with this change marriage took on new forms. Women became the property of their husbands; they ceased to hold property of their own, in their children or in anything else; and descent was traced through the males only. In the Patriarchal system marriage was closely akin to slavery. Polygamy and Monogamy were the two resulting institutions.

Polyandry may perhaps be looked upon as a survival of the group-marriage in a special form adapted to warrior races; but--as Engels remarks--both Polygamy and Polandry in any strict sense can only be regarded as exceptional institutions, since if they were general in any one country, that would imply a great preponderance of one sex over the other--unless indeed the two institutions existed side by side in the same country, which notoriously never happens. As a matter of fact in oriental countries Polygamy is confined to the rich, and is so to speak a luxury, within reach of the few only.

Thus it would appear that from the first, in oriental countries, the practices of polygamy and monogamy were intermixed. In Greece and Rome polygamy ceased to be recognized as an institution; though concubinage in one form or another remained. The Monogamic marriage became the legal institution; and the woman was handed over to the man as his chattel; was bought symbolically with his money, in the marriage ceremony; and had at first no more rights of her own than a chattel. In the later times, however, of the Roman Empire, with the institution of the dowry and the power granted to women of holding property, together with the great facilities of divorce allowed, the position of the Roman matron became much improved. And in modern European countries the monogamic institution seems to have passed or be passing through somewhat the same stages as in ancient Greece or Rome.

ON JEALOUSY

A GREAT disturber of the celestial order of Love is jealousy-that brand of physical passion which carried over into the emotional regions of the mind will sometimes rage there like a burning fire. One may distinguish two kinds of jealousy, a natural and an artificial. The first arises perhaps from the real uniqueness of the relationship between two persons--at any rate as it appears to one of them--and the endeavor to stamp this uniqueness on the whole relationship, sexual and moral-especially on the sexual relationship. This kind of jealousy seems in a sense natural and normal, at any rate for a period; but when the personal relation between the two parties has been fully and confessedly established, and is no more endangered, the feeling does often I think (equally naturally) die away; and may do so quite well without damaging the intimacy and uniqueness of the alliance. This jealousy is felt with terrible keenness and intensity by lovers before the consummation of their passion, and perhaps for a year or two afterwards--though it may be protracted rather indefinitely in the case where the alliance, on one side at any rate, is not quite satisfactory.

The other kind of jealousy rests on the sense of property, and is the kind that is often felt by the average husband and wife long after honeymooning days--by the husband not because of his especial devotion to his partner, but because he is furious at the idea of her disposing as she likes with what he considers *his property*; and by the wife because she is terrified at the thought that her matrimonial clothes-peg, from which depend all her worldly prospects, may vanish away or become the peg for another woman's clothes. This kind of jealousy is more especially the product of immediate social conditions, and is in that sense artificial. Though probably not quite so heart-rending as the other, it is often passionate enough, and lasts on indefinitely, like a chronic disease.

In early times, with the more communistic feeling of primitive societies, and with customs (like group-marriage) which allowed some latitude in sex-relation, jealousy though strong was not probably a very great force. But with the growth of individualism in life and in love, with the rise of the sense of property under civilization and the accentuation of every personal feeling in what may be called the *cellular* state of society, the passion became one of fearful and convulsive power and fury; as is borne witness to by numberless dramas and poems and romances of the historical period. In the communism and humanism of the future, as the sense of property declines, and as Love rises more and more out of mere blind confusion with the sex-act, we may fairly hope that the artificial jealousy will disappear altogether, and that the other form of the passion will subside again into a comparatively reasonable human emotion.

ON THE FAMILY

A CHANGE somewhat similar to that in the position of jealousy has taken place in the rôle of the Family during the progress of society into and through the period of civilization. In the primitive human association the Family was large in extent, and in outline vague; the boundaries of kinship, in cases where the woman might have several husbands, or the husband several wives, were hard to trace; paternal feeling was little or not at all developed; and the whole institution rested on the maternal instinct of care for the young. In the middle societies of civilization, and with monogamic arrangements, the Family grew exceedingly definite in form and circumscribed in extent. The growth of property and competition, and the cellular system of society, developed a kind of warfare between the units of which society was composed. These units were families. The essential communism and fraternity of society at large was dwarfed now and contracted into the limits of the family; and this institution acquired an extraordinary importance from the fact that it alone kept alive and showed in miniature (intensified by the darkness and chaos and warfare outside) the sacred fire of human fraternity. So great was this importance in fact that the Holy Family became one of the central religious conceptions of the civilized period, and it was commonly thought that society owed its existence to the Family--instead of, as was the case, the truth being the reverse, namely that the Family was the condensation of the principle which had previously existed, though diffused and unconscious, throughout society.

The third and future stage is of course easy to see--that is, the expansion again of the conception of the family *consciously* into the fraternity and communism of all society. It is obvious that as this takes place the family will once more lose its definition of outline and merge more and more again with the larger social groups in which it is embedded--but not into the old barbaric society in which the conception of human fellowship lay diffused and only dimly auroral, but into the newer society in which it shall be clear and all-illuminating as the sun.

Thus the Family institution in its present form, and as far as that form may be said to be artificial, will doubtless pass away. Nevertheless there remains of course, and must remain, its natural or physiological basis--namely the actual physical relation of the parents to each other and to the child. One perhaps of the most valuable results of the Monogamic family institution under civilization has been the development of the paternal feeling for the child, which in primitive society was so weak. To-day the love of man and wife for each other is riveted, as it never was in ancient days, by the tender beauty of the child-face, in which each parent sees with strange emotion his own features blended with the features of his loved one--the actual realization of that union which the lovers so desired, and which yet so often seemed to them after all not consummated. The little prolongation of oneself, carrying in its eyes the star-look of another's love, and descending a stranger into the world to face a destiny all its own, touches the most personal and mortal-close feelings (as well as perhaps the most impersonal) of the heart. And while to-day this sight often reconciles husband and wife to the legal chains which perforce hold them together, in a Free Society, we may hope, it will more often be the sign and seal of a love which neither requires nor allows any kind of mechanical bond.

ON PREVENTIVE CHECKS TO POPULATION

THIS is no doubt a complex and difficult subject. Nature from far back time has provided in the most determined and obstinate way for the perpetuation of organic life, and has endowed animals, and even plants, with a strong sexual instinct. By natural selection this instinct tends, it would seem, to be accentuated; and in the higher animals and man it sometimes attains a pitch almost of ferocity. In civilized man this effect is further increased by the intensity of consciousness, which reflects desire on itself, as well as by collateral conditions of life and luxury.

In the animal and plant world generally, and up to the realm of Man, Nature appears to be perfectly lavish in the matter, and careless of the waste of seed and of life that may ensue, provided her object of race-propagation is attained; and naturally when the time arrives that Man, objecting to this waste, faces up to the problem, he finds it no easy one to solve.

And not only Man (the male) objects to lower

Nature's method of producing superfluous individuals only to kill them off again in the struggle for existence; but Woman objects to being a mere machine for perpetual reproduction.

For meeting this difficulty, the only way commonly proposed--short of a continence and self-control almost amounting to total abstinence--is the adoption of some kind of artificial preventatives to conception. But it must be acknowledged that artificial checks to population are for the most part very unsatisfactory. Their uncertainty, their desperate matter-of-factness, so fatal to real feeling, the probability that they are in one way or another dangerous or harmful, and then their one-sidedness, since here-as so often in matters of sex--the man's satisfaction is largely at the cost of the woman: all these things are against them. One method however--that which consists in selecting, for sexual congress, a certain part of the woman's monthly cycle, can hardly be called artificial, and is altogether the least open to the objections cited. Its success truly is not absolutely certain, but is perhaps sufficiently nearly so for the general purpose of regulating the family; and if the method involves some self-control, it does not at any rate make an impracticable demand in that direction.

There is also another method which, while it may seem at first to demand considerable self-control, does really perhaps in the end yield fuller satisfaction than any. Late authors have pointed out that a distinction can and should be made between sexual intercourse for the definite purpose of race-propagation and sexual intercourse for simple union--that, in fact, the methods are different. Mrs. A. B. Stockham, in her little book "Karezza" (Stockham Publishing Co., Chicago), dwells on this subject. She indicates that for the latter purpose, *i.e.*, union, there may be complete and indeed prolonged bodily conjunction; but the whole process being kept (by the use of a certain amount of physical control) on the emotional plane and the plane of endearment and affection, there need be no actual emission, and the final orgasm may be avoided. "Given abundant time and mutual reciprocity, the interchange becomes satisfactory and complete without emission or crisis by either party." The result of this is really a more complete *soul-union*, a strange and intoxicating exchange of life, and transmutation of elements. "The whole being of each is submerged in the other, and an exquisite exaltation experienced. . . . In the course of an hour the physical tension subsides, the spiritual exaltation increases, and not uncommonly visions of a transcendent life are seen, and consciousness of new powers experienced." This "gives to the sexual relation an office entirely distinct from the propagative act--it is a union on the affectional plane, but at the same time it is a preparation for best possible conditions for procreation."

The importance of this distinction of the generative act from the act of union or conjunction can hardly be overrated. The two things have hitherto been undifferentiated. Though it may not be easy at once to establish the mental and other conditions necessary for the latter, yet they can be established; and the result is an avoidance of waste, and a great economy of vital forces--on the one side a more profound, helpful and satisfying union, and on the other a greater energy for procreation, when that is desired. We cannot help thinking that it is along this line that the solution of the marriage and population problem will, in time, be found. The overhanging dread of undesired child-birth, which so oppresses the life of many a young mother, will be removed; and marriage will be liberated at last from the tyranny of a brute need into the free and pleasurable exercise of a human and intelligent relationship.

THE END

IOLÄUS

AN ANTHOLOGY OF FRIENDSHIP

EDITED BY

EDWARD CARPENTER

"And as to the loves of Hercules it is difficult to record them because of their number. But some who think that Ioläus was one of them, do to this day worship and honour him; and make their loved ones swear fidelity at his tomb."

CONTENTS

PREFACE TO FIRST EDITION

THE degree to which Friendship, in the early history of the world, has been recognized as an institution, and the dignity ascribed to it, are things hardly realized to-day. Yet a very slight examination of the subject shows the important part it has played. In making the following collection I have been much struck by the remarkable manner in which the customs of various races and times illustrate each other, and the way in which they point to a solid and enduring body of human sentiment on the subject. By arranging the extracts in a kind of rough chronological and evolutionary order from those dealing with primitive races onwards, the continuity of these customs comes out all the more clearly, as well as their slow modification in course of time. But it must be confessed that the present collection is only incomplete, and a small contribution, at best, towards a large subject.

In the matter of quotation and translation, my best thanks are due to various authors and holders of literary copyrights for their assistance and authority. In cases where no reference is given the translations are by the Editor.

E. C.

I

FRIENDSHIP-CUSTOMS IN THE PAGAN AND EARLY WORLD

FRIENDSHIP-CUSTOMS, of a very marked and definite character, have apparently prevailed among a great many primitive peoples; but the information that we have about them is seldom thoroughly satisfactory. Travelers have been content to note external ceremonies, like the exchange of names between comrades, or the mutual tasting of each other's blood, but--either from want of perception or want of opportunity--have not been able to tell us anything about the inner meaning of these formalities, or the sentiments which may have inspired them. Still, we have material enough to indicate that comrade-attachment has been recognized as an important institution, and held in high esteem, among quite savage tribes; and some of the following quotations will show this. When we come to the higher culture of the Greek age the material fortunately is abundant--not only for the customs, but (in Greek philosophy and poetry) for the inner sentiments which inspired these customs. Consequently it will be found that the major part of this and the following two chapters deals with matter from Greek sources. The later chapters carry on the subject in loosely historical sequence through the Christian centuries down to modern times.

PRIMITIVE CEREMONY

THE Balonda are an African tribe inhabiting Londa land, among the Southern tributaries of the Congo River. They were visited by Livingstone, and the following account of their customs is derived from him:--

"The Balonda have a most remarkable custom of cementing friendship. When two men agree to be special friends they go through a singular ceremony. The men sit opposite each other holding hands, and by the side of each is a vessel of beer. Slight cuts are then made on the clasped hands, on the pit of the stomach, on the right cheek, and on the forehead. The point of a grass-blade is pressed against each of these cuts, so as to take up a little of the blood, and each man washes the grass-blade in his own beer vessel. The vessels are then exchanged and the contents drunk, so that each imbibes the blood of the other. The two are thenceforth considered as blood-relations, and are bound to assist each other in every possible manner. While the beer is being drunk, the friends of each of the men beat on the ground with clubs, and bawl out certain sentences as ratification of the treaty. It is thought correct for all the friends of each party to the contract to drink a little of the beer. The ceremony is called 'Kasendi.' After it has been completed, gifts are exchanged, and both parties always give their most precious possessions." *Natural History of Man. Rev. J. G. Wood. Vol: Africa*, p. 419.

Among the Manganjas and other tribes of the Zambesi region, Livingstone found the custom of changing names prevalent.

"Sininyane (a headman) had exchanged names with a Zulu at Shupanga, and on being called the next morning made no answer; to a second and third summons he paid no attention; but at length one of his men replied, 'He is not Sininyane now, he is Moshoshoma'; and to this name he answered promptly. The custom of exchanging names with men of other tribes is not uncommon; and the exchangers regard themselves as close comrades, owing special duties to each other ever after. Should one by chance visit his comrade's town, he expects to receive food, lodging, and other friendly offices from him." *Narrative of an Expedition to the Zambesi. By David and Charles Livingstone.* Murray, 1865, p. 148.

DAVID AND JONATHAN

IN the story of David and Jonathan, which follows, we have an example, from much the same stage of primitive tribal life, of a compact between two friends--one the son of the chief, the other a shepherd youth--only in this case, in the song of David ("I am distressed for thee, my brother Jonathan, thy love to me was wonderful") we are fortunate in having the inner feeling preserved for us. It should be noted that Jonathan gives to David his "most precious possessions."

"And when Saul saw David go forth against the Philistine (Goliath), he said unto Abner, the captain of the host, 'Abner, whose son is this youth?' And Abner said, 'As thy soul liveth, O King, I cannot tell.' And the King said, 'Inquire thou whose son the stripling is.' And as David returned from the slaughter of the Philistine, Abner took him and brought him before Saul, with the head of the Philistine in his hand. And Saul said to him, 'Whose son art thou, young man?' And David answered, 'The son of thy servant Jesse the Bethlehemite.'

"And it came to pass, when he had made an end of speaking unto Saul, that the soul of Jonathan was knit with the soul of David, and Jonathan loved him as his own soul. And Saul took him that day, and would let him go no more home to his father's house. Then Jonathan and David made a covenant, because he loved him as his own soul. And Jonathan stripped himself of the robe that was upon him, and gave it to David, and his garments, even to his sword, and to his bow, and to his girdle." 1 *Sam.* ch. xvii. 55.

FLOWER FRIENDS

With regard to the exchange of names, a slightly different custom prevails among the Bengali coolies. Two youths, or two girls, will exchange two flowers (of the same kind) with each other, in token of perpetual alliance. After that, one speaks of the other as "my flower," but never alludes to the other by *name* again--only by some roundabout phrase.

POLYNESIA TAHITI

HERMAN MELVILLE, who voyaged among the Pacific Islands in 1841-1845, gives some interesting and reliable accounts of Polynesian customs of that period. He says:--

"The really curious way in which all the Polynesians are in the habit of making bosom friends at the shortest possible notice is deserving of remark. Although, among a people like the Tahitians, vitiated as they are by sophisticating influences, this custom has in most cases degenerated into a mere mercenary relation, it nevertheless had its origin in a fine, and in some instances heroic, sentiment formerly entertained by their fathers. "In the annals of the island (Tahiti) are examples of extravagant friendships, unsurpassed by the story of Damon and Pythias, in truth, much more wonderful; for notwithstanding the devotion--even of life in some cases--to which they led, they were frequently entertained at first sight for some stranger from another island." *Omoo, Herman Melville*, ch. 39, p. 154.

"Though little inclined to jealousy in (ordinary) love-matters, the Tahitian will hear of no rivals in his friendship." *Ibid*, ch. 40.

MARQUESAS ISLANDS

Melville spent some months on one of the Marquesas Islands, in a valley occupied by a tribe called Typees; one day there turned up a stranger belonging to a hostile tribe who occupied another part of the island:--

"The stranger could not have been more than twenty-five years of age, and was a little above the ordinary height; had he been a single hair's breadth taller, the matchless symmetry of his form would have been destroyed. His unclad limbs were beautifully formed; whilst the elegant outline of his figure, together with his beardless cheeks, might have entitled him to the distinction of standing for the statue of the Polynesian Apollo; and indeed the oval of his countenance and the regularity of every feature reminded me of an antique bust. But the marble repose of art was supplied by a warmth and liveliness of expression only to be seen in the South Sea Islander under the most favorable developments of nature. . . . When I expressed my surprise (at his venturing among the Typees) he looked at me for a moment as if enjoying my perplexity, and then with his strange vivacity exclaimed—'Ah! me taboo-me go Nukuheva-me go Tior--me go Typee--me go everywhere--nobody harm me, me taboo.'

"This explanation would have been altogether unintelligible to me, had it not recalled to my mind something I had previously heard concerning a singular custom among these islanders. Though the country is possessed by various tribes, whose mutual hostilities almost wholly preclude any intercourse between them; yet there are instances where a person having ratified friendly relations with some individual belonging to the valley, whose inmates are at war with his own, may under particular restrictions venture with impunity into the country of his friend, where under other circumstances he would have been treated as an enemy. In this light are personal friendships regarded among them, and the individual so protected is said to be 'taboo,' and his person to a certain extent is held as sacred. Thus the stranger informed me he had access to all the valleys in the island." *Typee, Herman Melville*, ch. xviii.

TACITUS ON MILITARY COMRADESHIP

IN almost all primitive nations, warfare has given rise to institutions of military comradeship--including, for instance, institutions of instruction for young warriors, of personal devotion to their leaders, or of personal attachment to each other. In Greece these customs were specially defined, as later quotations will show.

Tacitus, speaking of the arrangement among the Germans by which each military chief was surrounded by younger companions in arms, says:--

"There is great emulation among the companions, which shall possess the highest place in the favor of their chief; and among the chiefs, which shall excel in the number and valor of his companions. It is their dignity, their strength, to be always surrounded with a large body of select youth, an ornament in peace, a bulwark in war. . . . In the field of battle, it is disgraceful for the chief to be surpassed in valor; it is disgraceful for the companions not to equal their chief; but it is reproach and infamy during the whole succeeding life to retreat from the field surviving him. To aid, to protect him; to place their own gallant actions to the account of his glory is their first and most sacred engagement." *Tacitus, Germania*, 13, 14, *Bohn Series.*

THE KHALIFA AT KHARTOUM

AMONG the Arab tribes very much the same thing may be found, every Sheikh having his bodyguard of young men, whom he instructs and educates, while they render to him their military and personal devotion. In the late expedition of the British to Khartoum (Nov., 1899), when Colonel Wingate and his troops mowed down the Khalifa and his followers with their Maxims, the death of the Khalifa was thus described by a correspondent of the daily papers:--

"In the centre of what was evidently the main attack on our right we came across a very large number of bodies all huddled together in a very small place; their horses lay dead behind them, the Khalifa lay dead on his furma, or sheepskin, the typical end of the Arab Sheikh who disdains surrender; on his right was the Khalifa Aly Wad Hila, and on his left Ahmed Fedil, his great fighting leader, whilst all around him lay his faithful emirs, all content to meet their death when he had chosen to meet his. His black Mulamirin, or bodyguard, all lay dead in a straight line about 40 yards in front of their master's body, with their faces to the foe and faithful to the last. It was truly a touching sight, and one could not help but feel that . . . their end was truly grand. . . . Amongst the dead were found two men tied together by the arms, who had charged towards the guns and had got nearer than any others. On enquiring of the prisoners Colonel Wingate was told these two were great friends, and on seeing the Egyptian guns come up had tied themselves by the arms with a cord, swearing to reach the guns or die together."

PRIMITIVE GERMANS

Compare also the following quotation from Ammianus Marcellinus (xvi. 13), who says that when Chonodomarus, "King of the Alamanni," was taken prisoner by the Romans,

"His companions, two hundred in number, and three friends peculiarly attached to him, thinking it infamous to survive their prince, or not to die for him, surrendered themselves to be put in bonds."

SOUTH AFRICAN TRIBES

The following passage from Livingstone shows the existence among the African tribes of his time of a system, which Wood rightly says "has a singular resemblance to the instruction of pages in the days of chivalry":--

"Monina (one of the confederate chiefs of the Banyai) had a great number of young men about him, from twelve to fifteen years of age. These were all sons of free men, and bands of young lads like them in the different districts leave their parents about the age of puberty and live with such men as Monina for the sake of instruction. When I asked the nature of the instruction I was told 'Bonyái,' which I suppose may be understood as indicating manhood, for it sounds as if we should say, 'to teach an American Americanism,' or, 'an Englishman to be English.' While here they are kept in subjection to rather stringent regulations. . . . They remain unmarried until a fresh set of youths is ready to occupy their place under the same instruction." *Missionary Travels and Researches in South Africa. By David Livingstone*, 1857, p. 618.

M. Foley (Bulln. Soc. d'Anthr. de Paris, 1879) speaks of fraternity in arms among the natives of New Caledonia as forming a close tie closer even than consanguinity.

GREEK FRIENDSHIP AND CHIVALRY

WITH regard to Greece, J. Addington Symonds has some interesting remarks, which are well worthy of consideration; he says:--

"Nearly all the historians of Greece have failed to insist upon the fact that fraternity in arms played for the Greek race the same part as the idealization of women for the knighthood of feudal Europe. Greek mythology and history are full of tales of friendship, which can only be paralleled by the story of David and Jonathan in the Bible. The legends of Herakles and Hylas, of Theseus and Peirithous, of Apollo and Hyacinth, of Orestes and Pylades, occur immediately to the mind. Among the noblest patriots, tyrannicides, lawgivers, and self-devoted heroes in the early times of Greece, we always find the names of friends and comrades received with peculiar honor. Harmodius and Aristogeiton, who slew the despot Hipparchus at Athens; Diocles and Philolaus, who gave laws to Thebes; Chariton and Melanippus, who resisted the sway of Phalaris in Sicily; Cratinus and Aristodemus, who devoted their lives to propitiate offended deities when a plague had fallen on Athens; these comrades, staunch to each other in their love, and elevated by friendship to the pitch of noblest enthusiasm, were among the favorite saints of Greek legend and history. In a word, the chivalry of Hellas found its motive force in friendship rather than in the love of women; and the motive force of all chivalry is a generous, soul-exalting, unselfish passion. The fruit which friendship bore among the Greeks was courage in the face of danger, indifference to life when honor was at stake, patriotic ardor, the love of liberty, and lion-hearted rivalry in battle. 'Tyrants,' said Plato, 'stand in awe of friends.'" *Studies of the Greek Poets. By J. A. Symonds*, vol. I, p. 97.

FRATERNITY IN ARMS IN SPARTA

THE customs connected with this fraternity in arms, in Sparta and in Crete, are described with care and at considerable length in the following extract from Müller's *History and Antiquities of the Doric Race*, book iv., ch. 4, par. 6:--

"At Sparta the party loving was called εἰσπνήλας, and his affection was termed a breathing in, or inspiring (εἰσπνεῖν); which expresses the pure and mental connection between the two persons, and corresponds with the name of the other, viz.: ἀίτας,*i.e.*, *listener* or *hearer*. Now it appears to have been the practice for every youth of good character to have his lover; and on the other hand every well-educated man was bound by custom to be the lover of some youth. Instances of this connection are furnished by several of the royal family of Sparta; thus, Agesilaus, while he still belonged to the herd (ἀγέλη) of youths, was the hearer (ἀίτας) of Lysander, and himself had in his turn also a hearer; his son Archidamus was the lover of the son of Sphodrias, the noble Cleonymus; Cleomenes III was when a young man the hearer of Xenares, and later in life the lover of the brave Panteus. The connection usually originated from the proposal of the lover; yet it was necessary that the listener should accept him with real affection, as a regard to the riches of the proposer was considered very disgraceful; sometimes, however, it happened that the proposal originated from the other party. The connection appears to have been very intimate and faithful; and was recognized by the State. If his relations were absent, the youth might be represented in the public assembly by his lover; in battle too they stood near one another, where their fidelity and affection were often shown till death; while at home the youth was constantly under the eyes of his lover, who was to him as it were a model and pattern of life; which explains why, for many faults, particularly want of ambition, the lover could be punished instead of the listener."

CRETE

"This ancient national custom prevailed with still greater force in Crete; which island was hence by many persons considered as the original seat of the connection in question. Here too it was disgraceful for a well-educated youth to be with out a lover; and hence the party loved was termed κλεινὸς, the praised; the lover being simply called φιλήτωϱ. It appears that the youth was always carried away by force, the intention of the ravisher being previously communicated to the relations, who, however, took no measures of precaution, and only made a feigned resistance; except when the ravisher appeared, either in family or talent, unworthy of the youth. The lover then led him away to his apartment (ἀνδϱεῖον), and afterwards, with any chance companions, either to the mountains or to his estate. Here they remained two months (the period prescribed by custom), which were passed chiefly in hunting together. After this time had expired, the lover dismissed the youth, and at his departure gave him, according to custom, an ox, a military dress, and brazen cup, with other things; and frequently these gifts were increased by the friends of the ravisher. The youth then sacrificed the ox to Jupiter, with which he gave a feast to his companions: and now he stated how he had been pleased with his lover; and he had complete liberty by law to punish any insult or disgraceful treatment. It depended now on the choice of the youth whether the connection should be broken off or not. If it was kept up, the companion in arms (παραστάτης), as the youth was then called, wore the military dress which had been given him, and fought in battle next his lover, inspired with double valor by the gods of war and love, according to the notions of the Cretans; and even in man's age he was distinguished by the first place and rank in the course, and certain insignia worn about the body.

DIOCLES

"Institutions, so systematic and regular as these, did not exist in any Doric State except Crete and Sparta; but the feelings on which they were founded seem to have been common to all the Dorians. The loves of Philolaus, a Corinthian of the family of the Bacchiadae, and the lawgiver of Thebes, and of Diocles the Olympic conqueror, lasted until death; and even their graves were turned towards one another in token of their affection; and another person of the same name was honored in Megara, as a noble instance of self-devotion for the object of his love." *Ibid.*

For an account of Philolaus and Diocles, Aristotle (Pol. ii. 9) may be referred to. The second Diocles was an Athenian who died in battle for the youth he loved.

"His tomb was honored with the ἐναγίσματα of heroes, and a yearly contest for skill in kissing formed part of his memorial celebration." *J. A. Symonds' "A Problem in Greek Ethics" privately printed*, 1883; see also *Theocritus*, Idyll xii. infra.

ALBANIAN CUSTOMS

HAHN, in his *Albanesische Studien*, says that the Dorian customs of comradeship still flourish in Albania "just as described by the ancients," and are closely entwined with the whole life of the people--though he says nothing of any military signification. It appears to be a quite recognized institution for a young man to take to himself a youth or boy as his special comrade. He instructs, and when necessary reproves, the younger; protects him, and makes him presents of various kinds. The relation generally, though not always ends with the marriage of the elder. The following is reported by Hahn as in the actual words of his informant (an Albanian):--

"Love of this kind is occasioned by the sight of a beautiful youth; who thus kindles in the lover a feeling of wonder and causes his heart to open to the sweet sense which springs from the contemplation of beauty. By degrees love steals in and takes possession of the lover, and to such a degree that all his thoughts and feelings are absorbed in it. When near the beloved he loses himself in the sight of him; when absent he thinks of him only." These loves, he continued, "are with a few exceptions as pure as sunshine, and the highest and noblest affections that the human heart can entertain." *Hahn*, vol. I, p. 166.

Hahn also mentions that troops of youths, like the Cretan and Spartan *agelae*, are formed in Albania, of twenty-five or thirty members each. The comradeship usually begins during adolescence, each member paying a fixed sum into a common fund, and the interest being spent on two or three annual feasts, generally held out of doors.

THE THEBAN BAND

THE Sacred Band of Thebes, or Theban Band, was a battalion composed entirely of friends and lovers; and forms a remarkable example of military comradeship. The references to it in later Greek literature are very numerous, and there seems no reason to doubt the general truth of the traditions concerning its formation and its complete annihilation by Philip of Macedon at the battle of Chaeronea (B.C. 338). Thebes was the last stronghold of Hellenic independence, and with the Theban Band Greek freedom perished. But the mere existence of this phalanx, and the fact of its renown, show to what an extent comradeship was recognized and prized as an institution among these peoples. The following account is taken from Plutarch's *Life of Pelopidas*, Clough's translation:--

"Gorgidas, according to some, first formed the Sacred Band of 300 chosen men, to whom as being a guard for the citadel the State allowed provision, and all things necessary for exercise; and hence they were called the city band, as citadels of old were usually called cities. Others say that it was composed of young men attached to each other by personal affection, and a pleasant saying of Pammenes is current, that Homer's Nestor was not well skilled in ordering an army, when he advised the Greeks to rank tribe and tribe, and family and family, together, that so 'tribe might tribe, and kinsmen kinsmen aid,' but that he should have joined lovers and their beloved. For men of the same tribe or family little value one another when dangers press, but a band cemented together by friendship grounded upon love is never to be broken, and invincible; since the lovers, ashamed to be base in sight of their beloved, and the beloved before their lovers, willingly rush into danger for the relief of one another. Nor can that be wondered at since they have more regard for their absent lovers than for others present; as in the instance of the man who, when his enemy was going to kill him, earnestly requested him to run him through the breast, that his lover might not blush to see him wounded in the back. It is a tradition likewise that Ioläus, who assisted Hercules in his labors and fought at his side, was beloved of him; and Aristotle observes that even in his time lovers plighted their faith at Ioläus' tomb. It is likely, therefore, that this band was called sacred on this account; as Plato calls a lover a divine friend. It is stated that it was never beaten till the battle at Chaeronea; and when Philip after the fight took a view of the slain, and came to the place where the three hundred that fought his phalanx lay dead together, he wondered, and understanding that it was the band of lovers, he shed tears and said, 'Perish any man who suspects that these men either did or suffered anything that was base.'

"It was not the disaster of Laius, as the poets imagine, that first gave rise to this form of attachment among the Thebans, but their law-givers, designing to soften whilst they were young their natural fickleness, brought for example the pipe into great esteem, both in serious and sportive occasions, and gave great encouragement to these friendships in the Palaestra, to temper the manner and character of the youth. With a view to this, they did well again to make Harmony, the daughter of Mars and Venus, their tutelar deity; since where force and courage is joined with gracefulness and winning behavior, a harmony ensues that combines all the elements of society in perfect consonance and order.

"Gorgidas distributed this sacred Band all through the front ranks of the infantry, and thus made their gallantry less conspicuous; not being united in one body, but mingled with many others of inferior resolution, they had no fair opportunity of showing what they could do. But Pelopidas, having sufficiently tried their bravery at Tegyrae, where they had fought alone, and around his own person, never afterwards divided them, but keeping them entire, and as one man, gave them the first duty in the greatest battles. For as horses run brisker in a chariot than single, not that their joint force divides the air with greater ease, but because being matched one against another circulation kindles and enflames their courage; thus, he thought, brave men, provoking one another to noble actions, would prove most serviceable and most resolute where all were united together."

ATHENÆUS

STORIES of romantic friendship form a staple subject of Greek literature, and were everywhere accepted and prized. The following quotations from Athenæus and Plutarch contain allusions to the Theban Band, and other examples:--

"And the Lacedæmonians offer sacrifices to Love before they go to battle, thinking that safety and victory depend on the friendship of those who stand side by side in the battle array. . . . And the regiment among the Thebans, which is called the*Sacred Band*, is wholly composed of mutual lovers, indicating the majesty of the God, as these men prefer a glorious death to a shameful and discreditable life." *Athenæus*, bk. xiii., ch. 12.

PLUTARCH ON LOVE

Ioläus, above-mentioned, is said to have been the charioteer of Hercules, and his faithful companion. As the comrade of Hercules he was worshipped beside him in Thebes, where the gymnasium was named after him. Plutarch alludes to this friendship again in his treatise on Love (*Eroticus*, par. 17):--

"And as to the loves of Hercules, it is difficult to record them because of their number; but those who think that Ioläus was one of them do to this day worship and honor him, and make their loved ones swear fidelity at his tomb."

And in this same treatise:--

"Consider also how love (Eros) excels in warlike feats, and is by no means idle, as Euripides called him, nor a carpet knight, nor 'sleeping on soft maidens' cheeks.' For a man inspired by Love needs not Ares to help him when he goes out as a warrior against the enemy, but at the bidding of his own god is 'ready' for his friend 'to go through fire and water and whirlwinds.' And in Sophocles' play, when the sons of Niobe are being shot at and dying, one of them calls out for no helper or assister but his lover.

"And you know of course how it was that Cleomachus, the Pharsalian, fell in battle. . . . When the war between the Eretrians and Chalcidians was at its height, Cleomachus had come to aid the latter with a Thessalian force; and the Chalcidian infantry seemed strong enough, but they had great difficulty in repelling the enemy's cavalry. So they begged that high-souled hero, Cleomachus, to charge the Eretrian cavalry first. And he asked the youth he loved, who was by, if he would be a spectator of the fight, and he saying he would, and affectionately kissing him and putting his helmet on his head, Cleomachus, with a proud joy, put himself at the head of the bravest of the Thessalians, and charged the enemy's cavalry with such impetuosity that he threw them into disorder and routed them; and the Eretrian infantry also fleeing in consequence, the Chalcidians won a splendid victory. However, Cleomachus got killed, and they show his tomb in the market place at Chalcis, over which a huge pillar stands to this day." *Eroticus*, par. 17, *trans. Bohn's Classics.*

And further on in the same:--

"And among you Thebans, Pemptides, is it not usual for the lover to give his boy-love a complete suit of armor when he is enrolled among the men? And did not the erotic Pammenes change the disposition of the heavy-armed infantry, censuring Homer as knowing nothing about love, because he drew up the Achæans in order of battle in tribes and clans, and did not put lover and love together, that so 'spear should be next to spear and helmet to helmet' (*Iliad*, xiii. 13 I), seeing that love is the only invincible general. For men in battle will leave in the lurch clansmen and friends, aye, and parents and sons, but what warrior ever broke through or charged through lover and love, seeing that when there is no necessity lovers frequently display their bravery and contempt of life."

ATHENÆUS ON LOVE

THE following is from the *Deipnosophists* of Athenæus (bk. xiii., ch. 78):--

But Hieronymus the peripatetic says that the loves of youths used to be much encouraged, for this reason, that the vigor of the young and their close agreement in comradeship have led to the overthrow of many a tyranny. For in the presence of his favorite a lover would rather endure anything than earn the name of coward; a thing which was proved in practice by the Sacred Band, established at Thebes under Epaminondas; as well as by the death of the Pisistratidæ, which was brought about by Harmodius and Aristogeiton.

"And at Agrigentum in Sicily the same was shown by the mutual love of Chariton and Melanippus--of whom Melanippus was the younger beloved, as Heraclides of Pontus tells in his Treatise on Love. For these two having been accused of plotting against Phalaris, and being put to torture in order to force them to betray their accomplices, not only did not tell, but even compelled Phalaris to such pity of their tortures that he released them with many words of praise. Whereupon Apollo, pleased at his conduct, granted to Phalaris a respite from death; and declared the same to the men who inquired of the Pythian priestess how they might best attack him. He also gave an oracular saying concerning Chariton. . . .

'Blessed indeed was Chariton and Melanippus,
Pioneers of Godhead, and of mortals the one most beloved.'"

Epaminondas, the great Theban general and statesman, so we are told by the same author, had for his young comrades Asopichus and Cephisodorus, "the latter of whom fell with him at Mantineia, and is buried near him."

PARMENIDES AND ZENO

THESE are mainly instances of what might he called "military comradeship," but as may be supposed, friendship in the early world did not rest on this alone. With the growth of culture other interests came in; and among the Greeks especially association in the pursuit of art or politics or philosophy became a common ground. Parmenides, the philosopher, whose life was held peculiarly holy, loved his pupil Zeno (see Plato *Parm*, 127A):--

"Parmenides and Zeno came to Athens, he said, at the great Panathenæan festival; the former was, at the time of his visit, about 65 years old, very white with age, but well-favored. Zeno was nearly 40 years of age, of a noble figure and fair aspect; and in the days of his youth he was reported to have been beloved of Parmenides."

PHÆDO

Pheidias, the sculptor, loved Pantarkes, a youth of Elis, and carved his portrait at the foot of the Olympian Zeus (Pausanias v. II), and politicians and orators like Demosthenes and Æschines were proud to avow their attachments. It was in a house of ill-fame, according to Diogenes Laertius (ii. 105) that Socrates first met Phædo:--

"This unfortunate youth was a native of Elis. Taken prisoner in war, he was sold in the public market to a slave dealer, who then acquired the right by Attic law to engross his earnings for his own pocket. A friend of Socrates, perhaps Cebes, bought him from his master, and he became one of the chief members of the Socratic circle. His name is given to the Platonic dialogue on immortality, and he lived to found what is called the Eleo-Socratic School. No reader of Plato forgets how the sage on the eve of his death stroked the beautiful long hair of Phædo, and prophesied that he would soon have to cut it short in mourning for his teacher." *J. J. Symonds, A Problem in Greek Ethics*, p. 58.

The relation of friendship to the pursuit of philosophy is a favourite subject with Plato, and is illustrated by some later quotations (see *infra* ch. 2).

HARMODIUS AND ARISTOGEITON

I CONCLUDE the present section by the insertion of three stories taken from classical sources. Though of a legendary character, it is probable that they enshrine some memory or tradition of actual facts. The story of Harmodius and Aristogeiton at any rate is treated by Herodotus and Thucydides as a matter of serious history. The names of these two friends were ever on the lips of the Athenians as the founders of the city's freedom, and to be born of their blood was esteemed among the highest of honors. But whether historical or not, these stories have much the same value for us, in so far as they indicate the ideals on which the Greek mind dwelt, and which it considered possible of realization.

"Now the attempt of Aristogeiton and Harmodius arose out of a love affair, which I will narrate at length; and the narrative will show that the Athenians themselves give quite an inaccurate account of their own tyrants, and of the incident in question, and know no more than other Hellenes. Pisistratus died at an advanced age in possession of the tyranny, and then, not as is the common opinion Hipparchus, but Hippias (who was the eldest of his sons) succeeded to his power.

"Harmodius was in the flower of his youth, and Aristogeiton, a citizen of the middle class, became his lover. Hipparchus made an attempt to gain the affections of Harmodius, but he would not listen to him, and told Aristogeiton. The latter was naturally tormented at the idea, and fearing that Hipparchus, who was powerful, would resort to violence, at once formed such a plot as a man in his station might for the overthrow of the tyranny. Meanwhile Hipparchus made another attempt; he had no better success, and thereupon he determined, not indeed to take any violent step, but to insult Harmodius in some underhand manner, so that his motive could not be suspected.

"When Hipparchus found his advances repelled by Harmodius he carried out his intention of insulting him. There was a young sister of his whom Hipparchus and his friends first invited to come and carry a sacred basket in a procession, and then rejected her, declaring that she had never been invited by them at all because she was unworthy. At this Harmodius was very angry, and Aristogeiton for his sake more angry still. They and the other conspirators had already laid their preparations, but were waiting for the festival of the great Panathenæa, when the citizens who took part in the procession assembled in arms; for to wear arms on any other day would have aroused suspicion. Harmodius and Aristogeiton were to begin the attack, and the rest were immediately to join in, and engage with the guards. The plot had been communicated to a few only, the better to avoid detection; but they hoped that, however few struck the blow, the crowd who would be armed, although not in the secret, would at once rise and assist in the recovery of their own liberties.

"The day of the festival arrived, and Hippias went out of the city to the place called the Ceramicus, where he was occupied with his guards in marshalling the procession. Harmodius and Aristogeiton, who were ready with their daggers, stepped forward to do the deed. But seeing one of the conspirators in familiar conversation with Hippias, who was readily accessible to all, they took alarm and imagined that they had been betrayed, and were on the point of being seized. Whereupon they determined to take their revenge first on the man who had outraged them and was the cause of their desperate attempt. So they rushed, just as they were, within the gates. They found Hipparchus near the Leocorium, as it was called, and then and there falling upon him with all the blind fury, one of an injured lover, the other of a man smarting under an insult, they smote and slew him. The crowd ran together, and so Aristogeiton for the present escaped the guards; but he was afterwards taken, and not very gently handled (*i.e.*, *tortured*). Harmodius perished on the spot." Thug: vi. 54-56, *trans. by B. Jowett.*

ORESTES AND PYLADES

"Phocis preserves from early times the memory of the union between Orestes and Pylades, who taking a god as witness of the passion between them, sailed through life together as though in one boat. Both together put to death Klytemnestra, as though both were sons of Agamemnon; and Ægisthus was slain by both. Pylades suffered more than his friend by the punishment which pursued Orestes. He stood by him when condemned, nor did they limit their tender friendship by the bounds of Greece, but sailed to the furthest boundaries of the Scythians--the one sick, the other ministering to him. When they had come into the Tauric land straightway they were met by the matricidal fury; and while the barbarians were standing round in a circle Orestes fell down and lay on the ground, seized by his usual mania, while Pylades 'wiped away the foam, tended his body, and covered him with his well-woven cloak'--acting not only like a lover but like a father.

"When it was determined that one should remain to be put to death, and the other should go to Mycenæ to convey a letter, each wishes to remain for the sake of the other, thinking that if he saves the life of his friend he saves his own life. Orestes refused to take the letter, saying that Pylades was more worthy to carry it, acting more like the lover than the beloved. 'For,' he said, 'the slaying of this man would be a great grief to me, as I am the cause of these misfortunes.' And he added, 'Give the tablet to him, for (turning to Pylades) I will send thee to Argos, in order that it may be well with thee; as for me, let any one kill me who desires it.'

"Such love is always like that; for when from boyhood a serious love has grown up and it becomes adult at the age of reason, the long-loved object returns reciprocal affection, and it is hard to determine which is the lover of which, for--as from a mirror--the affection of the lover is reflected from the beloved." *Trans. from Lucian's Amores, by W. J. Baylis.*

DAMON AND PYTHIAS

"Damon and Phintias, initiates in the Pythagorean mysteries, contracted so faithful a friendship towards each other, that when Dionysius of Syracuse intended to execute one of them, and he had obtained permission from the tyrant to return home and arrange his affairs before his death, the other did not hesitate to give himself up as a pledge of his friend's return. He whose neck had been in danger was now free; and he who might have lived in safety was now in danger of death. So everybody, and especially Dionysius, were wondering what would be the upshot of this novel and dubious affair. At last, when the day fixed was close at hand, and he had not returned, every one condemned the one who stood security, for his stupidity and rashness. But he insisted that he had nothing to fear in the matter of his friend's constancy. And indeed at the same moment and the hour fixed by Dionysius, he who had received leave, returned. The tyrant, admiring the courage of both, remitted the sentence which had so tried their loyalty, and asked them besides to receive him in the bonds of their friendship, saying that he would make his third place in their affection agreeable by his utmost goodwill and effort. Such indeed are the powers of friendship: to breed contempt of death, to overcome the sweet desire of life, to humanize cruelty, to turn hate into love, to compensate punishment by largess; to which powers almost as much veneration is due as to the cult of the immortal gods. For if with these rests the public safety, on those does private happiness depend; and as the temples are the sacred domiciles of these, so of those are the loyal hearts of men as it were the shrines consecrated by some holy spirit." *Valerius Maximus*, bk. iv. ch. 7. *De Amicitæ Vinculo.*

II

THE PLACE OF FRIENDSHIP IN GREEK LIFE AND THOUGHT

THE extent to which the idea of friendship (in a quite romantic sense) penetrated the Greek mind is a thing very difficult for us to realize; and some modern critics entirely miss this point. They laud the Greek culture to the skies, extolling the warlike bravery of the people, their enthusiastic political and social sentiment, their wonderful artistic sense, and so forth; and at the same time speak of the stress they laid on friendship as a little peculiarity of no particular importance--not seeing that the latter was the chief source of their bravery and independence, one of the main motives of their art, and so far an organic part of their whole polity that it is difficult to imagine the one without the other. The Greeks themselves never made this mistake; and their literature abounds with references to the romantic attachment as the great inspiration of political and individual life. Plato, himself, may almost be said to have founded his philosophy on this sentiment.

PLATONIC FRIENDSHIP

Nothing is more surprising to the modern than to find Plato speaking, page after page, of Love, as the safeguard of states and the tutoress of philosophy, and then to discover that what we call love, *i.e.*, the love between man and woman, is not meant at all--scarcely comes within his consideration--but only the love between men--what we should call romantic friendship. His ideal of this latter love is ascetic; it is an absorbing passion, but it is held in strong control. The other love--the love of women--is for him a mere sensuality. In this, to some extent, lies the explanation of his philosophical position.

But it is evident that in this fact--in the fact that among the Greeks the love of women was considered for the most part sensual, while the *romance* of love went to the account of friendship, we have the strength and the weakness of the Greek civilization. Strength, because by the recognition everywhere of romantic comradeship, public and private life was filled by a kind of divine fire; weakness, because by the non-recognition of woman's equal part in such comradeship, her saving, healing, and redeeming influence was lost, and the Greek culture doomed to be to that extent one-sided. It will, we may hope, be the great triumph of the modern love (when it becomes more of a true comradeship between man and woman than it yet is) to give both to society and to the individual the grandest inspirations, and perhaps in conjunction with the other attachment, to lift the modern nations to a higher level of political and artistic advancement than even the Greeks attained.

GREEK FRIENDSHIP

BISHOP THIRLWALL, that excellent thinker and scholar, in his *History of Greece* (vol. I, p. 176) says:--

"One of the noblest and most amiable sides of the Greek character is the readiness with which it lent itself to construct intimate and durable friendships; and this is a feature no less prominent in the earliest than in the latest times. It was indeed connected with the comparatively low estimation in which female society was held; but the devotedness and constancy with which these attachments were maintained was not the less admirable and engaging. The heroic companions whom we find celebrated, partly by Homer and partly in traditions, which if not of equal antiquity were grounded on the same feeling, seem to have but one heart and soul, with scarcely a wish or object apart, and only to live, as they are always ready to die, for one another. It is true that the relation between them is not always one of perfect equality: but this is a circumstance which, while it often adds a peculiar charm to the poetical description, detracts little from the dignity of the idea which it presents. Such were the friendships of Hercules and Ioläus, of Theseus and Pirithöus, of Orestes and Pylades: and though these may owe the greater part of their fame to the later epic or even dramatic poetry, the moral groundwork undoubtedly subsisted in the period to which the tradition referred. The argument of the Iliad mainly turns on the affection of Achilles for Patroclus--whose love for the greater hero is only tempered by reverence for his higher birth and his unequaled prowess. But the mutual regard which united Idomeneus and Meriones, Diomedes and Sthenelus--though, as the persons themselves are less important, it is kept more in the background--is manifestly viewed by the poet in the same light. The idea of a Greek hero seems not to have been thought complete, without such a brother in arms by his side."

LOVE COMPARED TO CHIVALRY

The following is from Ludwig Frey (*Der Eros und die Kunst*, p. 33):--

"Let it then be repeated: love for a youth was for the Greeks something sacred, and can only be compared with our German homage to women--say the chivalric love of mediæval times."

EDUCATIONAL AND POLITICAL VALUE

G. LOWES DICKINSON, in his *Greek View of Life*, noting the absence of romance in the relations between men and women of that civilization, says:--

"Nevertheless, it would be a mistake to conclude, from these conditions, that the element of romance was absent from Greek life. The fact is simply that with them it took a different form, that of passionate friendship between men. Such friendships, of course, occur in all nations and at all times, but among the Greeks they were, we might say, an institution. Their ideal was the development and education of the younger by the older man, and in this view they were recognized and approved by custom and law as an important factor in the state." *Greek View of Life*, p. 167.

"So much indeed were the Greeks impressed with the manliness of this passion, with its power to prompt to high thought and heroic action, that some of the best of them set the love of man for man far above that of man for woman. The one, they maintained, was primarily of the spirit, the other primarily of the flesh; the one bent upon shaping to the type of all manly excellence both the body and the soul of the beloved, the other upon a passing pleasure of the senses." *Ibid*, p. 172.

RELATION TO WOMEN

The following are some remarks of J. A. Symonds on the same subject:--

"Partly owing to the social habits of their cities, and partly to the peculiar notions which they entertained regarding the seclusion of free women in the home, all the higher elements of spiritual and mental activity, and the conditions under which a generous passion was conceivable, had become the exclusive privileges of men. It was not that women occupied a semi-servile station, as some students have imagined, or that within the sphere of the household they were not the respected and trusted helpmates of men. But circumstances rendered it impossible for them to excite romantic and enthusiastic passion. The exaltation of the emotions was reserved for the male sex." *A Problem in Greek Ethics*, p. 68.

J. A. SYMONDS ON SOCRATES

And he continues:--

"Socrates therefore sought to direct and moralize a force already existing. In the *Phædrus* he describes the passion of love between man and boy as a '*mania*,' not different in quality from that which inspires poets; and after painting that fervid picture of the lover, he declares that the true object of a noble life can only be attained by passionate friends, bound together in the chains of close yet temperate comradeship, seeking always to advance in knowledge, self-restraint, and intellectual illumination. The doctrine of the Symposium is not different, except that Socrates here takes a higher flight. The same love is treated as the method whereby the soul may begin her mystic journey to the region of essential beauty, truth, and goodness. It has frequently been remarked that Plato's dialogues have to be read as poems even more than as philosophical treatises; and if this be true at all, it is particularly true of both the *Phædrus* and the *Symposium*. The lesson which both essays seem intended to inculcate, is this: love, like poetry and prophecy, is a divine gift, which diverts men from the common current of their lives; but in the right use of this gift lies the secret of all human excellence. The passion which grovels in the filth of sensual grossness may be transformed into a glorious enthusiasm, a winged splendor, capable of soaring to the contemplation of eternal verities."

SPEECH OF PHÆDRUS

IN the *Symposium* or *Banquet* of Plato (B.C. 428-B.C. 347), a supper party is supposed, at which a discussion on love and friendship takes place. The friends present speak in turn--the enthusiastic Phædrus, the clear-headed

Pausanias, the grave doctor Eryximachus, the comic and acute Aristophanes, the young poet Agathon; Socrates, tantalizing, suggestive, and quoting the profound sayings of the prophetess Diotima; and Alcibiades, drunk, and quite ready to drink more;--each in his turn, out of the fulness of his heart, speaks; and thus in this most dramatic dialogue we have love discussed from every point of view, and with insight, acumen, romance and humor unrivalled.

Phædrus and Pausanias, in the two following quotations, take the line which perhaps most thoroughly represents the public opinion of the day--as to the value of friendship in nurturing a spirit of honor and freedom, especially in matters military and political:--

"Thus numerous are the witnesses who acknowledge love to be the eldest of the gods. And not only is he the eldest, he is also the source of the greatest benefits to us. For I know not any greater blessing to a young man beginning life than a virtuous lover, or to the lover than a beloved youth. For the principle which ought to be the guide of men who would nobly live--that principle, I say, neither kindred, nor honor, nor wealth, nor any other motive is able to implant so well as love. Of what am I speaking? of the sense of honor and dishonor, without which neither states nor individuals ever do any good or great work. And I say that a lover who is detected in doing any dishonorable act, or submitting through cowardice when any dishonor is done to him by another, will be more pained at being detected by his beloved than at being seen by his father, or by his companions, or by any one else. The beloved, too, when he is seen in any disgraceful situation, has the same feeling about his lover. And if there were only some way of contriving that a state or an army should be made up of lovers and their loves, they would be the very best governors of their own city, abstaining from all dishonor, and emulating one another in honor; and when fighting at one another's side, although a mere handful, they would overcome the world. For what lover would not choose rather to be seen by all mankind than by his beloved, either when abandoning his post or throwing away his arms? He would be ready to die a thousand deaths rather than endure this. Or who would desert his beloved, or fail him in the hour of danger? The veriest coward would become an inspired hero, equal to the bravest, at such a time; love would inspire him. That courage which, as Homer says, the god breathes into the soul of heroes, love of his own nature infuses into the lover." *Symposium of Plato, trans. B. Jowett.*

SPEECH OF PAUSANIAS

"In Ionia and other places, and generally in countries which are subject to the barbarians, the custom is held to be dishonorable; loves of youths share the evil repute of philosophy and gymnastics, because they are inimical to tyranny; for the interests of rulers require that their subjects should be poor in spirit, and that there should be no strong bond of friendship or society among them, which love above all other motives is likely to inspire, as our Athenian tyrants learned by experience." *Ibid.*

SPEECH OF ARISTOPHANES

ARISTOPHANES goes more deeply into the nature of this love of which they are speaking. He says it is a profound reality--a deep and intimate union, abiding after death, and making of the lovers "one departed soul instead of two." But in order to explain his allusion to "the other half" it must be premised that in the earlier part of his speech he: has in a serio-comic vein pretended that human beings were originally constructed double, with four legs, four arms, etc.; but that as a punishment for their sins Zeus divided them perpendicularly, "as folk cut eggs before they salt them," the males into two parts, the females into two, and the hermaphrodites likewise into two--since when, these divided people have ever pursued their lost halves, and "thrown their arms around and embraced each other, seeking to grow together again." And so, speaking of those who were originally males, he says:--

"And these when they grow up are our statesmen, and these only, which is a great proof of the truth of what I am saying. And when they reach manhood they are lovers of youth, and are not naturally inclined to marry or beget children, which they do, if at all, only in obedience to the law, but they are satisfied if they may be allowed to live with one another unwedded; and such a nature is prone to love and ready to return love, always embracing that which is akin to him. And when one of them finds his other half, whether he be a lover of youth or a lover of another sort, the pair are lost in an amazement of love and friendship and intimacy, and one will not be out of the other's sight, as I may say, even for a moment: they will pass their whole lives together; yet they could not explain what they desire of one another. For the intense yearning that each of them has towards the other does not appear to be the desire of lovers' intercourse, but of something else which the soul of either evidently desires and cannot tell, and of which she only has a dark and doubtful presentiment. Suppose Hephæstus, with his instruments, to come to the pair who are lying side by side and say to them, 'What do you people want of one another?' they would be unable to explain. And suppose further that when he saw their perplexity he said: 'Do you desire to be wholly one; always day and night to be in one another's company? for if this is what you desire, I am ready to melt you into one and let you grow together, so that being two you shall become one, and while you live, live a common life as if you were a single man, and after your death in the world below still be one departed soul instead of two--I ask whether this is what you lovingly desire, and whether you are satisfied to attain this?'--there is not a man of them who when he heard the proposal would deny or would not acknowledge that this meeting and melting in one another's arms, this becoming one instead of two, was the very expression of his ancient need." *Ibid.*

SPEECH OF SOCRATES

SOCRATES, in his speech, and especially in the later portion of it where he quotes his supposed tutoress Diotima, carries the argument up to its highest issue. After contending for the essentially creative, generative nature of love, not only in the Body but in the Soul, he proceeds to say that it is not so much the seeking of a lost half which causes the creative impulse in lovers, as the fact that in our mortal friends we are contemplating (though unconsciously) an image of the Essential and Divine Beauty; it is this that affects us with that wonderful "mania," and lifts us into the region where we become creators. And he follows on to the conclusion that it is by wisely and truly loving our visible friends that at last, after long, long experience, there dawns upon us the vision of that Absolute Beauty which by mortal eyes must ever remain unseen:--

"He who has been instructed thus far in the things of love, and who has learned to see the beautiful in due order and succession, when he comes towards the end will suddenly perceive a nature of wondrous beauty . . . beauty absolute, separate, simple and everlasting, which without diminution and without increase, or any change, is imparted to the ever-growing and perishing beauties of all other things. He who, from these ascending under the influence of true love, begins to perceive that beauty, is not far from the end." *Ibid.*

This is indeed the culmination, for Plato, of all existence-the ascent into the presence of that endless Beauty of which all fair mortal things are but the mirrors. But to condense this great speech of Socrates is impossible; only to persistent and careful reading (if even then) will it yield up all its treasures.

SOCRATES IN THE PHÆDRUS

IN the dialogue named *Phædrus* the same idea is worked out, only to some extent in reverse order. As in the *Symposium* the lover by rightly loving at last rises to the vision of the Supreme Beauty; so in the *Phædrus* it is explained that in reality every soul has at some time seen that Vision (at the time, namely, of its true initiation, when it was indeed winged)--but has forgotten it; and that it is the dim *reminiscence* of that Vision, constantly working within us, which guides us to our earthly loves and renders their effect upon us so transporting. Long ago, in some other condition of being, we saw Beauty herself:--

"But of beauty, I repeat again that we saw her there shining in company with the celestial forms; and coming to earth we find her here too, shining in clearness through the clearest aperture of sense. For sight is the keenest of our bodily senses; though not by that is wisdom seen; her loveliness would have been transporting if there had been a visible image of her, and the same is true of the loveliness of the other ideas as well. But this is the privilege of beauty, that she is the loveliest and also the most palpable to sight. Now he who is not newly initiated, or who has become corrupted, does not easily rise out of this world to the sight of true beauty in the other; he looks only at her earthly namesake, and instead of being awed at the sight of her, like a brutish beast he rushes on to enjoy and beget; he consorts with wantonness, and is not afraid or ashamed of pursuing pleasure in violation of nature. But he whose initiation is recent, and who has been the spectator of many glories in the other world, is amazed when he sees any one having a god-like face or form, which is the expression of Divine Beauty; and at first a shudder runs through him, and again the old awe steals over him; then looking upon the face of his beloved as of a god he reverences him, and if he were not afraid of being thought a downright madman, he would sacrifice to his beloved as to the image of a god." *The Phædrus of Plato, trans. B. Fowett.*

And again:--

"And so the beloved who, like a god, has received every true and loyal service from his lover, not in pretence but in reality, being also himself of a nature friendly to his admirer, if in former days he has blushed to own his passion and turned away his lover, because his youthful companions or others slanderously told him that he would be disgraced, now as years advance, at the appointed age and time, is led to receive him into communion. For fate which has ordained that there shall be no friendship among the evil has also ordained that there shall ever be friendship among the good. And when he has received him into communion and intimacy, then the beloved is amazed at the goodwill of the lover; he recognizes that the inspired friend is worth all other friendships or kinships, which have nothing of friendship in them in comparison. And when this feeling continues and he is nearer to him and embraces him, in gymnastic exercises and at other times of meeting, then does the fountain of that stream, which Zeus when he was in love with Ganymede named desire, overflow upon the lover, and some enters into his soul, and some when he is filled flows out again; and as a breeze or an echo rebounds from the smooth rocks and returns whence it came, so does the stream of beauty, passing the eyes which are the natural doors and windows of the soul, return again to the beautiful one; there arriving and quickening the passages of the wings, watering them and inclining them to grow, and filling the soul of the beloved also with love." *Ibid.*

For Plato the real power which ever moves the soul is this reminiscence of the Beauty which exists before all worlds. In the actual world the soul lives but in anguish, an exile from her true home; but in the presence of her friend, who reveals the Divine, she is loosed from her suffering and comes to her haven of rest.

"And wherever she [the soul] thinks that she will behold the beautiful one, thither in her desire she runs. And when she has seen him, and bathed herself with the waters of desire, her constraint is loosened, and she is refreshed, and has no more pangs and pains; and this is the sweetest of all pleasures at the time, and is the reason why the soul of the lover will never forsake his beautiful one, whom he esteems above all; he has forgotten mother and brethren and companions, and he thinks nothing of the neglect and loss of his property; the rules and proprieties of life, on which he formerly prided himself, he now despises, and is ready to sleep like a servant, wherever he is allowed, as near as he can to his beautiful one, who is not only the object of his worship, but the only physician who can heal him in his extreme agony." *Ibid.*

THE BANQUET OF XENOPHON

AT another time, in the Banquet of Xenophon, Socrates is again made to speak at length on the subject of Love--though not in so inspired a strain as in Plato:--

"Truly, to speak for one, I never remember the time when I was not in love; I know too that Charmides has had a great many lovers, and being much beloved has loved again. As for Critobulus, he is still of an age to love, and to be beloved; and Nicerates too, who loves so passionately his wife, at least as report goes, is equally beloved by her. . . . And as for you, Callias, you love, as well as the rest of us; (or who is it that is ignorant of your love for Autolycus? It is the town-talk; and foreigners, as well as our citizens, are acquainted with it. The reason for your loving him, I believe to be that you are both born of illustrious families; and at the same time are both possessed of personal qualities that render you yet more illustrious. For me, I always admired the sweetness and evenness of your temper; but much more when I consider that your passion for Autolycus is placed on a person who has nothing luxurious or affected in him; but in all things shows a vigor and temperance worthy of a virtuous soul; which is a proof at the same time that if he is infinitely beloved, he deserves to be so. I confess indeed I am not firmly persuaded whether there be but one Venus or two, the celestial and the vulgar; and it may be with this goddess, as with Jupiter, who has many different names though there is still but one Jupiter. But I know very well that both the Venuses have quite different altars, temples and sacrifices. The vulgar Venus is worshipped after a common negligent manner; whereas the celestial one is adored in purity and sanctity of life. The vulgar inspires mankind with the love of the body only, but the celestial fires the mind with the love of the soul, with friendship, and a generous thirst after noble actions. . . . Nor is it hard to prove, Callias, that gods and heroes have always had more passion and esteem for the charms of the soul, than those of the body: at least this seems to have been the opinion of our ancient authors. For we may observe in the fables of antiquity that Jupiter, who loved several mortals on account of their personal beauty only, never conferred upon them immortality. Whereas it was otherwise with Hercules, Castor, Pollux, and several others; for having admired and applauded the greatness of their courage and the beauty of their minds, he enrolled them in the number of the gods. . . . You are then infinitely obliged to the gods, Callias, who have inspired you with love and friendship for Autolycus, as they have inspired Critobulus with the same for Amandra; for real and pure friendship knows no difference in sexes." *Banquet of Xenophon* § viii. (*Bohn*).

PLUTARCH PHILOSOPHIZES

PLUTARCH, who wrote in the first century A.D. (nearly 500 years after Plato), carried on the tradition of his master, though with an admixture of later influences; and philosophized about friendship, on the basis of true love being a reminiscence.

"The rainbow is I suppose a reflection caused by the sun's rays falling on a moist cloud, making us think the appearance is in the cloud. Similarly erotic fancy in the case of noble souls causes a reflection of the memory from things which here appear and are called beautiful to what is really divine and lovely and felicitous and wonderful. But most lovers pursuing and groping after the semblance of beauty in youths and women, as in mirrors, 1 can derive nothing more certain than pleasure mixed with pain. And this seems the love-delirium of Ixion, who instead of the joy he desired embraced only a cloud, as children who desire to take the rainbow into their hands, clutching at whatever they see. But different is the behavior of the noble and chaste lover: for he reflects on the divine beauty that can only be felt, while he uses the beauty of the visible body only as an organ of the memory, though he embraces it and loves it, and associating with it is still more inflamed in mind. And so neither in the body do they sit ever gazing at and desiring this light, nor after death do they return to this world again, and skulk and loiter about the doors and bedchambers of newly-married people, disagreeable ghosts of pleasure-loving and sensual men and women, who do not rightly deserve the name of lovers. For the true lover, when he has got into the other world and associated with beauties as much as is lawful, has wings and is initiated and passes his time above in the presence of his Deity, dancing and waiting upon him, until he goes back to the meadows of the Moon and Aphrodite, and sleeping there commences a new existence. But this is a subject too high for the present occasion." *Plutarch's Eroticus* § xx. *trans. Bohn's Classics.*

ARISTOTLE

ARISTOTLE (Ethics, bk. viii.) says:--

"Friendship is a thing most necessary to life, since without friends no one would choose to live, though possessed of all other advantages." . . . "Since then his own life is, to a good man, a thing naturally sweet and ultimately desirable, for a similar reason is the life of his friend agreeable to him, and delightful merely on its own account, and without reference to any object beyond it; and to live without friends is to be destitute of a good, unconditioned, absolute, and in itself desirable; and therefore to be deprived of one of the most solid and most substantial of all enjoyments."

"Being asked 'What is Friendship?' Aristotle replied, 'One soul in two bodies.'" *Diog. Laertius.*

EPAMINONDAS AND PELOPIDAS

EPAMINONDAS and Pelopidas, the Theban statesmen and generals, were celebrated for their devotion to each other. In a battle (B.C. 385) against the Arcadians, Epaminondas is said to have saved his friend's life. Plutarch in his Life of Pelopidas relates of them:--

"Epaminondas and he were both born with the same dispositions to all kinds of virtues, but Pelopidas took more pleasure in the exercises of the body, and Epaminondas in the improvements of the mind; so that they spent all their leisure time, the one in hunting, and the pelestra, the other in learned conversation, and the study of philosophy. But of all the famous actions for which they are so much celebrated, the judicious part of mankind reckon none so great and glorious as that strict friendship which they inviolably preserved through the whole course of their lives, in all the high posts they held, both military and civil. . . . For being both in that battle, near one another in the infantry, and fighting against the Arcadians, that wing of the Lacedæmonians in which they were, gave way and was broken; which Pelopidas and Epaminondas perceiving, they joined their shields, and keeping close together, bravely repulsed all that attacked them, till at last Pelopidas, after receiving seven large wounds, fell upon a heap of friends and enemies that lay dead together. Epaminondas, though he believed him slain, advanced before him to defend his body and arms, and for a long time maintained his ground against great numbers of the

Arcadians, being resolved to die rather than desert his companion and leave him in the enemy's power; but being wounded in his breast by a spear, and in his arm by a sword, he was quite disabled and ready to fall, when Agesipolis, king of the Spartans, came from the other wing to his relief, and beyond all expectation saved both their lives."

POLEMON AND KRATES

POLEMON and Krates were followers of Plato in philosophy, and in their time (about 300 B.C.) leaders of the Platonic School. They were, according to Hesychius, devoted friends:--

"Krates and Polemon loved each other so well that they not only were occupied in life with the same work, but they almost drew breath simultaneously; and in death they shared the same grave. On account of which, Archesilaus, who visited them in company with Theophrastus (a pupil of. Aristotle), spoke of them as gods, or survivors from the Golden Age."

Hesychius xl.

ALEXANDER AND HEPHÆSTION

ALEXANDER, the great World-Conqueror, was born B.C. 356, and was King of Macedonia B.C. 336-323. His great favorite was Hephæstion, who had been brought up and educated with him.

"When Hephæstion died at Ecbatana (in 324) Alexander placed his weapons upon the funeral pyre, with gold and silver for the dead man, and a robe--which last, among the Persians is a symbol of great honor. He shore off his own hair, as in Homeric grief, and behaved like the Achilles of Homer. Indeed he acted more violently and passionately than the latter, for he caused the towers and strongholds of Ecbatana to be demolished all round. As long as he only dedicated his own hair, he was behaving, I think, like a Greek; but when he laid hands on the very walls, Alexander was already showing his grief in foreign fashion. Even in his clothing he departed from ordinary custom, and gave himself up to his mood, his love, and his tears."

Aelian's Varia Historia, vii, 8.

III

POETRY OF FRIENDSHIP AMONG GREEKS AND ROMANS

THE fact, already mentioned, that the romance of love among the Greeks was chiefly felt towards male friends, naturally led to their poetry being largely inspired by friendship; and Greek literature contains such a great number of poems of this sort, that I have thought it worth while to dedicate the main portion of the following section to quotations from them. No translations of course can do justice to the beauty of the originals, but the few specimens given may help to illustrate the depth and tenderness as well as the temperance and sobriety which on the whole characterized Greek feeling on this subject, at any rate during the best period of Hellenic culture. The remainder of the section is devoted to Roman poetry of the time of the Cæsars.

MOTIVE OF HOMER'S ILIAD

It is not always realized that the Iliad of Homer turns upon the motive of friendship, but the extracts immediately following will perhaps make this clear. E. F. M. Benecke in his *Position of Women in Greek Poetry* (p. 76) says of the Iliad:

"It is a story of which the main motive is the love of Achilles for Patroclus. This solution is astoundingly simple, and yet it took me so long to bring myself to accept it that I am quite ready to forgive any one who feels a similar hesitation. But those who do accept it cannot fail to observe, on further consideration, how thoroughly suitable a motive of this kind would be in a national Greek epic. For this is the motive running through the whole of Greek life, till that life was transmuted by the influence of Macedonia. The lover-warriors Achilles and Patroclus are the direct spiritual ancestors of the sacred Band of Thebans, who died to a man on the field of Chæronæa."

ACHILLES AND PATROCLUS

The following two quotations are from *The Greek Poets* by J. A. Symonds, ch. iii., p. 80 *et seq.*:--

"The Iliad therefore has for its whole subject the passion of Achilles--that ardent energy or μηνις of the hero which displayed itself first as anger against Agamemnon, and afterwards as love for the lost Patroclus. The truth of this was perceived by one of the greatest poets and profoundest critics of the modern world, Dante., When Dante, in the Inferno, wished to describe Achilles, he wrote, with characteristic brevity:--

"Achille
Che per amore at fine combatteo."

("Achilles
Who at the last was brought to fight by love.")

"In this pregnant sentence Dante sounded the whole depth of the *Iliad.* The wrath of Achilles for Agamemnon, which prevented him at first from fighting; the love of Achilles, passing the love of women, for Patroclus, which induced him to forego his anger and to fight at last; these are the two poles on which the *Iliad* turns."

HOMER'S VERSION

After his quarrel with Agamemnon, not even all the losses of the Greeks and the entreaties of Agamemnon himself will induce Achilles to fight--not till Patroclus is slain by Hector--Patroclus, his dear friend "whom above all my comrades I honored, even as myself." Then he rises up, dons his armor, and driving the Trojans before him revenges himself on the body of Hector. But Patroclus lies yet unburied; and when the fighting is over, to Achilles comes the ghost of his dead friend:--

"The son of Peleus, by the shore of the roaring sea lay, heavily groaning, surrounded by his Myrmidons; on a fair space of sand he lay, where the waves lapped the beach. Then slumber took him, loosing the cares of his heart, and mantling softly around him, for sorely wearied were his radiant limbs with driving Hector on by windy Troy. There to him came the soul of poor Patroclus, in all things like himself, in stature, and in the beauty of his eyes and voice, and on the form was raiment like his own. He stood above. the hero's head, and spake to him:--

"Sleepest thou, and me hast thou forgotten, Achilles? Not in my life wert thou neglectful of me, but in death. Bury me soon, that I may ass the gates of Hades. Far off the souls, the shadows of the dead, repel me, nor suffer me to join them on the river bank; but, as it is, thus I roam around the wide-doored house of Hades. But stretch to me thy hand I entreat; for never again shall I return from Hades when once e shall have given me the meed of funeral fire. Nay, never shall we sit in life apart from our dear comrades and take counsel together. But me hath hateful fate enveloped--fate that was mine at the moment of my birth. And for thyself, divine Achilles, it is doomed to die beneath the noble Trojan's wall. Another thing I say to thee, and bid thee do it if thou wilt obey me:--lay not my bones apart from thine, Achilles, but lay them together; for we were brought up together in house, when Menœtius brought me, a child, Opus to your house, because of woeful bloodshed on the day in which I slew the son of Amphidamas, myself a child, not willing it but in anger at our games. Then did the horseman, Peleus, take me, and rear me in his house, and cause me to be called thy squire. So then let one grave also hide the bones of both of us, the golden urn thy goddess-mother gave to thee.'

"Him answered swift-footed Achilles:--

'Why, dearest and most honored, hast thou hither come, to lay on me this thy behest? All things most certainly will I perform, and bow to what thou biddest. But stand thou near: even for one moment let us throw our arms upon each other's neck, and take our fill of sorrowful wailing.'

"So spake he, and with his outstretched hands he clasped, but could not seize. The spirit, earthward, like smoke, vanished with a shriek. Then all astonished arose Achilles, and beat his palms together, and spake a piteous word:--

'Heavens! is there then, among the dead, soul and the shade of life, but thought is theirs no more at all? For through the night the soul of poor Patroclus stood above my head, wailing and sorrowing loud, and bade me do his will; it was the very semblance of himself.'

So spake he, and in the hearts of all of them he raised desire of lamentation; and while they were yet mourning to them appeared rose-fingered dawn about the piteous corpse." *Iliad*, xxiii. 59 *et seq.*

PLATO'S VERSION

PLATO in the *Symposium* dwells tenderly on this relation between Achilles and Patroclus:--

[And great] "was the reward of the true love of Achilles towards his lover Patroclus--his lover and not his love (the notion that Patroclus was the beloved one is a foolish error into which Æschylus has fallen, for Achilles was surely the fairer of the two, fairer also than all the other heroes; and, as Homer informs us, he was still beardless, and younger far). And greatly as the gods honor the virtue of love, still the return of love on the part of the beloved to the lover is more admired and valued and rewarded by them, for the lover has a nature more divine and worthy of worship. Now Achilles was quite aware, for he had been told by his mother, that he might avoid death and return home, and live to a good old age, if he abstained from slaying Hector. Nevertheless he gave his life to revenge his friend, and dared to die, not only on his behalf, but after his death. Wherefore the gods honored him even above Alcestis, and sent him to the Islands of the Blest." *Symposium, speech of Phædrus, trans. by B. Fowett.*

And on this passage Symonds has the following note:--

"Plato, discussing the *Myrmidones* of Æschylus, remarks in the *Symposium* that the tragic poet was wrong to make Achilles the lover of Patroclus, seeing that Patroclus was the elder of the two, and that Achilles was the youngest and most beautiful of all the Greeks. The fact however is that Homer raises no question in our minds about the relation of lover and beloved. Achilles and Patroclus are comrades. Their friendship is equal. It was only the reflective activity of the Greek mind, working upon the Homeric legend by the light of subsequent custom, which introduced these distinctions." *The Greek Poets*, ch. iii. p. 103.

ATHENÆUS

From the time of Homer onwards, Greek literature was full of songs celebrating friendship:--

"And in fact there was such emulation about composing poems of this sort, and so far was any one from thinking lightly of the amatory poets, that

Æschylus, who was a very great poet, and Sophocles too introduced the subject of the loves of men on the stage in their tragedies: the one describing the love of Achilles for Patroclus, and the other, in his Niobe, the mutual love of her sons (on which account some have given an ill name to that tragedy); and all such passages as those are very agreeable to the spectators." *Athenæus*, bk. xlii. ch. 75.

FROM THEOGNIS

ONE of the earlier Greek poets was Theognis (B.C. 550) whose Gnomæ or Maxims were a series of verses mostly addressed to his young friend Kurnus, whom by this means he sought to guide and instruct out of the stores of his own riper experience. The verses are reserved and didactic for the most part, but now and then, as in the following passage, show deep underlying feeling:

"Lo, I have given thee wings wherewith to fly
  Over the boundless ocean and the earth;
Yea, on the lips of many shalt thou lie
  The comrade of their banquet and their mirth.
Youths in their loveliness shall make thee sound
  Upon the silver flute's melodious breath;
And when thou goest darkling underground
  Down to the lamentable house of death,
Oh yet not then from honor shalt thou cease,
  But wander, an imperishable name,
Kurnus, about the seas and shores of Greece,
  Crossing from isle to isle the barren main.
Horses thou shalt not need, but lightly ride
  Sped by the Muses of the violet crown,
And men to come, while earth and sun abide,
  Who cherish song shall cherish thy renown.
Yea, I have given thee wings I and in return
  Thou givest me the scorn with which I burn."

Theognis Gnomai, lines 237-254,
trans. by G. Lowes Dickinson.

SAPPHO

AS Theognis had his well-loved disciples, so had the poetess Sappho (600 B. c.). Her devotion to her girl-friends and companions is indeed proverbial.

"What Alcibiades and Charmides and Phædrus were to Socrates, Gyrinna and Atthis and Anactoria were to the Lesbian." *Max Tyrius, quoted in H. T. Wharton's Sappho*, p. 23.

Perhaps the few lines of Sappho, translated or paraphrased by Catullus under the title *To Lesbia*, form the most celebrated fragment of her extant work. They may be roughly rendered thus:--

"Peer of all the gods unto me appeareth
He of men who sitting beside thee heareth
Close at hand thy syllabled words sweet spoken,
Or loving laughter--

That sweet laugh which flutters my heart and bosom.
For, at sight of thee, in an instant fail me
Voice and speech, and under my skin there courses
Swiftly a thin flame;

Darkness is on my eyes, in my ears a drumming,
Drenched in sweat my frame, my body trembling;
Paler ev'n than grass--'tis, I doubt, but little
From death divides me."

ANACREON TO BATHYLLUS

SEVERAL of the odes of Anacreon (B.C. 520) are addressed to his young friend Bathyllus. The following short one has been preserved to us by Athenæus (bk. xiii. § 17):--

"O boy, with virgin-glancing eye,
I call thee, but thou dost not hear;
Thou know'st not how my soul doth cry
For thee, its charioteer."

Anacreon had not the passion and depth of Sappho, but there is a mark of genuine feeling in some of his poems, as in this simple little epigram:--

"On their hindquarters horses
  Are branded oft with fire,
And any one knows a Parthian
  Because he wears a tiar;
And I at sight of lovers
  Their nature can declare,
For in their hearts they too
  Some subtle flame-mark bear."

The following fragment is from Pindar's Ode to his young friend Theoxenos--in whose arms Pindar is said to have died (B.C. 442):--

"O soul, 'tis thine in season meet,
O pluck of love the blossom sweet,
When hearts are young:
But he who sees the blazing beams,
The light that from *that* forehead streams,
  And is not stung;--
Who is not storm-tossed with desire,--
Lo! he, I ween, with frozen fire,
Of adamant or stubborn steel
Is forged in his cold heart that cannot feel."
Trans. by F. Addington Symonds,
The Greek Poets, vol. I, p. 286.

EPIGRAMS OF PLATO

PLATO'S epigrams on Aster and Agathon are well known. The two first-quoted make a play of course on the name Aster (star).

To Aster.

"Thou wert the morning star among the living,
Ere thy fair light had fled;
Now, having died, thou art as Hesperus, giving
New splendor to the dead." (*Shelley.*)

To the same.

"Thou at the stars dost gaze, who art my star--O would that I were
Heaven, to gaze on thee, ever with thousands of eyes."

To Agathon:

"Thee as I kist, behold! on my lips my own soul was trembling;
For, bold one, she had come, meaning to find her way through."

MELEAGER

There are many other epigrams and songs on the same subject from the Greek writers. The following is by Meleager (a native of Gadara in Palestine) about 60 B. c., and one of the sweetest and most human of the lyric poets:--

"O mortals crossed in love! the Southwind, see!
That blows so fair for sailor folk, hath ta'en
Half of my soul, Andragathos, from me.
Thrice happy ships, thrice blesséd billowy main,
And four times favored wind that bears the youth,
O would I were a Dolphin! so, in truth,
High on my shoulders ferried he should come
To Rhodes, sweet haunt of boys, his island home."
From the Greek Anthology, ii. 402.

Also from the Greek Anthology:--

"O say, and again repeat, fair, fair--and still I will say it--
How fair, my friend, and good to see, thou art;
On pine or oak or wall thy name I do not blazon--
Love has too deeply graved it in my heart."

EPITAPH ANONYMOUS

Perhaps the most beautiful [says J. A. Symonds] of the sepulchral epigrams is one by an unknown writer, of which I here give a free paraphrase. *Anth. Pal.*, vii. 346:--

"'Of our great love, Parthenophil,
This little stone abideth still
  Sole sign and token:
I seek thee yet, and yet shall seek,
Tho' faint mine eyes, my spirit weak
  With prayers unspoken.

Meanwhile best friend or friends, do thou,
If this the cruel fates allow,
  By death's dark river,
Among those shadowy people, drink
No drop for me on Lethe's brink:
  Forget me never!'"
        The Greek Poets, Vol. 2, p. 298.

THEOCRITUS' IDYLS

THEOCRITUS, though coming late in the Greek age (about 300 B.C.) when Athens had yielded place to Alexandria, still carried on the Greek tradition in a remarkable way. A native of Syracuse, he caught and echoed in a finer form the life and songs of the country folk of that region--themselves descendants of Dorian settlers. Songs and ballads full of similar notes linger among the Greek peasants, shepherds and fisher-folk, even down to the present day.

The following poem (trans. by M. J. Chapman, 1836) is one of the best known and most beautiful of his Idyls:--

IDYL XII

"Art come, dear youth? two days and nights away!
(Who burn with love, grow aged in a day.)
As much as apples sweet the damson crude
Excel; the blooming spring the winter rude;
In fleece the sheep her lamb; the maiden in sweetness
The thrice-wed dame; the fawn the calf in fleetness;
The nightingale in song all feathered kind--
So much thy longed-for presence cheers my mind.
To thee I hasten, as to shady beech,
The traveller, when from the heaven's reach

The sun fierce blazes. May our love be strong,
To all hereafter times the theme of song!
'Two men each other loved to that degree,
That either friend did in the other see
A dearer than himself. They lived of old
Both golden natures in an age of gold.'

O father Zeus! ageless immortals all!
Two hundred ages hence may one recall,
Down-coming to the irremeable river,
This to my mind, and this good news deliver:
'E'en now from east to west, from north to south,
Your mutual friendship lives in every mouth.'
This, as they please, th' Olympians will decide: p. 77
Of thee, by blooming virtue beautified,
My glowing song shall only truth disclose;
With falsehood's pustules I'll not shame my nose.
If thou dost sometime grieve me, sweet the pleasure
Of reconcilement, joy in double measure
To find thou never didst intend the pain,
And feel myself from all doubt free again.

And ye Megarians, at Nisæa dwelling,
Expert at rowing, mariners excelling,
Be happy ever! for with honors due
Th' Athenian Diocles, to friendship true
Ye celebrate. With the first blush of spring
The youth surround his tomb: there who shall bring
The sweetest kiss, whose lip is purest found,
Back to his mother goes with garlands crowned.
Nice touch the arbiter must have indeed,
And must, methinks, the blue-eyed Ganymede
Invoke with many prayers--a mouth to own
True to the touch of lips, as Lydian stone
To proof of gold--which test will instant show
The pure or base, as money changers know."

The following Idyl, of which I append a rendering, is attributed to Theocritus:--

IDYL XXIX

They say, dear boy, that wine and truth agree;
And, being in wine, I'll tell the truth to thee--
Yes, all that works in secret in my soul.
'Tis this: thou dost not love me with thy whole
Untampered heart. I know; for half my time
Is spent in gazing on thy beauty's prime;
The other half is nought. When thou art good,
My days are like the gods'; but when the mood
Tormenting takes thee, 'tis my night of woe.
How were it right to vex a lover so?
Take my advice, my lad, thine elder friend,
'Twill make thee glad and grateful in the end:
In one tree build one nest, so no grim snake
May creep upon thee. For to-day thou'lt make
Thy home on one branch, and to-morrow changing
wilt seek another, to what's new still ranging;
And should a stranger praise your handsome face,
Him more than three-year-proven friend you'll grace,
While him who loved you first you'll treat as cold
As some acquaintanceship of three days old.
Thou fliest high, methinks, in love and pride;
But I would say: keep ever at thy side
A mate that is thine equal; doing so,
The townsfolk shall speak well of thee alway,
And love shall never visit thee with woe--
Love that so easily men's hearts can flay,
And mine has conquered that was erst of steel.
Nay, by thy gracious lips I make appeal:
Remember thou wert younger a year agone
And we grow grey and wrinkled, all, or e'er
We can escape our doom; of mortals none
His youth retakes again, for azure wings
Are on her shoulders, and we sons of care
Are all too slow to catch such flying things.

Mindful of this, be gentle, is my prayer,
And love me, guileless, ev'n as I love thee;
So when thou hast a beard, such friends as were
Achilles and Patroclus we may be."

BION

BION was a poet of about the same period as Theocritus, but of whom little is known. The following is a fragment translated by A. Lang:--

"Happy are they that love, when with equal love they are rewarded. Happy was Theseus, when Pirithous was by is side, yea tho' he went down to the house of implacable Hades. Happy among hard men and inhospitable was Orestes, for that Pylades chose to share his wanderings. And he was happy, Achilles Æacides, while his darling lived,--happy was he in his death, because he avenged the dread fate of Patroclus." *Theocritus, Bion and Moschus, Golden Treasury series*, p. 182.

LAMENT FOR BION BY MOSCHUS

The beautiful *Lament for Bion* by Moschus is interesting in this connection, and should be compared with Shelley's lament for Keats in *Adonais*--for which latter poem indeed it supplied some suggestions:--

Ye mountain valleys, pitifully groan!
Rivers and Dorian springs for Bion weep!
Ye plants drop tears! ye groves lamenting moan!
Exhale your life, wan flowers; your blushes deep
In grief, anemonies and roses, steep!
In softest murmurs, Hyacinth! prolong
The sad, sad woe thy lettered petals keep;
Our minstrel sings no more his friends among
Sicilian muses! now begin the doleful song."

M. F. Chapman trans. in the
Greek Pastoral Poets, 1836.

The allusion to Hyacinth is thus explained by Chapman:--

"Hyacinthus, a Spartan youth, the son of Clio, was in great favor with Apollo. Zephyrus, being enraged that he preferred Apollo to him, blew the discus when flung by Apollo, on a day that Hyacinthus was playing at discus-throwing with that god, against the head of the youth, and so killed him. Apollo, being unable to save his life, changed him into the flower which was named after him, and on whose petals the Greeks fancied they could trace the notes of grief. A festival called the Hyacinthia was celebrated for three days in each year at Sparta, in honor of the god and his unhappy favorite." *Note to Moschus*, Idyl iii.

TOLD BY OVID

The story of Apollo and Hyacinth is gracefully told by Ovid, in the tenth book of his Metamorphoses:--

"Midway betwixt the past and coming night
Stood Titan when the pair, their limbs unrobed,
And glistning with the olive's unctuous juice,
In friendly contest with the discus vied."

[The younger one is struck by the discus; and like a fading flower]

"To its own weight unequal drooped the head
Of Hyacinth; and o'er him wailed the god:--
Liest thou so, Œbalia's child, of youth
Untimely robbed, and wounded by my fault--
At once my grief and guilt?--This hand hath dealt
Thy death! 'Tis I who send thee to the grave!
And yet scarce guilty, unless guilt it were
To sport, or guilt to love thee! Would this life
Might thine redeem, or be with thine resigned!
But thou--since Fate denies a god to die--
Be present with me ever! Let thy name
Dwell ever in my heart and on my lips,
Theme of my lyre and burden of my song;
And ever bear the echo of my wail
Wt on thy new-born flower! The time shall come
When, with thyself associate, to its name
The mightiest of the Greeks shall link his own.
Prophetic as Apollo mourned, the blood
That with its dripping crimson dyed the turf
Was blood no more: and sudden sprang to life
A flower."

Ovid's Metamorphoses trans.
H. King, London, 1871.

VIRGIL ECLOGUE II

IN Roman literature, generally, as might be expected, with its more materialistic spirit, the romance of friendship is little dwelt upon; though the grosser side of the passion, in such writers as Catullus and Martial, is much in evidence. Still we find in Virgil a notable instance. His 2nd Eclogue bears the marks of genuine feeling; and, according to some critics, he there under the guise of Shepherd Corydon's love for Alexis celebrates his own attachment to the youthful Alexander:--

> Corydon, keeper of cattle, once loved the fair lad Alexis;
> But he, the delight of his master, permitted no hope to the shepherd.
> Corydon, lovesick swain, went into the forest of beeches,
> And there to the mountains and woods--the one relief of his passion--
> With useless effort outpoured the following artless complainings:--
> Alexis, barbarous youth, say, do not my mournful lays move thee?
> Showing me no compassion, thou'lt surely compel me to perish.
> Even the cattle now seek after places both cool and shady;
> Even the lizards green conceal themselves in the thorn-bush.
> Thestylis, taking sweet herbs, such as garlic and thyme, for the reapers
> Faint with the scorching noon, doth mash them and bray in a mortar.
> Alone in the heat of the day am I left with the screaming cicalas,
> While patients in tracking thy path, I ever pursue thee, Belovéd."
>
> *Trans. by J. W. Baylis.*

CORYDON AND ALEXIS

There is a translation of this same 2nd Eclogue, by Abraham Fraunce (1591), which is interesting not only on account of its felicity of phrase, but because, as in the case of some other Elizabethan hexameters, the metre is ruled by *quantity*, *i.e.*, length of syllables, instead of by *accent*. The following are the first five lines of Fraunce's translation:--

> "Silly shepherd Corydon lov'd hartyly fayre lad Alexis,
> His master's dearling, but saw noe matter of hoping;
> Only amydst darck groves thickset with broade shadoe beech-trees
> Dayly resort did he make, thus alone to the woods, to the mountyns
> With broken speeches fond thoughts there vaynly revealing."

CATULLUS also (b. B.C. 87) has some verses of real feeling:--

> "Quintius, if 'tis thy wish and will
> That I should owe my eyes to thee,
> Or anything that's dearer still,
> If aught that's dearer there can be;
>
> Then rob me not of that I prize,
> Of the dear form that is to me,
> Oh! far far dearer than my eyes,
> Or aught, if dearer aught there be."
> *Catullus, trans. Hon. F. Lamb*, 1821.

> "If all complying, thou would'st grant
> Thy lovely eyes to kiss, my fair,
> Long as I pleased; oh! I would plant
> Three hundred thousand kisses there.
>
> Nor could I even then refrain,
> Nor satiate leave that fount of blisses,
> Tho' thicker than autumnal grain
> Should be our growing crop of kisses."
> *(Ibid.)*

TO LICINIUS

> "Long at our leisure yesterday
> Idling, Licinius, we wrote
> Upon my tablets verses gay,

Or took our turns, as fancy smote,
At rhymes and dice and wine.

But when I left, Licinius mine,
Your grace and your facetious mood
Had fired me so, that neither food
Would stay my misery, nor sleep
My roving eyes in quiet keep.
But still consumed, without respite,
I tossed about my couch in vain
And longed for day--if speak I might,
Or be with you again.

But when my limbs with all the strain
Worn out, half dead lay on my bed,
Sweet friend to thee this verse I penned,
That so thou mayest condescend
To understand my pain.

So now, Licinius, beware!
And be not rash, but to my prayer
A gracious hearing tender;
Lest on thy head pounce Nemesis:
A goddess sudden and swift she is
Beware lest thou offend her!"

MARTIAL TO DIADUMENOS

The following little poem is taken from Martial:--

"As a vineyard breathes, whose boughs with grapes are bending,
Or garden where are hived Sicanian bees;
As upturned clods when summer rain's descending
Or orchards rich with blossom-laden trees;
So, cruel youth, thy kisses breathe--so sweet--
Would'st thou but grant me all their grace, complete!"

IV

FRIENDSHIP IN EARLY CHRISTIAN AND MEDIÆVAL TIMES

THE quotations we have given from Plato and others show the very high ideal of friendship which obtained in the old world, and the respect accorded to it. With the incoming of the Christian centuries, and the growth of Alexandrian and Germanic influences, a change began to take place. Woman rose to greater freedom and dignity and influence than before. The romance of love began to centre round her. The days of chivalry brought a new devotion into the world, and the Church exalted the Virgin Mother to the highest place in heaven. Friendship between men ceased to be regarded in the old light--*i.e.*, as a thing of deep feeling, and an important social institution. It was even, here and there, looked on with disfavor--and lapses from the purity or chastity of its standard were readily suspected and violently reprobated. Certainly it survived in the monastic life for a long period; but though inspiring this to a great extent, its influence was not generally acknowledged. The Family, in the modern and more limited sense of the word (as opposed to the clan), became the recognized unit of social life, and the ideal centre of all good influences (as illustrated in the worship of the Holy Family). At the same time, by this very shrinkage of the Family, as well as by other influences, the solidarity of society became to some extent weakened, and gradually the more communistic forms of the early world gave place to the individualism of the commercial period.

The special sentiment of comrade-love or attachment (being a thing inherent in human nature) remained of course through the Christian centuries, as before, and unaltered--except that being no longer recognized it became a private and personal affair, running often powerfully enough beneath the surface of society, but openly unacknowledged, and so far deprived of some of its dignity and influence. Owing to this fact there is nothing, for this period, to be quoted in the way of general ideal or public opinion on the subject of friendship, and the following sections therefore become limited to the expression of individual sentiments and experiences, in prose and poetry.

These we find, during the mediæval period, largely colored by religion; while at the Renaissance and afterwards they are evidently affected by Greek associations.

SAINT AUGUSTINE

FOLLOWING are some passages from S. Augustine:--

"In those years when I first began to teach in my native town, I had made a friend, one who through having the same interests was very dear to me, one of my own age, and like me in the first flower of youth. We had grown up together, and went together to school, and used to play together. But he was not yet so great a friend as afterwards, nor even then was our friendship true; for friendship is not true unless Thou cementest it between those who are united to Thee by that 'love which is shed abroad in our hearts by the Holy Ghost which is given unto us.' Yet our friendship was but too sweet, and fermented by the pursuit of kindred studies. For I had turned him aside from the true faith (of which as a youth he had but an imperfect grasp) to pernicious and superstitious fables, for which my mother grieved over me. And now in mind he erred with me, and my soul could not endure to be separated from him. But lo, Thou didst follow close behind Thy fugitives, Thou--both God of vengeance and fountain of mercies-- didst convert us by wonderful ways; behold, Thou didst take him out of this life, when scarcely a ear had our close intimacy lasted--sweet to me beyond the sweetness of my whole life. . . .

No ray of light pierced the gloom with which my heart was enveloped by this grief, and wherever I looked I beheld death. M native place was a torment to me, and my father's house strangely joyless; and whatever I had shared with him, without him was now turned into a huge torture. My longing eyes sought him everywhere, and found him not; and I hated the very places, because he was not in them, neither could they say to me 'he is coming,' as they used to do when he was alive and was absent. And I became a great puzzle to myself, and I asked my soul why it was so sad, and why so disquieted within me; and it knew not what to answer. And if I said 'Trust thou in God,' it rightly did not obey; for that dearest one whom it had lost was both truer and better than that phantasm in which it was bidden to trust. Weeping was the only thing which was sweet to me, and it succeeded my friend in the dearest place in my heart." *S. Augustine, Confessions,* bk. 4, ch. iv. *Trans. by Rev. W. H. Hutchings, M.A.*

"I was miserable, and miserable is every soul which is fettered by the love of perishable things; he is torn to pieces when he loses them, and then he perceives how miserable he was in reality while he possessed them. And so was I then, and I wept most bitterly, and in that bitterness I found rest. Thus was I miserable, and that miserable life I held dearer than my friend. For though I would fain have changed it, yet to it I clung even more than to him; and I cannot say whether I would have parted with it for his sake, as it is related, if true, that Orestes and Pylades were willing to do, for they would gladly have died for each other, or together, for they preferred death to separation from each other. But in me a feeling which I cannot explain, and one of a contradictory nature had arisen; for I had at once an unbearable weariness of living, and a fear of dying. For I believe the more I loved him, the more I hated and dreaded death which had taken him from me, and regarded it as a most cruel enemy; and I felt as if it would soon devour all men, now that its power had reached him. . . . For I marveled that other mortals lived, because he whom I had loved, without thought of his ever dying, was dead; and that I still lived--I who was another self--,when he was gone, was a greater marvel still. Well said a certain one of his friend, 'Thou half of my soul;' for I felt that his soul and mine were 'one soul in two bodies:' and therefore life was to me horrible, because I hated to live as half of a life; and therefore perhaps I feared to die, lest he should wholly die whom I had loved so greatly." *Ibid*, ch. vi.

MONTALEMBERT ON THE MONKS

IT is interesting to see, in these extracts from S. Augustine, and in those which follow from Montalembert, the points of likeness and difference between the Christian ideal of love and that of Plato. Both are highly transcendental, both seem to contemplate an inner union of souls, beyond the reach of space and time; but in Plato the union is in contemplation of the Eternal Beauty, while in the Christian teachers it is in devotion to a personal God.

"If inanimate nature was to them an abundant source of pleasure they had a life still more lively and elevated in the life of the heart, in the double love which burned in them--the love of their brethren inspired and consecrated by the love of God." *Monks of the West*, introdn., ch. v.

"Everything invited and encouraged them to choose one or several souls as the intimate companions of their life. . . . And to prove how little the divine love, thus understood and practiced, tends to exclude or chill the love of man for man, never was human eloquence more touching or more sincere than in that immortal elegy by which S. Bernard laments a lost brother snatched by death from the cloister:--'Flow, flow my tears, so eager to flow! he who prevented your flowing is here no more! It is not he who is dead, it is I who now live only to die. Why, O why have we loved, and why have we lost each other.'" *Ibid.*

"The mutual affection which reigned among the monks flowed as a mighty stream through the annals of the cloister. It has left its trace even in the 'formulas,' collected with care by modern eruditions. . . . The correspondence of the most illustrious, of Geoffrey de Vendôme, of Pierre le Vénérable, and of S. Bernard, give proofs of it at every page." *Ibid.*

SAINT ANSELM

SAINT ANSELM'S letters to brother monks are full of expressions of the same ardent affection. Montalembert gives several examples:--

"Souls well-beloved of my soul," he wrote to two near relatives whom he wished to draw to Bec, "my eyes ardently desire to behold you; my arms expand to embrace you; my lips sigh for your kisses; all the life that remains to me is consumed with waiting for you. I hope in praying, and, I pray in hoping--come and taste how gracious the Lord is--you cannot fully know it while you find sweetness in the world."

"'Far from the eyes, far from the heart,' say the vulgar. Believe nothing of it; if it was so, the farther you were distant from me the cooler my love for you would be; whilst on the contrary, the less I can enjoy your presence, the more the desire of that pleasure burns in the soul of your friend."

TO GONDULPH

To Gondulf, Anselm ------ I put no other or longer salutations at the head of my letter, because I can say nothing more to him whom I love. All who know Gondulph and Anselm know well what this means, and how much love is understood in these two names." . . . "How could I forget thee? Can a man forget one who is placed like a seal upon his heart? In thy silence I know that thou lovest me; and thou also, when I say nothing, thou knowest that I love thee. Not only have I no doubt of thee, but I answer for thee that thou art sure of me. What can my letter tell thee that thou knowest not already, thou who art my second soul? Go into the secret place of thy heart, look there at thy love for me, and thou shalt see mine for thee." . . . "Thou knewest how much I love thee, but I knew it not. He who has separated us has alone instructed me how dear to me thou wert. No, I knew not before the experience of thy absence how sweet it was to have thee, how bitter to have thee not. Thou hast another friend whom thou hast loved as much or more than me to console thee, but I have no longer thee I--thee I thee I thou understandest? and nothing to replace thee. Those who rejoice in the possession of thee may perhaps be offended by what I say. Ah I let them content themselves with their joy, and permit me to weep for him whom I ever love."

THE STORY OF AMIS AND AMILE

THE story of Amis and Amile, a mediæval legend, translated by William Morris (as well as by Walter Pater) from the *Bibliotheca Elzeviriana*, is very quaint and engaging in its old-world extravagance and supernaturalism:--

Amis and Amile were devoted friends, twins in resemblance and life. On one occasion, having strayed apart, they ceased not to seek each other for two whole years. And when at last they met "they lighted down from their horses, and embraced and kissed each other, and gave thanks to God that they were found. And they swore fealty and friendship and fellowship perpetual, the one to the other, on the sword of Amile, wherein were relics." Thence they went together to the court of "Charles, king of France."

Here soon after, Amis took Amile's place in a tournament, saved his life from a traitor, and won for him the King's daughter to wife. But so it happened that, not long after, he himself was stricken with leprosy and brought to Amile's door. And when Amile and his royal bride knew who it was they were sore grieved, and they brought him in and placed him on a fair bed, and put all that they had at his service. And it came to pass one night "when as Amis and Amile lay in one chamber without other company) that God sent to Amis Raphael his angel, who said to him: 'Sleepest thou, Amis?' And he, who deemed that Amile had called to him, answered: 'I sleep not, fair sweet fellow.' Then the angel said to him: 'Thou hast answered well, for thou art the fellow of the citizens of heaven, and thou hast followed after job, and Thoby in patience. Now I am Raphael, an angel of our Lord, and am come to tell thee of a medicine for thine healing, whereas he hath heard thy prayers. Thou shalt tell to Amile thy fellow, that he slay his two children and wash thee in their blood, and thence thou shalt get the healing of thy body.'"

Amis was shocked when he heard these words, and at first refused to tell Amile; but the latter had also heard the angel's voice, and pressed him to tell. Then, when he knew, he too was sorely grieved. But at last he determined in his mind not even to spare his children for the sake of his friend, and going secretly to their chamber he slew them, and bringing some of their blood washed Amis--who immediately was healed. He then arrayed Amis in his best clothes and, after going to the church to give thanks, they met Amile's wife who (not knowing all) rejoiced greatly too. But Amile, going apart again to the children's chamber to weep over them, found them at play in bed, with only a thread of crimson round their throats to mark what had been done!

The two knights fell afterwards and were killed in the same battle; "for even as God had joined them together by good accord in their life-days, so in their death they were not sundered." And a miracle was added, for even when they were buried apart from each other the two coffins leapt together in the night and were found side by side in the morning.

Of this story Mr. Jacobs, in his introduction to William Morris' translation, says: "Amis and Amil were the David and Jonathan, the Orestes and Pylades, of the mediæval world." There were some thirty other versions of the legend "in almost all the tongues of Western and Northern Europe"-- their "peerless friendship" having given them a place among the mediæval saints. (See *Old French Romances*, trans. by William Morris, London, 1896.)

EASTERN POETS

IT may not be out of place here, and before passing on to the times of the Renaissance and Modern Europe, to give one or two extracts relating to Eastern countries. The honor paid to friendship in Persia, Arabia, Syria and other Oriental lands has always been great, and the tradition of this attachment there should be especially interesting to us, as having arisen independently of classic or Christian ideals. The poets of Persia, Saadi and Jalalu-ddin Rumi (13th cent.), Hafiz (14th cent.), Jami (15th cent.), and others, have drawn much of their inspiration from this source; but unfortunately for those who cannot read the originals, their work has been scantily translated, and the translations themselves are not always very reliable. The extraordinary way in which, following the method of the Sufis, and of Plato, they identify the mortal and the divine love, and see in their beloved an image or revelation of God himself, makes their poems difficult of comprehension to the Western mind. Apostrophes to Love, Wine, and Beauty often, with them, bear a frankly twofold sense, material and spiritual. To these poets of the mid-region of the earth, the bitter antagonism between matter and spirit, which like an evil dream has haunted so long both the extreme Western and the extreme Eastern mind, scarcely exists; and even the body "which is a portion of the dustpit" has become perfect and divine.

JALALU-DDIN RUMI

"Every form you see has its archetype in the placeless world. . .
From the moment you came into the world of being
A ladder was placed before you that you might escape (ascend)
First you were mineral, later you turned to plant,
Then you became an animal: how should this be a secret to you?
Afterwards you were made man, with knowledge, reason, faith;
Behold the body, which is a portion of the dustpit, how perfect it has grown I
When you have traveled on from man, you will doubtless become an angel;
After that you are done with earth: your station is in heaven.
Pass again even from angelhood: enter that ocean,
That your drop may become a sea which is a hundred seas of 'Oman.'"

From the Divani Shamsi Tabriz of Jalalu-ddin Rumi, trans. by R. J. Nicholson.

"'Twere better that the spirit which wears not true love as a garment
Had not been: its being is but shame.
Be drunken in love, for love is all that exists. . . .
Dismiss cares and be utterly clear of heart,
Like the face of a mirror, without image or picture.
When it becomes clear of images, all images are contained in it." *Ibid.*

"Happy the moment when we are seated in the palace, thou and I,
With two forms and with two figures, but with one soul, thou and I." *Ibid.*

Once a man came and knocked at the door of his friend.
His friend said, 'Who art thou, O faithful one?'
He said, "Tis I.' He answered, 'There is no admittance.
There is no room for the raw at my well-cooked feast.
Naught but fire of separation and absence
Can cook the raw one and free him from hypocrisy!
Since thy *self* has not yet left thee,
Thou must be burned in fiery flames.'
The poor man went away, and for one whole year
Journeyed burning with grief for his friend's absence.
His heart burned till it was cooked; then he went again
And drew near to the house of his friend.
He knocked at the door in fear and trepidation
Lest some careless word should fall from his lips.
His friend shouted, 'Who is that at the door?'
He answered, "Tis thou who art at the door, O beloved!'
The friend said, 'Since 'tis I, let me come in,
There is not room for two I's in one house.'

From the Masnavi of Jalalu-ddin Rumi, trans. by E. H. Whinfield.

HAFIZ AND SAADI

SOME short quotations here following are taken from *Flowers culled from Persian Gardens* (Manchester, 1872):--

"Everyone, whether he be abstemious or self-indulgent is searching after the Friend. Every place may be the abode of love, whether it be a mosque or a synagogue. . . . On thy last day, though the cup be in thy hand, thou may'st be borne away to Paradise even from the corner of the tavern." *Hafiz.*

"I have heard a sweet word which was spoken by the old man of Canaan (Jacob)—'No tongue can express what means the separation of friends.'" *Hafiz.*

"Neither of my own free will cast I myself into the fire; for the chain of affection was laid upon my neck. I was still at a distance when the fire began to glow, nor is this the moment that it was lighted up within me. Who shall impute it to me as a fault, that I am enchanted by my friend, that I am content in casting myself at his feet?" *Saadi.*

FROM SAADI'S ROSE-GARDEN

VON KUPFFER, in his Anthology, *Lieblingminne und Freundes liebe in der Weltliteratur*, gives the following three poems from Saadi and Hafiz:--

A youth there was of golden heart and nature,
Who loved a friend, his like in every feature;
Once, as upon the ocean sailed the pair,
They chanced into a whirlpool unaware.
A fisherman made haste the first to save,
Ere his young life should meet a watery grave;
But crying from the raging surf, he said:
'Leave me, and seize my comrade's hand instead.'
E'en as he spoke the mortal swoon o'ertook him,
With that last utterance life and sense forsook him.

Learn not love's temper from that shallow pate
Who in the hour of fear forsakes his mate;
True friends will ever act like him above
(Trust one who is experienced in love);
For Sadi knows full well the lover's part,
And Bagdad understands the Arab heart.
More than all else thy loved one shalt thou prize,
Else is the whole world hidden from thine eyes.

Lov'st thou a being formed of dust like thee--
Peace and contentment from thy heart shall flee;
Waking, fair limbs and features shall torment thee;
Sleeping, thy love in dreams shall hold and haunt thee.
Under his feet thy head is bowed to earth;
Compared with him the world's a paltry crust;
If to thy loved one gold is nothing worth,
Why, then to thee is gold no more than dust.

Hardly a word for others canst thou find,
For no room's left for others in thy mind.

Dear Friend, since thou hast passed the whole
Of one sweet night, till dawn, with me,
I were scarce mortal, could I spend
Another hour apart from thee.
The fear of death, for all of time
Hath left me since my soul partook
The water of true Life, that wells
In sweet abundance from thy brook.

NESIM BEY

Hahn in his *Albanesische Studien*, already quoted, gives some of the verses of Neçin or Nesim Bey, a Turco-Albanian poet, of which the following is an example:--

"Whate'er, my friend, or false or true,
  The world may tell thee, give no ear,
  For to separate us, dear,
The world will say that one is two.
Who should seek to separate us
  May he never cease to weep.
The rain at times may cease; but he
  In Summer's warmth or Winter's sleep
  May he never cease to weep."

SULEYMAN AND IBRAHIM

BESIDES literature there is no doubt a vast amount of material embedded in the customs and traditions of these countries and awaiting adequate recognition and interpretation.

The following quotations may afford some glimpses of interest.

Suleyman the Magnificent.--The Story of Suleyman's attachment to his Vezir Ibrahim is told as follows by Stanley Lane-Poole:--

"Suleyman, great as he was, shared his greatness with a second mind, to which his reign owed much of its brilliance. The Grand Vezir Ibrahim was the counterpart of the Grand Monarch Suleyman. He was the son of a sailor at Parga, and had been captured by corsairs, by whom he was sold to be the slave of a widow at Magnesia. Here he passed into the hands of the young prince Suleyman, then Governor of Magnesia, and soon his extraordinary talents and address brought him promotion. . . . From being Grand Falconer on the accession of Suleyman, he rose to be first minister and almost co-Sultan in 1523.

He was the object of the Sultan's tender regard: an emperor knows better than most men how solitary is life without friendship and love, and Suleyman loved this man more than a brother. Ibrahim was not only a friend, he was an entertaining and instructive companion. He read Persian, Greek and Italian; he knew how to open unknown worlds to the Sultan's mind, and Suleyman drank in his Vezir's wisdom with assiduity. They lived together: their meals were shared in common; even their beds were in the same room. The Sultan gave his sister in marriage to the sailor's son, and Ibrahim was at the summit of power." *Turkey, Story of Nations series*, p. 174.

STORY OF A BAGDAD DERVISH

T. S. BUCKINGHAM, in his "Travels in Assyria, Media and Persia," speaking of his guide whom he had engaged at Bagdad, and who was supposed to have left his heart behind him in that city, says:--

"Amidst all this I was at a loss to conceive how the Dervish could find much enjoyment [in the expedition] while laboring under the strong passion which I supposed he must then be feeling for the object of his affections at Bagdad, whom he had quitted with so much reluctance. What was my surprise, however, on seeking an explanation of this seeming inconsistency, to find it was the son, and not the daughter, of his friend Elias who held so powerful a hold on his heart. I shrank back from the confession as a man would recoil from a serpent on which he had unexpectedly trodden . . . but in answer to enquiries naturally suggested by the subject he declared he would rather suffer death than do the slightest harm to so pure, so innocent, so heavenly a creature as this. . . .

I took the greatest pains to ascertain by a severe and minute investigation, how far it might be possible to doubt of the purity of the passion by which this Affgan Dervish was possessed, and whether it deserved to be classed with that described as prevailing among the ancient Greeks; and the result fully satisfied me that both were the same. Ismael was, however, surprised beyond measure when I assured him that such a feeling was not known at all among the peoples of Europe." *Travels, &c.*, 2nd edition, vol. 1, p. 159.

ANOTHER STORY

"The Dervish added a striking instance of the force of these attachments, and the sympathy which was felt in the sorrows to which they led, by the following fact from his own history. The place of his residence, and of his usual labor, was near the bridge of the Tigris, at the gate of the Mosque of the Vizier. While he sat here, about five or six years since, surrounded by several of his friends who came often to enjoy his conversation and beguile the tedium of his work, he observed, passing among the crowd, a young and beautiful Turkish boy, whose eyes met his, as if by destiny and they remained fixedly gazing on each other for some time. The boy, after 'blushing like the first hue of a summer morning,' passed on, frequently turning back to look on the person who had regarded him so ardently. The Dervish felt his heart 'revolve within him,' for such was his expression, and a cold sweat came across his brow. He hung his head upon his graving-tool in dejection, and excused himself to those about him by saying he felt suddenly ill. Shortly afterwards the boy returned, and after walking to and fro several times, drawing nearer and nearer, as if under the influence of some attracting charm, he came up to his observer and said, 'Is it really true, then, that you love me?' 'This,' said Ismael, 'was a dagger in my heart; I could make no reply.' The friends who were near him, and now saw all explained, asked him if there had been any previous acquaintance existing between them. He assured them that they had never seen each other before. 'Then,' they replied, 'such an event must be from God.'

The boy continued to remain for a while with this party, told with great frankness the name and rank of his parents, as well as the place of his residence, and promised to repeat his visit on the following day. He did this regularly for several months in succession, sitting for hours by the Dervish, and either singing to him or asking him interesting questions, to beguile his labors, until as Ismael expressed himself, 'though they were still two bodies they became one soul.' The youth at length fell sick, and was confined to his bed, during which time his lover, Ismael, discontinued entirely his usual occupations and abandoned himself completely to the care of his beloved.

He watched the changes of his disease with more than the anxiety of a parent, and never quitted his bedside, night or day. Death at length separated them; but even when the stroke came the Dervish could not be prevailed on to quit the corpse. He constantly visited the grave that contained the remains of all he held dear on earth, and planting myrtles and flowers there after the manner of the East, bedewed them daily with his tears. His friends sympathized powerfully in his distress, which he said 'continued to feed his grief' until he pined away to absolute illness, and was near following the fate of him whom he deplored." *Ibid*, p. 160.

"From all this, added to many other examples of a similar kind, related as happening between persons who had often been pointed out to me in Arabia and Persia, I could no longer doubt the existence in the East of an affection for male youths, of as pure and honorable a kind as that which is felt in Europe for those of the other sex . . . and it would be as unjust to suppose that this necessarily implied impurity of desire as to contend that no one could admire a lovely countenance and a beautiful form in the other sex, and still be inspired with sentiments of the most pure and honorable nature towards the object of his admiration." *Ibid*, p. 163.

EXPLANATION

"One powerful reason why this passion may exist in the East, while it is quite unknown in the West, is probably the seclusion of women in the former, and the freedom of access to them in the latter. . . . Had they [the Asiatics] the unrestrained intercourse which we enjoy with such superior beings as the virtuous and accomplished females of our own country they would find nothing in nature so deserving of their love as these." *Ibid*, p. 165.

V

THE RENAISSANCE AND MODERN TIMES

WITH the Renaissance, and the impetus it gave at that time to the study of Greek and Roman models, the exclusive domination of Christianity and the Church was broken. A literature of friendship along classic lines began to spring up. Montaigne (b. 1533) was saturated with classic learning. His essays were doubtless largely formed upon the model of Plutarch. His friendship with Stephen de la Boëtie was evidently of a romantic and absorbing character. It is referred to in the following passage by William Hazlitt; and the description of it occupies a large part of Montaigne's Essay on Friendship.

MONTAIGNE AND STEPHEN DE LA BOËTIE

"The most important event of his counselor's life at Bordeaux was the friendship which he there formed with Stephen de la Boëtie, an affection which makes a streak of light in modern biography almost as beautiful as that left us by Lord Brook and Sir Philip Sydney. Our essayist and his friend esteemed, before they saw, each other. La Boëtie had written a little work in which Montaigne recognized sentiments congenial with his own, and which indeed bespeak a soul formed in the mould of classic times. Of Montaigne, le Boëtie had also heard accounts, which made him eager to behold him, and at length they met at a large entertainment given by one of the magistrates of Bordeaux. They saw and loved, and were thenceforward all in all to each other. The picture that Montaigne in his essays draws of this friendship is in the highest degree beautiful and touching; nor does la Boëtie's idea of what is due to this sacred bond betwixt soul and soul fall far short of the grand perception which filled the exalted mind of his friend. . . . Montaigne married at the age of 33, but as he informs us, not of his own wish or choice. 'Might I have had my wish,' says he, 'I would not have married Wisdom herself if she would have had me.'" *Life of Montaigne, by Wm. Hazlitt.*

MONTAIGNE ON FRIENDSHIP

The following is from Montaigne's Essay, bk. I, ch. xxvii:--

"As to marriage, besides that it is a covenant, the making of which is only free, but the continuance in it forced and compelled, having another dependence than that of our own free will, and a bargain moreover commonly contracted to other ends, there happen a thousand intricacies in it to unravel, enough to break the thread, and to divert the current, of a lively affection: whereas friendship has no manner of business or traffic with anything but itself. . . . For the rest, what we commonly call friends and friendships are nothing but an acquaintance and connection, contracted either by accident or upon some design, by means of which there happens some little intercourse betwixt our souls: but, in the friendship I speak of, they mingle and melt into one piece, with so universal a mixture that there is left no more sign of the seam by which they were first conjoined. If any one should importune me to give a reason why I loved him [Stephen de la Boëtie] I feel it could no otherwise be expressed than by making answer, 'Because it was he; because it was I.' There is, beyond what I am able to say, I know not what inexplicable and inevitable power that brought on this union. We sought one another long before we met, and from the characters we heard of one another, which wrought more upon our affections than in reason mere reports should do, and, as I think, by some secret appointment of heaven; we embraced each other in our names; and at our first meeting, which was accidentally at a great city entertainment, we found ourselves so mutually pleased with one another--we became at once mutually so endeared--that thenceforward nothing was so near to us as one another. . . .

"Common friendships will admit of division, one may love the beauty of this, the good humor of that person, the liberality of a third, the paternal affection of a fourth, the fraternal love of a fifth, and so on. But this friendship that possesses the whole soul, and there rule s and sways with an absolute sovereignty, can admit of no rival. . . . In good earnest, if I compare all the rest of my life with the four years I had the happiness f to enjoy the sweet society of this excellent man, 'tis nothing but smoke, but an obscure and tedious night. From the day that I lost him I have only led a sorrowful and languishing life; and the very pleasures that present themselves to me, instead of administering anything of consolation, double my affliction for his loss. We were halves throughout, and to that degree that, methinks, by outliving him I defraud him of his part."

SIDNEY, GREVILLE AND DYER

PHILIP SIDNEY, born 1554, was remarkable for his strong personal attachments. Chief among his allies were his school-mate and distant relative, Fulke Greville (born in the same year as himself), and his college friend Edward Dyer (also about his own age). He wrote youthful verses to both of them. The following, according to the fashion of the age, are in the form of an invocation to the pastoral god Pan:--

> "Only for my two loves' sake,
> In whose love I pleasure take;
> Only two do me delight
> With their ever-pleasing sight;
> Of all men to thee retaining
> Grant me with these two remaining."

PHILIP SIDNEY AND HUBERT LANGUET

An interesting friendship existed also between Sidney and the well-known French Protestant, Hubert Languet--many years his senior--whose conversation and correspondence helped much in the formation of Sidney's character. These two had shared together the perils of the massacre of S. Bartholomew, and had both escaped from France across the Rhine to Germany, where they lived in close intimacy at Frankfort for a length of time; and after this a warm friendship and steady correspondence--varied by occasional meetings--continued between the two until Languet's death. Languet had been Professor of Civil Law at Padua, and from 1550 forwards was recognized as one of the leading political agents of the Protestant Powers.

"The elder man immediately discerned in Sidney a youth of no common quality, and the attachment he conceived for him savored of romance. We possess a long series of Latin letters from Languet to his friend, which breathe the tenderest spirit of affection, mingled with wise counsel and ever watchful thought for the young man's higher interests. . . . There must have been something inexplicably attractive in his [Sidney's] person and his genius at this time; for the tone of Languet's correspondence can only be matched by that of Shakespeare in the sonnets written for his unknown friend." *Sir Philip Sidney, English Men of Letters Series*, pp. 27, 28.

Of this relation Fox Bourne says:--

"No love-oppressed youth can write with more earnest passion and more fond solicitude, or can be troubled with more frequent fears and more causeless jealousies, than Languet, at this time 55 years old, shows in his letters to Sidney, now 19."

MICHELANGELO

IT may be appropriate here to introduce two or three sonnets from Michel Angelo (b. 1475). Michel Angelo, one of the greatest, perhaps the greatest, artist of the Italian Renaissance, was deeply imbued with the Greek spirit. His conception of Love was close along the line of Plato's. For him the body was the symbol, the expression, the dwelling place of some divine beauty. The body may be loved, but it should only be loved as a symbol, not for itself. Diotima in the *Symposium* has said that in our mortal loves we first come to recognize (dimly) the divine form of beauty which is Eternal. Maximus Tyrius (Dissert. xxvi. 8) commenting on this, confirms it, saying that nowhere else but in the human form, "the loveliest and most intelligent of body creatures," does the light of divine beauty shine so clear. Michel Angelo carried on the conception, gave it noble expression, and held to it firmly in the midst of a society which was certainly willing enough to love the body (or try to love it) merely for its own sake.

GIORDANO BRUNO

And Giordano Bruno (b. 1550) as a later date wrote as follows:--

"All the loves--if they be heroic and not purely animal, or what is called natural, and slaves to generation as instruments in some way of nature--have for object the divinity, and tend towards divine beauty, which first is communicated to, and shines in, souls, and from them or rather through them is communicated to bodies; whence it is that well-ordered affection loves the body or corporeal beauty, insomuch as it is an indication of beauty of spirit." *Gli Eroici Furori* (dial. iii. 13), *trans. L. Williams.*

MICHELANGELO'S SONNETS

THE labors of Von Scheffler and others have now pretty conclusively established that the love-poems of Michel Angelo were for the most part written to male friends--though this fact was disguised by the pious frauds of his nephew, who edited them in the first instance. Following are three of his sonnets, translated by J. A. Symonds.

It will be seen that the last line of the first contains a play on the name of his friend:--

To Tommaso de' Cavalieri:

A CHE PIU DEBB'IO

"Why should I seek to ease intense desire
With still more tears and windy words of grief,
When heaven, or late or soon, sends no relief
To souls whom love hath robed around with fire.
Why need my aching heart to death aspire,
When all must die? Nay death beyond belief
Unto these eyes would be both sweet and brief,
Since in my sum of woes all joys expire!

Therefore because I cannot shun the blow
I rather seek, say who must rule my breast,
Gliding between her gladness and her woe?
If only chains and bands can make me blest,
No marvel if alone and bare I go
An armèd Knight's captive and slave confessed."

NON VIDER GLI OCCHI MIEI

"No mortal thing enthralled these longing eyes
When perfect peace in thy fair face I found;
But far within, where all is holy ground,
My soul felt Love, her comrade of the skies:
For she was born with God in Paradise;
Nor all the shows of beauty shed around
This fair false world her wings to earth have bound;
Unto the Love of Loves aloft she flies.

Nay things that suffer death quench not the fire
  Of deathless spirits; nor eternity
  Serves sordid Time, that withers all things rare.
Not love but lawless impulse is desire:
  That slays the soul; our love makes still more fair
  Our friends on earth, fairer in death on high."

VEGGIO NEL TUO BEL VISO

"From thy fair face I learn, O my loved lord,
  That which no mortal tongue can rightly say;
  The soul imprisoned in her house of clay,
  Holpen by thee to God hath often soared:
And tho' the vulgar, vain, malignant horde
  Attribute what their grosser wills obey,
  Yet shall this fervent homage that I pay,
  This love, this faith, pure joys for us afford.

Lo, all the lovely things we find on earth,
  Resemble for the soul that rightly sees,
  That source of bliss divine which gave us birth:
Nor have we first fruits or remembrances
  Of heaven elsewhere. Thus, loving loyally,
  I rise to God and make death sweet by thee."

RICHARD BARNFIELD

RICHARD BARNFIELD, one of the Elizabethan singers (b. 1574) wrote a long poem, dedicated to "The Ladie Penelope Rich" and entitled "The Affectionate Shepheard," which he describes as "an imitation of Virgil in the 2nd Eclogue, of Alexis." I quote the first two stanzas:--

I

"Scarce had the morning starre hid from the light
Heaven's crimson Canopie with stars bespangled,
But I began to rue th' unhappy sight
Of that fair boy that had my heart intangled;
  Cursing the Time, the Place, the sense, the sin;
  I came, I saw, I view'd, I slippèd in.

II

If it be sin to love a sweet-fac'd Boy,
(Whose amber locks trust up in golden tramels
Dangle adown his lovely cheeks with joye
When pearle and flowers his faire haire enamels)
  If it be sin to love a lovely Lad,
  Oh then sinne I, for whom my soule is sad."

These stanzas, and the following three sonnets (also by Barnfield) from a series addressed to a youth, give a fair sample of a considerable class of Elizabethan verses, in which classic conceits were mingled with a certain amount of real feeling:--

BARNFIELD'S SONNETS

SONNET IV

"Two stars there are in one fair firmament
(Of some intitled Ganymede's sweet face)
  Which other stars in brightness do disgrace,
As much as Po in cleanness passeth Trent.
Nor are they common-natur'd stars; for why,
  These stars when other shine vaile their pure light,
  And when all other vanish out of sight
They add a glory to the world's great eie:

By these two stars my life is only led,
  In them I place my joy, in them my pleasure,
  Love's piercing darts and Nature's precious treasure,
With their sweet food my fainting soul is fed:
  Then when my sunne is absent from my sight
  How can it chuse (with me) but be darke night?"

SONNET XVIII

"Not Megabetes, nor Cleonymus
  (Of whom great Plutarch makes such mention,
  Praysing their faire with rare invention),
As Ganymede were halfe so beauteous.
They onely pleased the eies of two great kings,

But all the world at my love stands amazed,
Nor one that on his angel's face hath gazed,
But (ravisht with delight) him presents bring:

Some weaning lambs, and some a suckling kyd,
Some nuts, and fil-beards, others peares and plums;
Another with a milk-white heyfar comes;
As lately Ægon's man (Damœtas) did;
But neither he nor all the Nymphs beside,
Can win my Ganymede with them t' abide."

SONNET XIX

"Ah no; nor I my selfe: tho' my pure love
(Sweete Ganymede) to thee hath still been pure,
And ev'n till my last gaspe shall aie endure,
Could ever thy obdurate beuty move:
Then cease, oh goddesse sonne (for sure thou art
A Goddesse sonne that can resist desire),
Cease thy hard heart, and entertain love's fire
Within thy sacred breast: by Nature's art.

And as I love thee more than any Creature
(Love thee, because thy beautie is divine,
Love thee, because my selfe, my soule, is thine:
Wholie devoted to thy lovely feature),
Even so of all the vowels, I and U
Are dearest unto me, as doth ensue."

FRANCIS BACON ON FRIENDSHIP

FRANCIS BACON'S essay *Of Friendship* is known to everybody. Notwithstanding the somewhat cold and pragmatic style and genius of the author, the subject seems to inspire him with a certain enthusiasm; and some good things are said.

"But we may go farther and affirm most truly that it is a mere and miserable solitude to want true friends, without which the world is but a wilderness; and even in this scene also of solitude, whosoever in the frame of his nature and affections is unfit for friendship, he taketh it of the beast, and not from humanity. A principal fruit of friendship is the ease and discharge of the fulness of the heart, which passions of all kinds do cause and induce. We know diseases of stoppings and suffocations are the most dangerous in the body; and it is not much otherwise in the mind: you may take sarza to open the liver, steel to open the spleen, flower of sulphur for the lungs, castoreum for the brain; but no receipt openeth the heart but a true friend, to whom you may impart griefs, joys, fears, hopes, suspicions, counsels, and whatsoever lieth upon the heart to oppress it, in a kind of civil shrift or confession. . . .

Certainly if a man would give it a hard phrase, those that want friends to open themselves unto, are cannibals of their own hearts; but one thing is most admirable (wherewith I will conclude this first fruit of friendship) which is, that this communicating of a man's self to his friend worketh two contrary effects, for it redoubleth joys, and cutteth griefs in halfs; for there is no man that imparteth his joys to his friend, but he joyeth the more, and no man that imparteth his griefs to his friend, but he grieveth the less." Essay 27, *Of Friendship*.

SHAKESPEARE'S SONNETS

SHAKESPEARE'S sonnets have been much discussed, and surprise and even doubt have been expressed as to their having been addressed (the first 126 of them) to a man friend; but no one who reads them with open mind can well doubt this conclusion; nor be surprised at it, who knows anything of Elizabethan life and literature. "Were it not for the fact," says F. T. Furnivall, "that many critics really deserving the name of Shakespeare students, and not Shakespeare fools, have held the Sonnets to be merely dramatic, I could not have conceived that poems so intensely and evidently autobiographic and self-revealing, poems so one with the spirit and inner meaning of Shakespeare's growth and life, could ever have been conceived to be other than what they are the records of his own loves and fears."

SONNET XVIII

"Shall I compare thee to a summer's day?
Thou art more lovely and more temperate:
Rough winds do shake the darling buds of May,
And summer's lease hath all too short a date.

Some time too hot the eye of heaven shines,
And often is his gold complexion dimmed;
And every fair from fair sometime declines,
By chance, or nature's changing course, untrimmed;

But they eternal summer shall not fade,
Nor lose possession of that fair thou owest;
Nor shall death brag thou wander'st in his shade,
When in eternal lines to time thou growest.
So long as men can breathe, or eyes can see,
So long lives this, and this gives life to thee."

SONNET XX

"A woman's face, with Nature's own hand painted,
Hast thou, the master-mistress of my passion;
A woman's gentle heart, but not acquainted
With shifting change, as is false women's fashion;
An eye more bright than theirs, less false in rolling,
Gilding the object whereupon it gazeth;
A man in hue, all hues in his controlling,
Which steals men's eyes, and women's souls amazeth;

And for a woman wert thou first created,
Till Nature, as she wrought thee, fell a-doting,
And by addition me of thee defeated,
By adding one thing to my purpose nothing.
But since she pricked thee out for women's pleasure,
Mine be thy love, and thy love's use their treasure."

SONNET CIV

"To me, fair friend, you never can be old,
For as you were when first your eye, I ey'd ,
Such seems your beauty still. Three winters' cold
Have from the forest shook three summers' pride;
Three beauteous springs to yellow autumn turned
In process of the seasons I have seen;

Three April perfumes in three hot Junes burned,
Since first I saw you fresh, which yet are green.

Ah! yet doth beauty, like a dial hand,
Steal from his figure, and no pace perceived;
So your sweet hue, which methinks still doth stand,
Hath motion, and mine eye may be deceived;
  For fear of which, hear this, thou age unbred,
  Ere you were born was beauty's summer dead."

SONNET CVIII

"What's in the brain that ink may character,
Which hath not figur'd to thee my true spirit?
What's new to speak, what new to register,
That may express my love, or thy dear merit?
Nothing, sweet boy; but yet, like prayers divine,
I must each day say o'er the very same,
Counting no old thing old, thou 'mine, I thine,
Even as when first I hallow'd thy fair name.

So that eternal love, in love's fresh case,
Weighs not the dust and injury of age;
Nor gives to necessary wrinkles place,
But makes antiquity for aye his page;
  Finding the first conceit of love there bred,
  Where time and outward form would show it dead."

MERCHANT OF VENICE

THAT Shakespeare, when the drama needed it, could fully and warmly enter into the devotion which one man may feel for another, as well as into the tragedy which such devotion may entail, is shown in his *Merchant of Venice* by the figure of Antonio, over whom from the first line of the play ("In sooth I know not why I am so sad") there hangs a shadow of destiny. The following lines are from Act iv. sc. 1:--

Antonio: "Commend me to your honorable wife;
Tell her the process of Antonio's end;

Say how I loved you, speak me fair in death;
And when the tale is told, bid her be judge,
Whether Bassanio had not once a love.
Repent not you that you shall lose your friend,
And he repents not that he pays your debt;
For, if the Jew do cut but deep enough,
I'll pay it instantly with all my heart.

Bassanio: Antonio, I am married to a wife,
Who is as dear to me as life itself;
But life itself, my wife, and all the world,
Are not with me esteem'd above thy life:
I would lose all, ay, sacrifice them all,
Here to this devil, to deliver you."

HENRY THE FIFTH

We may also, in this connection, quote his *Henry the Fifth* (act iv. scene 6) for the deaths of the Duke of York and the Earl of Suffolk at the battle of Agincourt. Exeter, addressing Henry, says:--

"Suffolk first died; and York, all haggled over,
Comes to him, where in gore he lay insteep'd,
And takes him b y the beard, kisses the gashes,
That bloodily did yawn upon his face;
He cries aloud,--'Tarry, dear cousin Suffolk!
My soul shall thine keep company to heaven:
Tarry, sweet soul, for min; then fly abreast,
As in this glorious and well-foughten field
We kept together in our chivalry!'
Upon these words I came and cheered him up:
He smiled me in the face, raught me his hand,
And, with a feeble gripe, says, 'Dear my Lord,
Commend my service to my sovereign.'
So did he turn, and over Suffolk's neck
He threw his wounded arm, and kissed his lips;
And so, espoused to death, with blood he seal'd
A testament of noble-ending love."

SIR THOMAS BROWNE

Shakespeare, with his generous many-sided nature was, as the Sonnets seem to show, and as we should expect, capable of friendship, passionate friendship, towards both men and women. Perhaps this marks the highest reach of temperament. That there are cases in which devotion to a man-friend altogether replaces the love of the opposite sex is curiously shown by the following extract from Sir Thomas Browne:--

"I never yet cast a true affection on a woman; but I have loved my friend as I do virtue, my soul, my God. . . . I love my friend before myself, and yet methinks I do not love him enough: some few months hence my multiplied affection will make me believe I have not loved him at all. When I am from him, I am dead till I be with him; when I am with him, I am not satisfied, but would be still nearer him. . . . This noble affection falls not on vulgar and common constitutions, but on such as are marked for virtue: he that can love his friend with this noble ardor, will in a competent degree affect all." *Sir Thomas Browne, Religio Medici*, 1642.

BEAUMONT AND FLETCHER

BEAUMONT and Fletcher are two names which time and immortal friendship have sealed in one. Francis Beaumont was son of a judge, and John Fletcher, who was some four or five years the elder of the two, son of a bishop. The one went to Oxford, the other to Cambridge. Both took to writing at an early age; they probably met at the Mermaid Tavern, about the year 1604, and a friendship sprang up between them of the closest character. "The intimacy which now commenced was one of singular warmth even for that romantic age." (Chambers' Biog. Dict.) For many years they lived in the same house as bachelors, writing plays together, and sharing everything in common. Then in 1613 Beaumont married, but died in 1616. Fletcher lived on unmarried, till 1625, when he died of the plague.

J. St. L. Strachey, in his introduction to the works of Beaumont and Fletcher in the Mermaid Series, says:--

"In the whole range of English literature, search it from Chaucer till to-day, there is no figure more fascinating or more worthy of attention than 'the mysterious double personality' of Beaumont and Fletcher. Whether we bow to the sentiment of the first Editor, who, though he knew the secret of the poets, 'yet since never parted while they lived' conceived it not equitable to 'separate their ashes,' and so refuse to think of them apart; whether we adopt the legendary union of the comrade-poets who dwelt on the Bankside, who lived and worked together, their thoughts no less in common than the cloak and bed o'er which tradition has grown fond; whether we think of them as two minds so married that to divorce or disunite them were a sacrilegious deed; or whether we yield to the subtler influences of the critical fancy, and delight to discover and explore each from its source, the twin fountains of inspiration that feed the majestic stream of song that flows through 'The Lost Aspatia's' tragedy, etc. . . . whether we treat the poets as a mystery to which love and sympathy are the initiation, or as a problem for the tests and reagents of critical analysis to solve, the double name of Beaumont and Fletcher will ever strike the fancy and excite the imagination as does no other name in the annals of English song."

George Varley, in his Introduction to the works of B. and F. (London, E. Moxon, 1839), says:--

"The story of their common life, which scandalizes some biographers, contains much that is agreeable to me, as offering a picture of perfect union whose heartiness excuses its homeliness . . . but when critics would explain away the community of cloak and clothes by accident or slander, methinks their fastidiousness exceeds their good feeling."

SWEET FLETCHER'S BRAIN

Beaumont was a man of great personal beauty and charm. Ben Jonson was much attracted to him. Fletcher delighted to do him honor and to put his name first on their title page; though it is probable that Beaumont's share in the plays was the lesser one. See following verses by Sir Aston Cokaine in the 1st Collection of their works, published in 1647:--

> "In the large book of playes you late did print,
> In Beaumont and in Fletcher's name, why in't
> Did you not justice? Give to each his due?
> For Beaumont of those many writ in few,
> And Massinger in other few; the main
> Being sole issues of sweet Fletcher's brain.
> But how came I, you ask, so much to know?
> Fletcher's chief bosome-friend inform'd me so."

AN EPITAPH

The following lines were written by Fletcher on the death of Beaumont:--

"Come, sorrow, come I bring all thy cries,
All thy laments, and all thy weeping eyes!
Burn out, you living monuments of woe!
Sad, sullen griefs, now rise and overflow!
Virtue is dead;
Oh! cruel fate!
All youth is fled;
All our laments too late.
Oh, noble youth, to thy ne'er dying name,
Oh, happy youth, to thy still growing fame,
To thy long peace in earth, this sacred knell
Our last loves ring--farewell, farewell, farewell!
Go, happy soul, to thy eternal birth!
And press his body lightly, gentle Earth."

And among the poems attributed to Francis Beaumont is one generally supposed to be addressed to Fletcher, and speaking of an alliance hidden from the world--of which the last five lines run:--

"If when I die, physicians doubt
What caused my death, and these to view
Of all their judgments, which was true,
Rip up my heart; O, then I fear
The world will see thy picture there."

--though it is perhaps more probable that it was addressed to Beaumont by Fletcher, and has accidentally found place among the former's writings.

In the *Maid's Tragedy* by B. and F. (Act I. Scene i.), we have Melantius speaking about his companion Amintor, a young nobleman:--

"All joys upon him I for he is my friend.
Wonder not that I call a man so young my friend:
His worth is great; radiant he is, and temperate;
And one that never thinks his life his own,
If his friend need it."

VAUVENARGUES ON DE SEYTRES

THE devotion of Vauvenargues to his friend De Seytres is immortalized by the *éloge* he wrote on the occasion of the latter's death. V., a youth of noble family, born in S. France in 1715, entered military service and the regiment of the King at an early age. He seems to have been a gentle, wise character, much beloved by his comrades. During the French invasion of Bohemia, in 174r, when he was about 26, he met Hippolyte de Seytres, who belonged to the same regiment, and who was only 18 years of age. A warm friendship sprang up between the two, but lasted for a brief time only. DeSeytres died during the privations of the terrible Siege of Prague in 1742. Vauvenargues escaped, but with the loss of his health, as well as of his friend. He took to literature, and wrote some philosophic works, and became correspondent and friend of Voltaire, but died in 1747 at the early age of 32. In his *éloge* he speaks of his friend as follows:--

"By nature full of grace, his movements natural, his manners frank, his features noble and grave, his expression sweet and penetrating; one could not look upon him with indifference. From the first his loveable exterior won all hearts in his favor, and whoever was in the position to know his character could not but admire the beauty of his disposition. Never did he despise or envy or hate any one. He understood all the passions and opinions, even the most singular, that the world blames. They did not surprise him; he penetrated their cause, and found in his own reflexions the means of explaining them."

"And so Hippolyte," he continues, "I was destined to be the survivor in our friendship--just when I was hoping that it would mitigate all the sufferings and ennui of my life even to my latest breath. At the moment when my heart, full of security, placed blind confidence in thy strength and youth, and abandoned itself to gladness--O Misery! in that moment a mighty hand was extinguishing the sources of life in thy blood. Death was creeping into thy heart, and harboring in thy bosom! . . O pardon me once more; for never canst thou have doubted the depth of my attachment. I loved thee before I was able to know thee. I have never loved but thee . . . I was ignorant of thy very name and life, but my heart adored thee, spoke with thee, saw thee and sought thee in solitude. Thou knewest me but for a moment; and when we did become acquainted, already a thousand times had I paid homage in secret to thy virtues. . . . Shade worthy of heaven, whither hast thou fled! Do my sighs reach thee? I tremble--O abyss profound, O woe, O death, O grave! Dark veil and viewless night, and mystery of Eternity!"

(It is said that Vauvenargues thought more of this memorial inscription to his friend than of any other of his works, and constantly worked at and perfected it.)

WILLIAM PENN

WILLIAM PENN (b. 1644) the founder of Pennsylvania, and of Philadelphia, "The city of brotherly love" was a great believer in friendship. He says in his *Fruits of Solitude*:--

"A true friend unbosoms freely, advises justly, assists readily, adventures boldly, takes all patiently, defends courageously, and continues a friend unchangeably. . . . In short, choose a friend as thou dost a wife, till death separate you. . . . Death cannot kill what never dies. Nor can spirits ever be divided that love and live in the same Divine Principle; the Root and Record of their friendship. . . . This is the comfort of friends, that though they may be said to die, yet their friendship and society are, in the best sense, ever present, because immortal."

PRINCE WILLIAM AND BENTINCK

IT may be worth while here to insert two passages from Macaulay's History of England. The first deals with the remarkable intimacy between the Young Prince William of Orange and "a gentleman of his household" named Bentinck. William's escape from a malignant attack of small-pox

"was attributed partly to his own singular equanimity, and partly to the intrepid and indefatigable friendship of Bentinck. From the hands of Bentinck alone William took food and medicine--by Bentinck alone William was lifted from his bed and laid down in it. 'Whether Bentinck slept or not while I was ill,' said William to Temple with great tenderness, 'I know not. But this I know, that through sixteen days and nights, I never once called for anything but that Bentinck was instantly at my side.' Before the faithful servant had entirely performed this task, he had himself caught the contagion." (But he recovered.)*History of England*, ch. vii.

PRINCESS ANNE AND LADY CHURCHILL

The second passage describes the devotion of the Princess Anne (daughter of James II and afterwards Queen Anne) to Lady Churchill--a devotion which had considerable influence on the political situation.

"It is a common observation that differences of taste, understanding, and disposition are no impediments to friendship, and that the closest intimacies often exist between minds, each of which supplies what is wanting in the other. Lady Churchill was loved and even worshipped by Anne. The princess could not live apart from the object of her romantic fondness. She married, and was a faithful and even an affectionate wife; but Prince George, a dull man, whose chief pleasures were derived from his dinner and his bottle, acquired over her no influence comparable to that exercised by her female friend, and soon gave himself up with stupid patience to the dominion of that vehement and commanding spirit by which his wife was governed." *History of England*, ch. vii.

ARCHBISHOP POTTER

THAT the tradition of Greek thought was not quite obliterated in England by the Puritan movement is shown by the writings of Archbishop Potter, who speaks with approval of friendship as followed among the Greeks, "not only in private, but by the public allowance and encouragement of their laws; for they thought there could be no means more effectual to excite their youth to noble undertakings, nor any greater security to their commonwealths, than this generous passion." He then quotes Athenæus, saying that "free commonwealths and all those states that consulted the advancement of their own honor, seem to have been unanimous in establishing laws to encourage and reward it." John Potter, *Antiquities of Greece*, 1698.

WINCKELMANN'S LETTERS

The eighteenth century however in England, with its leaning towards formalism, was perhaps not favorable to the understanding of the Greek spirit. At any rate there is not much to show in that direction. In Germany the classical tradition in art was revived by Raphael Mengs, while Winckelmann, the art critic, showed himself one of the best interpreters of the Hellenic world that has ever lived. His letters, too, to his personal friends, breathe a spirit of the tenderest and most passionate devotion: "Friendship," he says, "without love is mere acquaintanceship." Winckelmann met, in 1762, in Rome, a young nobleman, Reinhold von Berg, to whom he became deeply attached:--

"Almost as first there sprang up, on Winckelmann's side, an attachment as romantic, emotional and passionate as love. In a letter to his friend he said, 'From the first moment an indescribable attraction towards you, excited by something more than form and feature, caused me to catch an echo of that harmony which passes human understanding and which is the music of the everlasting concord of things. . . . I was aware of the deep consent of our spirits, the instant I saw you., And in a later letter: 'No name by which I might call you would be sweet enough or sufficient for my love; all that I could say would be far too feeble to give utterance to my heart and soul. Truly friendship came from heaven and was not created by mere human impulses. . . . My one friend, I love you more than any living thing, and time nor chance nor age can ever lessen this love." *Ludwig Frey, Der Eros und die Kunst, Leipzig*, 1898, p. 211.

GOETHE ON WINCKELMANN

GOETHE, that universal genius, has some excellent thoughts on this subject; speaking of Winckelmann he says:--

"The affinities of human beings in Antiquity give evidence of an important distinction between ancient and modern times. The relation to women, which among us has become so tender and full of meaning, hardly aspired in those days beyond the limits of vulgar necessity. The relation of parents to their children seems in some respects to have been tenderer. More to them than all other feelings was the friendship between persons of the male sex (though female friends, too, like Chloris and Thyia, were inseparable, even in Hades). In these cases of union between two youths, the passionate fulfilment of loving duties, the joys of inseparableness, the devotion of one for the other, the unavoided companionship in death, fill us with astonishment; indeed one feels oneself ashamed when poets, historians, philosophers and orators overwhelm us with legends, anecdotes, sentiments. and ideas, containing such meaning and feeling. Winckelmann felt himself born for a friendship of this kind--not only as capable of it, but in the highest degree in need of it; he became conscious of his true self only under the form of friendship." *Goethe on Winckelmann.*

POEM BY GOETHE

Some of Goethe's poems further illustrate this subject. In the Saki Nameh of his West-Oestlichen Divan he has followed the style of a certain class of Persian love-songs. The following poem is from a Cupbearer to his Master:--

"In the market-place appearing
  None thy Poet-fame dispute;
I too gladly hear thy singing,
  I too hearken when thou'rt mute.

Yet I love thee, when thou printest
  Kisses not to be forgot,
Best of all, for words may perish,
  But a kiss lives on in thought.

Rhymes on rhymes fair meaning carry,
  Thoughts to think bring deeper joy;
Sing to other folk, but tarry
  Silent with thy serving-boy."

HERDER ON GREEK FRIENDSHIP

JOHANN GOTTFRIED VON HERDER (1744-1803) as theologian, philosopher, friend of Goethe, Court preacher at Weimar, and author of *Ideas on the Philosophy of History*, has had a great and enduring reputation. The following extract is from the just-mentioned book:--

"Never has a branch born finer fruit than that little branch of Olive, Ivy, and Pine, which was the victor's crown among the Greeks. It gave to the young men good looks, good health, and good spirits; it made their limbs nimble, graceful and well-formed; in their souls it lighted the first sparks of the desire for good name, the love of fame even, and stamped on them the inviolable temper of men who live for their city and their country. Finally, what was most precious, it laid the foundation in their characters of that predilection for male society and friendship which so markedly distinguishes the Greeks. In Greece, woman was not the one prize of life for which the young man fought and strove; the loveliest Helen could only mould the spirit of one Paris, even though her beauty might be the coveted object of all manly valor. The feminine sex, despite the splendid examples of every virtue that it exhibited in Greece, as elsewhere, remained there only a secondary object of the manly life. The thoughts of aspiring youths reached towards something higher. The bond of friendship which they knitted among themselves or with grown men, compelled them into a school which Aspasia herself could hardly have introduced them to; so that in many of the states of Greece manly love became surrounded and accompanied by those intelligent and educational influences, that permanence of character and devotion, whose sentiment and meaning we read of in Plato almost as if in a romance from some far planet."

FROM SCHILLER'S DON KARLOS

SCHILLER, the great German poet, had an enthusiastic appreciation of friendship-love, as can be seen from his poems, "Freundschaft" and "Die Burgschaft," and others of his writings. His tragedy Don Karlos turns upon the death of one friend for the sake of another. The young Infanta of Spain, Don Karlos, alienated by the severities of his father, Phillip II, enters into plots and intrigues, from the consequences of which he is only saved by his devoted companion, the Marquis of Posa, who, by making himself out the guilty party, dies in the Prince's stead. Early in the play (Act I., Scene ii.) the attachment between the two is outlined:--

Karlos. Oh, if indeed 'tis true--
What my heart says--that out of millions, thou
Hast been decreed at last to understand me;
If it be true that Nature all-creative
In moulding Karlos copied Roderick,
And strung the tender chords of our two souls
Harmonious in the morning of our lives;
If even a tear that eases thus my sorrow
Is dearer to thee than my father's favor--

Marquis of Posa. Oh, dearer than the world!

Karlos. So low, so low
Have I now fallen, have become so needy,
That of our early childish years together
I must remind thee--Must indeed entreat
Thy payment of those long-forgotten debts
Which thou, while yet in sailor garb, contractedst;
When thou and I, two boys of venturous habit,
Grew up, and side by side, in brotherhood.
No grief oppressed me then--save that thy spirit
Seemed so eclipsing mine--until at length
I boldly dared to *love* thee without limit,
Since to be *like* thee was beyond my dreams.
Then I began, with myriad tenderness
And brother-love most loyal, to torment thee;
And thou, proud heart, returned it all so coldly.
Oft would I stand there--and thou saw'st it not!
And hot and heavy tear-drops from my eyes
Hung, when perchance, thou, Roderick, hastening past me,
Would'st throw thy arms about some lesser playmate.
"Why only these?" I cried, and wept aloud
"Am I not also worthy of thy heart?"
But thou--
So cold and serious before me kneeling,
"Homage" thou said'st, "to the King's son is due."

Marquis. A truce, O Prince, to all these tales of childhood,
Thy make my cheeks red even now with shame!

Karlos. And this from thee indeed I did not merit.
Contemn thou could'st, and even rend my heart,
But ne'er estrange. Three times thou did'st repulse
The young Prince from thee; thrice again he came
As suppliant to thee--to entreat thy love,
And urgently to press his love upon thee.
But that which Karlos could not, chance effected.

(The story is then related of how as a boy he took on himself the blame for a misdemeanor of Roderick's, and was severely punished by his royal father)--

Under the pitiless strokes my blood flowed red;
I looked on thee and wept not. But the King

Was angered by my boyish heroism,
And for twelve terrible hours emprisoned me
In a dark dungeon, to repent thereof.
So proud and fierce was my determination
By Roderick to be beloved. Thou cam'st,
And loudly weeping at my feet did'st fall,
"Yes, yes," did'st cry, "my pride is overcome,
One day, when thou art king, I will repay thee."

Marquis (giving his hand.)
I will so, Karl. My boyish affidavit
As man I now renew; I will repay;
My hour will also strike, perchance.

(The hour comes, when Roderick takes on himself the blame for an intrigue of Don Karlos with the Queen and William of Orange. He writes a letter to the latter, and allows it purposely to fall into the King's hands. He is assassinated by order of the King; and the following speech over his body (Act V., Scene iv.) is made to the King by Don Karlos, who thenceforth abjures all love except for the memory of his friend.)

Karlos (to the King.)
The dead man was my friend. And would you know
Wherefore he died? He perished for my sake.
Yes, Sire, for we were brothers I brothers by
A nobler chain than Nature ever forges.
Love was his glorious life-career. And love
For me, his great, his glorious death. Mine was he.
What time his lowly bearing puffed you up,
What time his gay persuasive eloquence
Made easy sport of your proud giant-spirit.
You thought to dominate him quite-and were
The obedient creature of his deeper plans.
That I am prisoner, is the schemed result
Of his great friendship. To achieve my safety
He wrote that letter to the Prince of Orange--
O God! the first, last falsehood of his life.
To rescue me he went to meet the Fate
Which he has suffered. With your gracious favors
You loaded him. He died for me. On him
You pressed the favors of your heart and Friendship.

Your sceptre was the plaything of his hands;
He threw it from him, and for me he died.

FRITZ OF PRUSSIA AND VON KATTE

THERE is little, I believe, in the historical facts relating to Don Karlos to justify this tale of friendship; but there seems great probability that the incidents were transferred by Schiller from the history of Frederick the Great, of Prussia, when a youth at his father's court. The devotion that existed between the young Frederick and Lieut. Von Katte, the anger and severities of the royal parent, the supposed conspiracy, the imprisonment of Frederick, and the execution of Von Katte, are all reproduced in Schiller's play.

Von Katte was a young man of good family and strange but charming personality, who, as soon as he came to Court, being three or four years older than Frederick, exercised a strong attraction upon the latter. The two were always together, and finally, enraged by the harshness of the royal father, they plotted flight to England. They were arrested, and Katte, accused of treason to the throne, was condemned to death. That this sentence was pronounced, not so much for political reasons, as in order to do despite to the affection between him and the Crown Prince, is strongly suggested by the circumstances. Von Katte was sent from a distance in order to be executed at Cüstrin, in the fortress where the Prince was confined, and with instructions that the latter should witness his execution. Carlyle, in his life of Frederick II, says:--

DEATH OF VON KATTE

"Katte wore, by order, a brown dress exactly like the Prince's; the Prince is already brought down into a lower room to see Katte as he passes (to see Katte die has been the royal order, but they smuggled that into abeyance), and Katte knows he shall see him." [Besserer, the chaplain of the Garrison, quoted by Carlyle, describing the scene as they approached the Castle, says:-- 'Here, after long wistful looking about, he did get sight of his beloved Jonathan at a window in the Castle, from whom, he, with politest and most tender expression, speaking in French, took leave, with no little emotion of sorrow.] "*Pardonnez moi, mon cher Katte,*" cried Friedrich. "*La mort est douce pour un si aimable Prince,*" said Katte, and fared on; round some angle of the

Fortress it appears; not in sight of Friedrich, who sank in a faint, and had seen his last glimpse of Katte in this world."

Life of Frederick II, Vol. 2, p. 489.

FREDERICK THE GREAT

Frederick's grief and despair were extreme for a time. Then his royal father found him a wife, in the Princess Elizabeth of Brunswick, whom he obediently married, but in whom he showed little interest--their meetings growing rarer and rarer till at last they became merely formal. Later, and after his accession, he spent most of his leisure time when away from the cares of war and political reorganization, at his retreat at Sans-Souci, afar from feminine society (a fact which provoked Voltaire's sarcasms), and in the society of his philosophic and military friends, to many of whom he was much attached. Von Kupffer has unearthed from his poems printed at Sans-Souci in 1750 the following, addressed to Count Von Kaiserlinck, a favorite companion, on whom he bestowed the by-name of Cesarion:--

"Cesarion, let us keep unspoiled
    Our faith, and be true friends,
    And pair our lives like noble Greeks,
    And to like noble ends!
That friend from friend may never hide
A fault through weakness or thro' pride,
    Or sentiment that cloys.
Thus gold in fire the brighter glows,
And far more rare and precious grows,
    Refined from all alloys."

There is also in the same collection a long and beautiful ode "To the shades of Cesarion," of which the following are a few lines:--

"O God! how hard the word of Fate!
    Cesarion dead! His happy days
Death to the grave has consecrate.
    His charm I mourn and gentle grace.
He's dead--my tender, faithful mate!
A thousand daggers pierce my heart;
It trembles, torn with grief and pain.

He's gone! the dawn comes not again!
Thy grave's the goal of my heart's strife;
Holy shall thy remembrance be;
To thee I poured out love in life;
And love in death I vow to thee."

VON KUPFFER ON ETHICS AND POLITICS

ELISAR VON KUPFFER, in the introduction to his Anthology, from which I have already quoted a few extracts, speaks at some length on the great ethical and political significance of a loving comradeship. He says:--

"In open linkage and attachment to each other ought youth to rejoice in youth. In attachment to another, one loses the habit of thinking only of self. In the love and tender care and instruction that the youth receives from his lover he learns from boyhood up to recognize the good of self-sacrifice and devotion; and in the love which he shows, whether in the smaller or the greater offerings of an intimate friendship, he accustoms himself to self-sacrifice for another. In this way the young man is early nurtured into a member of the Community--to a useful member and not one who has self and only self in mind. And how much closer thus does unit grow to unit, till indeed the whole comes to feel itself a whole! . . .

The close relationship between two men has this further result--that folk instinctively and not without reason judge of one from the other; so that should the one be worthy and honorable, he naturally will be anxious that the other should not bring a slur upon him. Thus there arises a bond of moral responsibility with regard to character. And what can be of more advantage to the community than that the individual members should feel responsible for each other? Surely it is just that which constitutes national sentiment, and the strength of a people, namely, that it should form a complete whole in itself, where each unit feels locked and linked with the others. Such unions may be of the greatest social value, as in the case of the family. And it is especially in the hour of danger that the effect of this unity of feeling shows itself; for where one man stands or falls with another, where glad self-sacrifice, learnt in boyhood, becomes so to speak, a warm-hearted instinct, there is developed a power of incalculable import, a power that folly alone can hold cheap. Indeed, the unconquerable force of these unions has already been practically shown, as, in the Sacred Band of the Thebans who fought to its bitter end the battle of Leuctra; and, psychologically speaking, the explanation is most natural; for where one person feels himself united, body and soul to another, is it not natural that he should put forth all his powers in order to help the other, in order to manifest his love for him in every way? If any one cannot or will not perceive this we may indeed well doubt either the intelligence of his head or the morality of his heart."

FRIEDRICH RUCKERT TO HIS FRIEND

FRIEDRICH RUCKERT (1788-1866), Professor of Oriental Literature in Berlin, wrote verses in memory of his friend Joseph Kopp:--

"How shall I know myself without thee,
Who knew myself as part of thee?
I only know one half is vanished,
And half alone is left, of me.
Never again my proper mind
I'll know; for thee I'll never find.

Never again, out there in space,
I'll find thee; but here, deep within.
I see, tho' not in dreams, thy face;
My waking eyes thy presence win,
And all my thought and poesy
Are but my offering to thee.

. . . .
My Jonathan, now hast thou fled,
And I to weep thy loss remain;
If David's harp might grace my hands
O might it help to ease my pain!
My friend, my Joseph, true of faith,
In life so loved--so loved in death."

ROUGH WEATHER FRIENDS

And the following are by Joseph Kitir, an Austrian poet:--

"Not where breathing roses bless
The night, or summer airs caress;
Not in Nature's sacred grove;
No, but at a tap-room table,
Sitting in the window-gable
Did we plight our troth of love.

No fair lime tree's roofing shade
By the spring wind gently swayed
Formed for us a bower of bliss;
No, stormbound, but love-intent,
There against the damp wall bent
We two bartered kiss for kiss.

Therefore shalt thou, Love so rare
(Child of storms and wintry air),
Not like Spring's sweet fragrance fade.
Even in sorrow thou shalt flourish,
Frost shall not make thee afraid,
And in storms thou shalt not perish."

AUGUST VON PLATEN

COUNT AUGUST VON PLATEN (born at Ansbach in Bavaria, 1796) was in respect of style one of the most finished and perfect of German poets. His nature (which was refined and self-controlled) led him from the first to form the most romantic attachments with men. He freely and openly expressed his feelings in his verses; of which a great number are practically love-poems addressed to his friends. They include a series of twenty-six sonnets to one of his friends, Karl Theodor German. Of these Raffalovich says (*Uranisme*, Lyons, 1896, p. 351):--

"These sonnets to Karl Theodor German are among the most beautiful in German literature. Platen in the sonnet surpasses all the German poets, including even Goethe. In them perfection of form, and poignancy or wealth of emotion are illustrated to perfection. The sentiment is similar to that of the sonnets of Shakespeare (with their personal note), and the form that of the Italian or French sonnet."

Platen, however, was unfortunate in his affairs of the heart, and there is a refrain of suffering in his poems which comes out characteristically in the following sonnet:--

"Since pain is life and life is only pain,
  Why he can feel what I have felt before,
  Who seeing joy sees it again no more
The instant he attempts his joy to gain;
Who, caught as in a labyrinth unaware,
  The outlet from it never more can find;
  Whom love seems only for this end to bind--
In order to hand over to Despair;

Who prays each dizzy lightning-flash to end him,
  Each star to reel his thread of life away
With all the torments which his heart are rending;
  And envies even the dead their pillow of clay,
Where Love no more their foolish brains can steal.
He who knows this, knows me, and what I feel."

ON THE DEATH OF PINDAR

One of Platen's sonnets deals with an incident, referred to in an earlier page, namely, the death of the poet Pindar in the theatre, in the arms of his young friend Theoxenos:--

"Oh I when I die, would I might fade away
  Like the pale stars, swiftly and silently,
  Would that death's messenger might come to me,
As once it came to Pindar--so they say.
Not that I would in Life, or in my Verse,
  With him, the great Incomparable, compare;
  Only his Death, my friend, I ask to share:
But let me now the gracious tale rehearse.

Long at the play, hearing sweet Harmony,
  He sat; and wearied out at last, had lain
His cheek upon his dear one's comely knee;
  Then when it died away--the choral strain--

He who thus cushioned him said: Wake and come!
But to the Gods above he had gone home."

WAGNER AND LUDWIG II

THE correspondence of Richard Wagner discloses the existence of a very warm friendship between him and Ludwig II, the young king of Bavaria. Ludwig as a young man appears to have been a very charming personality, good looking, engaging and sympathetic; every one was fond of him. Yet his tastes led him away from "society," into retirement, and the companionship of Nature and a few chosen friends--often of humble birth. Already at the age of fifteen he had heard Lohengrin, and silently vowed to know the composer. One of his first acts when he came to the throne was to send for Wagner; and from the moment of their meeting a personal intimacy sprang up between them, which in due course led to the establishment of the theatre at Bayreuth, and to the liberation of Wagner's genius to the world. Though the young king at a later time lost his reason--probably owing to his over-sensitive emotional nature--this does not detract from the service that he rendered to Music by his generous attachment. How Wagner viewed the matter may be gathered from Wagner's letters.

"He, the king, loves me, and with the deep feeling and glow of a first love; he perceives and knows everything about me, and understands me as my own soul. He wants me to stay with him always. . . . I am to be free and my own master, not his music-conductor--only my very self and his friend." *Letters to Mme. Eliza Wille*, 4th May, 1864.

It is true that I have my young king who genuinely adores me. You cannot form an idea of our relations. I recall one of the dreams of my youth. I once dreamed that Shakespeare was alive: that I really saw and spoke to him: I can never forget the impression that dream made on me. Then I would have wished to see Beethoven, though he was already dead. Something of the same kind must pass in the mind of this lovable man when with me. He says he can hardly believe that he really possesses me. None can read without astonishment, without enchantment, the letters he writes to me." *Ibid*, 9th Sept., 1864.

"I hope now for a long period to gain strength again by quiet work. This is made possible for me by the love of an unimaginably beautiful and thoughtful being: it seems that it *had* to be even so greatly gifted a man and one so destined for me, as this young King of Bavaria. What he is to me no one can imagine. My guardian! In his love I completely rest and fortify myself towards the completion of my task." *Letter to his brother-in-law*, 10th Sept., 1865.

LUDWIG II TO RICHARD WAGNER

BELOW are some of the actual letters of Ludwig to Wagner. (See Prof. C. Beyer's book, *Ludwig II, König von Bayern.*)

"Dear Friend, O I see clearly that your sufferings are deep-rooted! You tell me, beloved friend, that you have looked deep into the hearts of men, and seen there the villainy and corruption that dwells within. Yes, I believe you, and I can well understand that moments come to you of disgust with the human race; yet always will we remember (will we not, beloved?) that there are yet many noble and good people, for whom it is a real pleasure to live and work. And yet you say you are no use for this world!--I pray you, do not despair, your true friend conjures you; have Courage: 'Love helps us to bear and suffer all things, love brings at last the victor's crown!' Love recognizes, even in the most corrupt, the germ of good; she alone overcomes all!--Live on, darling of my soul. I recall your own words to you. To learn to forget is a noble work!--Let us be careful to hide the faults of others; it was for all men indeed that the Saviour died and suffered. And now, what a pity that 'Tristan' can not be presented to-day; will it perhaps to-morrow? Is there any chance?

Unto death, your faithful friend,
LUDWIG."

15*th May*, 186S.

"*Purschling*, 4*th Aug.*, 1865.

My one, my much-loved Friend,--You express to me your sorrow that, as it seems to you, each one of our last meetings has only brought pain and anxiety to me.--Must I then remind my loved one of Brynhilda's words?--Not only in gladness and enjoyment, but in suffering also Love makes man blest. . . . When does my friend think of coming to the 'Hill-Top,' to the woodland's aromatic breezes?--Should a stay in that particular spot not altogether suit, why, I beg my dear one to choose any of my other mountain-cabins for his residence.--What is mine is his! Perhaps we may meet on the way between the Wood and the World, as my friend expressed it! . . . To thee I am wholly devoted; for thee, for thee only to live!

Unto death your own, your faithful
"LUDWIG."

"*Hohenschwangau*, 2*nd Nov.*, 1865.

My one Friend, my ardently beloved! This afternoon, at 3.30, I returned from a glorious tour in Switzerland! How this land delighted me!--There I found your dear letter; deepest warmest thanks for the same. With new and burning enthusiasm has it filled me; I see that the beloved marches boldly and confidently forward, towards our great and eternal goal.

All hindrances I will victoriously like a hero overcome. I am entirely at thy disposal; let me now dutifully prove it.--Yes, we must meet and speak together. I will banish all evil clouds; Love has strength for all. You are the star that shines upon my life, and the sight of you ever wonderfully strengthens me.--Ardently I long for you, O my presiding Saint, to whom I pray! I should be immensely pleased to see my friend here in about a week; oh, we have plenty to say!

If only I could quite banish from me the curse of which you speak, and send it back to the deeps of night from whence it sprang!--How I love, how I love you, my one, my highest good! . . . "My enthusiasm and love for you are boundless. Once more I swear you faith till death!

Ever, ever your devoted
"LUDWIG."

WAGNER ON GREEK COMRADESHIP

IN these letters we see chiefly, of course, the passionate sentiments of which Ludwig was capable; but that Wagner fully understood the feeling and appreciated it may be gathered from various passages in his published writings--such as the following, in which he seeks to show how the devotion of comradeship became the chief formative influence of the Spartan State:--

"This beauteous naked man is the kernel of all Spartanhood; from genuine delight in the beauty of the most perfect human body--that of the male--

arose that spirit of comradeship which pervades and shapes the whole economy of the Spartan State: This love of man to man, in its primitive purity, proclaims itself as the noblest and least selfish utterance of man's sense of beauty, for it teaches man to sink and merge his entire self in the object of his affection"; and again:--"The higher element of that love of man to man consisted even in this: that it excluded the motive of egoistic physicalism. Nevertheless it not only included a purely spiritual bond of friendship, but this spiritual friendship was the blossom and the crown of the physical friendship. The latter sprang directly from delight in the beauty, aye in the material bodily beauty of the beloved comrade; yet this delight was no egoistic yearning, but a thorough stepping out of self into unreserved sympathy with the comrade's joy in himself; involuntarily betrayed by his life-glad beauty-prompted bearing. This love, which had its basis in the noblest pleasures of both eye and soul--not like our modern postal correspondence of sober friendship, half business-like, half sentimental--was the Spartan's only tutoress of youth, the never-ageing instructress alike of boy and man, the ordainer of common feasts and valiant enterprises; nay the inspiring helpmeet on the battlefield. For this it was that knit the fellowship of love into battalions of war, and fore-wrote the tactics of death-daring, in rescue of the imperilled or vengeance for the slaughtered comrade, by the infrangible law of the soul's most natural necessity." *The Art-work of the Future, trans. by W. A. Ellis.*

HÆCKEL'S VISIT TO CEYLON

FRNST HÆCKEL, in his "Visit to Ceylon,", describes the devotion entertained for him by his Rodiya serving-boy at Belligam, near Galle. The keeper of the rest-house at Belligam was an old and philosophically-minded man, whom Hæckel, from his likeness to a well known head, could not help calling by the name of Socrates. And he continues:--

"It really seemed as though I should be pursued by the familiar aspects of classical antiquity from the first moment of my arrival at my idyllic home. For, as Socrates led me up the steps of the open central hall of the rest-house, I saw before me, with uplifted arms in an attitude of prayer, a beautiful naked brown figure, which could be nothing else than the famous statue of the 'Youth adoring.' How surprised I was when the graceful bronze statue suddenly came to life, and dropping his arms fell on his knees, and, after raising his black eyes imploringly to mine, bowed his handsome face so low at my feet that his long black hair fell on the floor! Socrates informed me that this boy was a Pariah, a member of the lowest caste, the Rodiyas, who had lost his parents at an early age, so he had taken pity on him. He was told off to my exclusive service, had nothing to do the livelong day but obey my wishes, and was a good boy, sure to do his duty punctually. In answer to the question what I was to call my new body-servant, the old man informed me that his name was Gamameda. Of course I immediately thought of Ganymede, for the favorite of Jove himself could not have been more finely made, or have had limbs more beautifully proportioned and molded. As Gamameda also displayed a peculiar talent as butler, and never allowed any one else to open me a cocoa-nut or offer me a glass of palm wine, it was no more than right that I should dub him Ganymede.

Among the many beautiful figures which move in the foreground of my memories of the paradise of Ceylon, Ganymede remains one of my dearest favorites. Not only did he fulfill his duties with the greatest attention and conscientiousness, but he developed a personal attachment and devotion to me which touched me deeply. The poor boy, as a miserable outcast of the Rodiya caste, had been from his birth the object of the deepest contempt of his fellow-men, and subjected to every sort of brutality and ill-treatment. With the single exception of old Socrates, who was not too gentle with him either, no one perhaps had ever cared for him in any way. He was evidently as much surprised as delighted to find me willing to be kind to him from the first. . . . I owe many beautiful and valuable contributions to my museum to Ganymede's unfailing zeal and dexterity. With the keen eye, the neat hand, and the supple agility of the Cinghalese youth, he could catch a fluttering moth or a gliding fish with equal promptitude; and his nimbleness was really amazing, when, out hunting, he climbed the tall trees like a cat, or scrambled through the densest jungle to recover the prize I had killed."

My Visit to Ceylon, by Ernst Hæckel, p. 200. (Kegan Paul, Trench & Co., 1883).

Hæckel stayed some weeks in and around Belligain; and continues (p. 272):--

"On my return to Belgium I had to face one of the hardest duties of my whole stay in Ceylon: to tear myself away from this lovely spot of earth, where I had spent six of the happiest and most interesting weeks in my life. . . . But hardest of all was the parting from my faithful Ganymede; the poor lad wept bitterly, and implored me to take him with me to Europe. In vain had I assured him that it was impossible, and told him of our chill climate and dull skies. He clung to my knees and declared that he would follow me unhesitatingly wherever I would take him. I was at last almost obliged to use force to free myself from his embrace. I got into the carriage which was waiting, and as I waved a last farewell to my good brown friends, I almost felt as if I had been expelled from Paradise."

K. H. ULRICHS

WE may close this record of celebrated Germans with the name of K. H. Ulrichs, a Hanoverian by birth, who occupied for a long time an official position in the revenue department at Vienna, and who became well known about 1866 through his writings on the subject of friendship.

He gives, in his pamphlet *Memnon*, an account of the "story of his heart" in early years. In an apparently quite natural way, and independently of outer influences, his thoughts had from the very first been of friends of his own sex. At the age of 14, the picture of a Greek hero or god, a statue, seen in a book, woke in him the tenderest longings.

"This picture (he says), put away from me, as it was, a hundred times, came again a hundred times before the eyes of my soul. But of course for the origin of my special temperament it is in no way responsible. It only woke up what was already slumbering there--a thing which might have been done equally well by something else."

From that time forward the boy worshipped with a kind of romantic devotion elder friends, young men in the prime of early manhood; and later still his writings threw a flood of light on the "urning" temperament--as he called it--of which he was himself so marked an example.

Some of Ulrich's verses are scattered among his prose writings:--

To his friend Eberhard

"And so farewell! perchance on Earth
  God's finger--as 'twixt thee and me--
Will never make that wonder clear
  Why thus It drew me unto thee."

And this:--

"It was the day of our first meeting--
  That happy day, in Davern's grove--
I felt the Spring wind's tender greeting,

And April touched my heart to love.
Thy hand in mine lay kindly mated;
Thy gaze held mine quite fascinated--
So gracious wast, and fair!
Thy glance my life-thread almost severed;
My heart for joy and gladness quivered,
Nigh more than it could bear.

There in the grove at evening's hour
The breeze thro' budding twigs hath ranged,
And lips have learned to meet each other,
And kisses mute exchanged."
Memnon, p. 23.

BYRON'S LETTERS

T0 return to England. With the beginning of the 19th century we find two great poets, Byron and Shelley, both interested in and even writing in a romantic strain on the subject in question.

Byron's attachment, when at Cambridge, to Eddleston the chorister, a youth two years younger than himself, is well known. In a youthful letter to Miss Pigot he, Byron, speaks of it in enthusiastic terms:--

"Trin. Coll., Camb., *July* 5*th*, 1807.

I rejoice to hear you are interested in my protégé; he has been my *almost constant* associate since October, 1805, when I entered Trinity College. His *voice* first attracted my attention, his *countenance* fixed it, and his *manners* attached me to him for ever. He departs for a mercantile house in town in October, and we shall probably not meet till the expiration of my minority, when I shall leave to his decision either entering as a partner through my interest or residing with me altogether. Of course he would in his present frame of mind prefer the latter, but he may alter his opinion previous to that period; however, he shall have his choice. I certainly love him more than any human being, and neither time nor distance have had the least effect on my (in general) changeable disposition. In short we shall put Lady E. Butler and Miss Ponsonby to the blush, Pylades and Orestes out of countenance, and want nothing but a catastrophe like Nisus and Euryalus to give Jonathan and David the 'go by.' He certainly is more attached to *me* than even I am in return. During the whole of my residence at Cambridge we met every day, summer and winter, without passing *one* tiresome moment, and separated each time with increasing reluctance."

THE ADIEU

Eddleston gave Byron a cornelian (brooch-pin) which Byron prized very much, and is said to have kept all his life. He probably refers to it, and to the inequality of condition between him and Eddleston, in the following stanza from his poem, *The Adieu*, written about this time:--

"And thou, my friend, whose gentle love
  Yet thrills my bosom's chords,
How much thy friendship was above
  Description's power of words!
Still near my breast thy gift I wear
Which sparkled once with Feeling's tear,
  Of Love, the pure, the sacred gem;
Our souls were equal, and our lot
In that dear moment quite forgot;
  Let pride alone condemn."

THE LADIES OF LLANGOLLEN

THE Lady Eleanor Butler and Miss Sarah Ponsonby mentioned in the above letter were at that time living at Llangollen, in Wales, and were known as the "Ladies of Llangollen," their romantic attachment to each other having already become proverbial. When Miss Ponsonby was seventeen, and Lady E. Butler some twenty years older, they had run away from their respective and respectable homes in Ireland, and taking a cottage at Llangollen lived there, inseparable companions, for the rest of their lives. Letters and diaries of contemporary celebrities mention their romantic devotion. (The Duke of Wellington was among their visitors.) Lady Eleanor died in 18 29, at the age of ninety; and Miss Ponsonby only survived her "beloved one" (as she always called her) by two years.

BYRON'S NISUS AND EURYALUS

AS to the allusion to Nisus and Euryalus, Byron's paraphrase of the episode (from the 9th book of Virgil's Æneid) serves to show his interest in it:--

"Nisus, the guardian of the portal, stood,
Eager to gild his arms with hostile blood;
Well-skilled in fight the quivering lance to wield,
Or pour his arrows thro' the embattled field:
From Ida torn, he left his Sylvan cave,
And sought a foreign home, a distant grave.
  To watch the movements of the Daunian host,
With him Euryalus sustains the post;
No lovelier mien adorn'd the ranks of Troy,
And beardless bloom yet graced the gallant boy;
Tho' few the seasons of his youthful life,
A yet a novice in the martial strife,
'Twas his, with beauty, valor's gifts to share--
A soul heroic, as his form was fair.
These burn with one pure flame of generous love;
In peace, in war, united still they move;
Friendship and glory form their joint reward;
And now combined they hold their nightly guard."

[The two then carry out a daring raid on the enemy, in which Euryalus is slain. Nisus, coming to his rescue is--after performing prodigies of valor--slain too.]

"Thus Nisus all his fond affection proved--
Dying, revenged the fate of him he loved;
Then on his bosom sought his wonted place,
And death was heavenly in his friend's embrace!
Celestial pair! if aught my verse can claim,
Wafted on Time's broad pinion, yours is fame!
Ages on ages shall your fate admire,
No future day shall see your names expire,
While stands the Capitol, immortal dome!
And vanquished millions hail their empress, Rome!"

BYRON'S CALMAR AND ORLA

BYRON'S "Death of Calmar and Orla: an Imitation of Ossian," is, like his "Nisus and Euryalus," a story of two hero-friends who, refusing to be separated, die together in battle:--

"In Morven dwelt the chief; a beam of war to Fingal. His steps in the field were marked in blood. Lochlin's sons had fled before his angry spear; but mild was the eye of Calmar; soft was the flow of his yellow locks: they streamed like the meteor of the night. No maid was the sigh of his soul: his thoughts were given to friendship--to dark-haired Orla, destroyer of heroes! Equal were their swords in battle; but fierce was the pride of Orla--gentle alone to Calmar. Together they dwelt in the cave of Oithona." [Orla is sent by the King on a mission of danger amid the hosts of the enemy. Calmar insists on accompanying him, in spite of all entreaties to the contrary. They are discovered. A fight ensues, and they are slain.] "Morn glimmers on the hills: no living foe is seen; but the sleepers are many; grim they lie on Erin. The breeze of ocean lifts their locks; yet they do not awake. The hawks scream above their prey.

Whose yellow locks wave o'er the breast of a chief? Bright as the gold of the stranger they mingle with the dark hair of his friend. 'Tis Calmar: he lies on the bosom of Orla. Theirs is one stream of blood. Fierce is the look of gloomy Orla. He breathes not, but his eye is still aflame. It glares in death unclosed. His hand is grasped in Calmar's; but Calmar lives! He lives, though low. 'Rise,' said the King, 'Rise, son of Mora: 'tis mine to heal the wounds of heroes. Calmar may yet bound on the hills of Morven.'

'Never more shall Calmar chase the deer of Morven with Orla,' said the hero. 'What were the chase to me alone? Who should share the spoils of battle with Calmar? Orla is at rest. Rough was thy soul, Orla! Yet soft to me as the dew of morn. It glared on others in lightning: to me a silver beam of night. Bear my sword to blue-eyed Mora; let it hang in my empty hall. It is not pure from blood: but it could not save Orla. Lay me with my friend. Raise the song when I am dead.'" [So they are laid by the stream of Lubar, and four grey stones mark the dwelling of Orla and Calmar.]

MOORE ON BYRON

Byron's friendships, in fact, with young men were so marked that Moore in his *Life and Letters of Lord Byron* seems to have felt it necessary to mention and, to some extent, to explain them:--

"During his stay in Greece (in 1810) we find him forming one of those extraordinary friendships-if attachment to persons so interior to himself can be called by that name--of which I have already mentioned two or three instances in his younger days, and in which the pride of being a protector and the pleasure of exciting gratitude seem to have contributed to his mind the chief, pervading charm. The person whom he now adopted in this manner, and from similar feelings to those which had inspired his early attachments to the cottage boy near Newstead and the young chorister at Cambridge, was a Greek youth, named Nicolo Giraud, the son, I believe, of a widow lady in whose house the artist Lusieri lodged. In this young man he seems to have taken the most lively and even brotherly interest.'"

SHELLEY ON FRIENDSHIP

SHELLEY, in his fragmentary *Essay on Friendship*--stated by his friend Hogg to have been written "not long before his death" says:--

"I remember forming an attachment of this kind at school. I cannot recall to my memory the precise epoch at which this took place; but I imagine it must have been at the age of eleven or twelve. The object of these sentiments was a boy about my own age, of a character eminently generous, brave and gentle, and the elements of human feeling seemed to have been, from his birth, genially compounded within him. There was a delicacy and a simplicity in his manners, inexpressibly attractive. It has never been my fortune to meet with him since my schoolboy days; but either I confound my present recollections with the delusions of past feelings, or he is now a source of honor and utility to every one around him. The tones of his voice were so soft and winning, that every word pierced into m heart; and their pathos was so deep that in listening to him the tears have involuntarily gushed from my eyes. Such was the being for whom I first experienced the sacred sentiments of friendship."

It may be noted that Hogg takes the reference as to himself!

LEIGH HUNT ON SCHOOL-LIFE

WITH this passage we may compare the following from Leigh Hunt:--

"If I had reaped no other benefit from Christ Hospital, the school would be ever dear to me from the recollection of the friendships I formed in it, and of the first heavenly taste it gave me of that most spiritual of the affections. . . . If ever I tasted a disembodied transport on earth, it was in those friendships which I entertained at school, before I dreamt of any maturer feeling. I shall never forget the impression it made on me. I loved my friend for his gentleness, his candor, his truth, his good repute, his freedom even from my own livelier manner, his calm and reasonable kindness. It was not any particular talent that attracted me to him, or anything striking whatsoever. I should say, in one word, it was his goodness. I doubt whether he ever had a conception of a tithe of the regard and respect I entertained for him; and I smile to think of the perplexity (though he never showed it) which he probably felt sometimes at my enthusiastic expressions; for I thought him a kind of angel. It is no exaggeration to say, that, take away the unspiritual part of it--the genius and the knowledge--and there is no height of conceit indulged in by the most romantic character in Shakespeare, which surpassed what I felt towards the merits I ascribed to him, and the delight which I took in his society. With the other boys I played antics, and rioted in fantastic jests; but in his society, or whenever I thought of him, I fell into a kind of Sabbath state of bliss; and I am sure I could have died for him.

I experienced this delightful affection towards three successive school-fellows, till two of them had for some time gone out into the world and forgotten me; but it grew less with each, and in more than one instance became rivalled by a new set of emotions, especially in regard to the last, for I fell in love with his sister--at least, I thought so. But on the occurrence of her death, not long after, I was startled at finding myself assume an air of greater sorrow than I felt, and at being willing to be relieved by the sight of the first pretty face that turned towards me. . . . My friend, who died himself not long after his quitting the University, was of a German family in the service of the court, very refined and musical." *Autobiography of Leigh Hunt, Smith and Elder*, 1870, p. 75.

LORD BEACONSFIELD'S "CONINGSBY"

ON this subject of boy-friendships and their intensity Lord Beaconsfield has, in *Coningsby*, a quite romantic passage, which notwithstanding its sentimental setting may be worth quoting; because, after all, it signalizes an often forgotten or unconsidered aspect of school-life:--

"At school, friendship is a passion. It entrances the being; it tears the soul. All loves of after-life can never bring its rapture, or its wretchedness; no bliss so absorbing, no pangs of jealousy or despair so crushing and so keen! What tenderness and what devotion; what illimitable confidence, infinite revelations of inmost thoughts; what ecstatic present and romantic future; what bitter estrangements and what melting reconciliations; what scenes of wild recrimination, agitating explanations, passionate correspondence; what insane sensitiveness, and what frantic sensibility; what earthquakes of the heart and whirlwinds of the soul are confined in that simple phrase, a schoolboy's friendship!"

FITZGERALD AND POSH

EDWARD FITZGERALD, the interpreter and translator of *Omar Khayyam*, was a man of the deepest feeling and sensibility, with a special gift for friendship. Men like Tennyson and Thackeray declared that they loved him best of all their friends. He himself said in one of his letters, "My friendships are more like loves." A. C. Benson, his biographer, writes of him:--

"He was always taking fancies, and once under the spell he could see no faults in his friend. His friendship for Browne arose out of one of these romantic impulses. So too his affection for Posh, the boatman; for Cowell, and for Alfred Smith, the farmer of Farlingay and Boulge, who had been his protégé as a boy. He seems to have been one of those whose best friendships are reserved for men; for though he had beloved women friends like Mrs. Cowell and Mrs. Kemble, yet these are the exceptions rather than the rule. The truth is, there was a strong admixture of the feminine in Fitzgerald's character." *Fitzgerald, English Men of Letters Series*, ch. viii.

The friendship with Posh, the fisherman, at Lowestoft and at Woodbridge, lasted over many years. Fitzgerald had a herring-lugger built for him, which he called the *Meum and Tuum*, and in which they had many a sail together. Benson, speaking of their first meeting, says:--

"In the same year [1864] came another great friendship. He made the acquaintance of a stalwart sailor named Joseph Fletcher, commonly called Posh. It was at Lowestoft that he was found, where Fitzgerald used, as he wrote in 1850, 'to wander about the shore at night longing for some fellow to accost me who might give some promise of filling up a very vacant place in my heart.' Posh had seen the melancholy figure wandering about, and years after, when Fitz used to ask him why he had not been merciful enough to speak to him, Posh would reply that he had not thought of it becoming. Posh was, in Fitzgerald's own words, 'a man of the finest Saxon type, with a complexion, *vif*, *mâle et flamboyant*, blue eyes, a nose less than Roman, more than Greek, and strictly auburn hair that woman might sigh to possess.' He was too, according to Fitz, 'a a man of simplicity of soul, justice of thought, tenderness of nature, a gentleman of Nature's grandest type.' Fitz became deeply devoted to this big-handed, soft-hearted, grave fellow, then 24 years of age."

Ibid., ch. iii.

ALFRED TENNYSON'S "IN MEMORIAM"

ALFRED TENNYSON, in his great poem, *In Memoriam*, published about the middle of the 19th century, gives superb expression to his love for his lost friend, Arthur Hallam. Reserved, dignified, in sustained meditation and tender sentiment, yet half revealing here and there a more passionate feeling; expressing in simplest words the most difficult and elusive thoughts (*e.g.*, Cantos 128 and 129), as well as the most intimate and sacred moods of the soul; it is indeed a great work of art. Naturally, being such, it was roundly abused by the critics on its first appearance. The *Times* solemnly rebuked its language as unfitted for any but amatory tenderness, and because young Hallam was a barrister spent much wit upon the poet's "Amaryllis of the Chancery bar." Tennyson himself, speaking of *In Memoriam*, mentioned (see *Memoir* by his son, p. 800) "the number of shameful letters of abuse he had received about it!"

CANTO XIII

"Tears of the widower, when he sees,
  A late-lost form that sleep reveals,
  And moves his doubtful arms, and feels
Her place is empty, fall like these;

Which weep a loss for ever new,
  A void where heart on heart reposed;
  And, where warm hands have prest and closed,
Silence, till I be silent too.

Which weep the comrade of my choice,
  An awful thought, a life removed,
  The human-hearted man I loved,
A spirit, not a breathing voice.

Come Time, and teach me, many years,
  I do not suffer in a dream;
  For now so strange do these things seem,
Mine eyes have leisure for their tears;

My fancies time to rise on wing,
  And glance about the approaching sails,
  As tho' they brought but merchant's bales,
And not the burden that they bring."

CANTO XVIII

"'Tis well, 'tis something, we may stand
  Where he in English earth is laid,
  And from his ashes may be made
The violet of his native land.

'Tis little; but it looks in truth
  As if the quiet bones were blest
  Among familiar names to rest
And in the places of his youth.

Come then, pure hands, and bear the head
  That sleeps, or wears the mask of sleep,
  And come, whatever loves to weep,
And hear the ritual of the dead.

Ah yet, ev'n yet, if this might be,
  I, falling on his faithful heart,
  Would breathing thro' his lips impart
The life that almost dies in me:

That dies not, but endures with pain,
  And slowly forms the firmer mind,
  Treasuring the look it cannot find,
The words that are not heard again."

CANTO LIX

"If, in thy second state sublime,
  Thy ransom'd reason change replies
  With all the circle of the wise,
The perfect flower of human time;

And if thou cast thine eyes below,
  How dimly character'd and slight,
  How dwarf'd a growth of cold and night,
How blanch'd with darkness must I grow!

Yet turn thee to the doubtful shore,
  Where thy first form was made a man;
  I loved thee, Spirit, and love, nor can
The soul of Shakspeare love thee more."

CANTO CXXVII

"Dear friend, far off, my lost desire,
  So far, so near, in woe or weal;
  O loved the most when most I feel
There is a lower and a higher;

Known and unknown, human, divine!
  Sweet human hand and lips and eye,
  Dear heavenly friend that canst not die,
Mine, mine, for ever, ever, mine!

Strange friend, past, present and to be;
  Loved deeplier, darklier understood;
  Behold I dream a dream of good
And mingle all the world with thee."

CANTO CXXVIII

"Thy voice is on the rolling air;
  I hear thee where the waters run;
  Thou standest in the rising sun,
And in the setting thou art fair.

What are thou then? I cannot guess;
  But tho' I seem in star and flower
  To feel thee some diffusive power,
I do not therefore love thee less:

My love involves the love before;
  My love is vaster passion now;
  Tho' mixed with God and Nature thou,
I seem to love thee more--and more.

Far off thou art, but ever nigh;
  I have thee still, and I rejoice;
  I prosper, circled with thy voice;
I shall not lose thee tho' I die."

BROWNING'S "MAY AND DEATH"

FOLLOWING is a little poem by Robert Browning, entitled *May and Death*, which may well be placed near the stanzas of *In Memoriam*:--

"I wish that when you died last May,
  Charles, there had died along with you
Three parts of Spring's delightful things;
  Ay, and for me the fourth part too.

A foolish thought, and worse, perhaps!
  There must be many a pair of friends

Who arm-in-arm deserve the warm
  Moon-births and the long evening-ends.

So, for their sake, be May still May!
  Let their new time, as mine of old,
Do all it did for me; I bid
  Sweet sights and sounds throng manifold.

Only one little sigh, one plant
  Woods have in May, that starts up green
Save a sole streak which, so to speak,
  Is Spring's blood, split its leaves between--

That, they might spare; a certain wood
  Might miss the plant; their loss were small;
But I--whene'er the leaf grows there--
  It's drop comes from my heart, that's all."

RALPH WALDO EMERSON

BETWEEN Browning and Whitman we may insert a few lines from R. W. Emerson:--

"The only way to have a friend is to be one. . . . In the last analysis love is only the reflection of a man's own worthiness from other men. Men have sometimes exchanged names with their friends, as if they would signify that in their friend each loved his own soul.

The higher the style we demand of friendship, of course the less easy to establish it with flesh and blood. . . . Friends, such as we desire, are dreams and fables. But a sublime hope cheers ever the faithful heart, that elsewhere, in other regions of the universal power, souls are now acting, enduring, and daring, which can love us, and which we can love." *Essay on Friendship.*

HENRY D. THOREAU

These also from Henry D. Thoreau:--

"No word is oftener on the lips of men than Friendship, and indeed no thought is more familiar to their aspirations. All men are dreaming of it, and its drama, which is always a tragedy, is enacted daily. It is the secret of the universe. You may thread the town, you may wander the country, and none shall ever speak of it, yet thought is everywhere busy about it, and the idea of what is possible in this respect affects our behavior towards all new men and women, and a great many old ones. Nevertheless I can remember only two or three essays on this subject in all literature. . . . To say that a man is your friend, means commonly no more than this, that he is not your enemy. Most contemplate only what would be the accidental and trifling advantages of friendship, as that the friend can assist in time of need, by his substance, or his influence, or his counsel; but he who foresees such advantages in this relation proves himself blind to its real advantage, or indeed wholly inexperienced in the relation itself. . . . What is commonly called Friendship is only a little more honor among rogues. But sometimes we are said to *love* another, that is, to stand in a true relation to him, so that we give the best to, and receive the best from, him. Between whom there is hearty truth there is love; and in proportion to our truthfulness and confidence in one another our lives are divine and miraculous, and answer to our ideal. There are passages of affection in our intercourse with mortal men and women, such as no prophecy had taught us to expect, which transcend our earthly life, and anticipate heaven for us." *From On the Concord River.*

WALT WHITMAN

I CONCLUDE this collection with a few quotations from Whitman, for whom "the love of comrades" perhaps stands as the most intimate part of his message to the world—"Here the frailest leaves of me and yet my strongest lasting." Whitman, by his great power, originality and initiative, as well as by his deep insight and wide vision, is in many ways the inaugurator of a new era to mankind; and it is especially interesting to find that this idea of comradeship, and of its establishment as a social institution, plays so important a part with him. We have seen that in the Greek age, and more or less generally in the ancient and pagan world, comradeship was an institution; we have seen that in Christian and modern times, though existent, it was socially denied and ignored, and indeed to a great extent fell under a kind of ban; and now Whitman's attitude towards it suggests to us that it really is destined to pass into its third stage, to arise again, and become a recognized factor of modern life, and even in a more extended and perfect form than at first.

"It is to the development, identification, and general prevalence of that fervid comradeship (the adhesive love, at least rivaling the amative love hitherto possessing imaginative literature, if not going beyond it), that I look for the counterbalance and offset of our materialistic and vulgar American Democracy, and for the spiritualization thereof. Many will say it is a dream, and will not follow my inferences; but I confidently expect a time when there will be seen, running like a half-hid warp through all the myriad audible and visible worldly interests of America, threads of manly friendship, fond and loving, pure and sweet, strong and lifelong, carried to degrees hitherto unknown--not only giving tone to individual character, and making it unprecedently emotional, muscular, heroic, and refined, but having deepest relations to general politics. I say Democracy infers such loving comradeship, as its most inevitable twin or counterpart, without which it will be incomplete, in vain, and incapable of perpetuating itself." *Democratic Vistas, note.*

"LEAVES OF GRASS"

The three following poems are taken from *Leaves of Grass*:--

"Recorders ages hence,
Come, I will take you down underneath this impassive exterior,
I will tell you what to say of me,
Publish my name and hang up my picture as that of the tenderest lover,
The friend the lover's portrait, of whom his friend his lover was fondest,
Who was not proud of his Songs, but of the measureless ocean of love within him, and freely pour'd it forth,
Who often walk'd lonesome walks thinking of his dear friends, his lovers,
Who pensive away from one he lov'd often lay sleepless and dissatisfied at night,
Who knew too well the sick, sick dread lest the one he lov'd might secretly be indifferent to him,
Whose happiest days were far away through fields, in woods, on hills, he and another wandering hand in hand, they twain apart from other men,
Who oft as he saunterd the streets curv'd with his arm the shoulder of his friend, while the arm

of his friend rested upon him also."
Leaves of Grass, 1891, 2 edn., p. 102.

"When I heard at the close of the day how my name had been receiv'd with plaudits in the capitol, still it was not a happy night for me that follow'd,
And else when I carous'd, or when my plans were accomplish'd, still I was not happy,
But the day when I rose at dawn from the bed of perfect health, refresh'd, singing, inhaling the ripe breath of autumn,
When I saw the full moon in the west grow pale and disappear in the morning light,
When I wander'd alone over the beach, and undressing bathed, laughing with the cool waters, and saw the sun rise,
And when I thought how my dear friend my lover was on his way coming, O then I was happy,
O then each breath tasted sweeter, and all that day my food nourish'd me more, and the beautiful day pass'd well,
And the next came with equal and with the joy, next at evening came my friend,
And that night while all was still I heard the waters roll slowly continuously up the shores,
I heard the hissing rustle of the liquid and sands as directed to me whispering to congratulate me,
For the one I love most lay sleeping by me under the same cover in the cool night,
In the stillness in the autumn moonbeams his face was inclined toward me,
And his arm lay lightly around my breast--and that night I was happy."
Ibid, p. 103.

"I hear it was charged against me that I sought to destroy institutions,
But really I am neither for nor against institutions,
(What indeed have I in common with them? or what with the destruction of them?)
Only I will establish in the Mannahatta and in every city of these States inland and seaboard,
And in the fields and woods, and above every keel little or

large that dents the water,
Without edifices or rules or trustees or any argument,
The institution of the dear love of comrades."

Ibid, p. 107.

SEX = LOVE,

AND ITS PLACE IN A FREE SOCIETY

SEX = LOVE

The subject of Sex is most difficult to deal with, not only on account of a certain prudery as well as a natural reticence on the subject, but doubtless also because the passion itself being so tremendously strong and occupying such a large part of human thought—and words being so scanty and inadequate on the subject—everything that *is* said is liable to be misunderstood; the most violent inferences are made, and equivocations surmised, from the simplest remarks; qualified admissions of liberty are interpreted into recommendations of unbridled license; and generally the perspective of literary expression is turned upside down by the effect of the unfamiliarity of the topic on the reader's mind.

There is indeed a vast deal of fetishism in the current treatment of Sex; and the subject is dealt with as though it lay quite out of line with any other need or faculty of human nature. Nor can one altogether be surprised at this when one perceives of what vast import Sex is in the scheme of things, and how deeply it has been associated since the earliest times not only with man's personal impulses but even with his religious sentiments and ceremonials.

Next to hunger this is doubtless the most primitive and imperative of our needs. But in modern civilized life Sex enters probably even more into *consciousness* than hunger. For the hunger-needs of the human race are in the later societies fairly well satisfied, but the sex-desires are strongly restrained, both by law and custom, from satisfaction—and so assert themselves all the more in thought.

To find the place of these desires, their utterance, their control, their personal import, their social import, is a tremendous problem to every youth and girl, man and woman.

There are a few of both sexes, doubtless, who hardly feel the passion—who have never been "in love," and who experience no strong sexual appetite—but these are rare. Practically the passion is a matter of universal experience; and speaking broadly and generally we may say it is a matter on which it is quite desirable that every adult at some time or other *should* have experience—actual and physical, as well as emotional. There may be exceptions; but, as said, the sex-instinct lies so deep and is so universal, that for the understanding of life—of one's own life, of that of others, and of human nature in general—as well as for the proper development of one's own capacities, such experience is almost indispensable.

While the glory of Sex pervades and suffuses all Nature; while the flowers are rayed and starred out towards the sun in the very ecstasy of generation; while the nostrils of the animals dilate, and their forms become instinct, under the passion, with a proud and fiery beauty; while even the human lover is transformed, and in the great splendors of the mountains and the sky perceives something to which he had not the key before—yet it is curious that just here, in Man, we find the magic wand of Nature suddenly broken, and doubt and conflict and division entering in, where a kind of unconscious harmony had erst prevailed.

Heine I think says somewhere that the man who loves unsuccessfully knows himself to be a god. It is not perhaps till the great current of sexual love is checked and brought into conflict with the other parts of his being that the whole nature of the man, sexual and moral, under the tremendous stress rises into consciousness and reveals in fire its god-like quality. This is the work of the artificer who makes immortal souls—who out of the natural love evolves even a more perfect love. "In tutti gli amanti," says Giordano Bruno, "é questo fabro vulcano" ("in all lovers is this Olympian blacksmith present").

To teach the child first, quite openly, its physical relation to its own mother, its long indwelling in her body, and the deep and sacred bond of tenderness between mother and child in consequence; then, after a time, to explain the work of fatherhood, and how the love of the parents for each other was the cause of its own (the child's) existence: these things are easy and natural—at least they are so to the young mind—and excite in it no surprise, or sense of unfitness, but only gratitude and a kind of tender wonderment. Then, later on, as the special sexual needs and desires develop, to instruct the girl or boy in the further details of the matter, and the care and right conduct of her or his own sexual nature; on the meaning and the dangers of solitary indulgence—if this habit has been contracted; on the need of self-control and the presence of affection in all relations with others, and (without asceticism) on the possibility of deflecting physical desire to some degree into affectional and emotional channels, and the great gain so resulting: all these are things which an ordinary youth of either sex will easily understand and appreciate, and which may be of priceless value, saving such an one from years of struggle in foul morasses, and waste of precious life-strength. Finally, with the maturity of * (See Appendix.)

The moral nature, the supremacy of the pure human relation should be taught—not the extinguishment of desire, but the attainment of the real kernel of it, its dedication to the well-being of another—the evolution of the *human* element in love, balancing the natural—till at last the snatching of an unglad pleasure, regardless of the other from whom it is snatched, or the surrender of one's body to another, for any reason except that of love, become things impossible.

Between lovers then a kind of hardy temperance is much to be recommended—for all reasons, but especially because it lifts their satisfaction and delight in each other out of the region of ephemeralities (which too soon turn to dull indifference and satiety) into the region of more lasting things—one step nearer at any rate to the Eternal Kingdom. How intoxicating indeed, how penetrating—like a most precious wine—is that love which is the sexual transformed by the magic of the will into the emotional and spiritual! And what a loss on the merest grounds of prudence and the economy of pleasure is its unbridled waste along physical channels! So nothing is so much to be dreaded between lovers as just this—the vulgarization of love—and this is the rock upon which marriage so often splits.

There is a kind of illusion about physical desire similar to that which a child suffers from when, seeing a beautiful flower, it instantly snatches the same, and destroys in a few moments the form and fragrance which attracted it. He only gets the full glory who holds himself back a little, and truly possesses who is willing if need be not to possess.

On the other hand it must not be pretended that the physical passions are by their nature abhorrent, or anything but admirable and desirable in their place. Any attempt to absolutely disown or despite them, carried out over long periods either by individuals or bodies of people, only ends in the *thinning out* of the human nature—by the very consequent stinting of the supply of its growth-material, and is liable to stultify itself in time by leading to reactionary excesses. It must never be forgotten that the physical basis throughout life is of the first importance, and supplies the nutrition and food-stuff without which the higher powers cannot exist or at least manifest themselves. Intimacies founded on intellectual and moral affinities alone are seldom very deep and lasting; if the physical or sexual basis is quite absent, the acquaintanceship is liable to die away again like an ill-rooted plant. In many cases (especially of women) the nature is never really understood or disclosed till the sex-feeling is touched—however lightly. Besides it must be remembered that in order for a perfect intimacy between two people their bodies must by the nature of the case be free to each other. The sexual and bodily intimacy may not be the object for which they come together; but if it is denied, its denial will bar any real sense of repose and affiance, and make the relation restless, vague, tentative and unsatisfied.

In these lights it will be seen that what we call asceticism and what we call libertinism are two sides practically of the same shield. So long as the tendency towards mere pleasure-indulgence is strong and uncontrolled, so long will the instinct towards asceticism assert itself—and rightly, else we might speedily find ourselves in headlong Phaethonian career. Asceticism is in its place (as the word would indicate) as an *exercise*; but let it not be looked upon as an end in itself, for that is a mistake of the same kind as going to the opposite extreme. Certainly if the welfare and happiness of the beloved one were always really the main purpose in our minds we should have plenty of occasion for self-control, and an artificial asceticism would not be needed. We look for a time doubtless when the hostility between these two parts of man's unperfected nature will be merged in the perfect love; but at present and until this happens their conflict is certainly one of the most pregnant things in all our experience; and must not by any means be blinked or evaded, but boldly faced. It is in itself almost a sexual act. The mortal nature through it is, so to speak, torn asunder; and through the rent so made in his mortality does it sometimes happen that a new and immortal man is born.

The Sex-act affords the type of all pleasures. The dissatisfaction which at times follows on it is the same as follows on all pleasure which is *sought,* and which does not come unsought. The dissatisfaction is not in the nature of pleasure itself but in the nature of *seeking.* In consciously surrendering oneself to the pursuit of things external, the "I" (since it really has everything and needs nothing) deceives itself, goes out from its true home, tears itself asunder, and admits a gap or rent in its own being. This is what is meant by *sin*—the separation or sundering (German *Sünde*) of one's being—and all the pain that goes therewith. It all consists in *seeking* those external things and pleasures; not (a thousand times be it said) in those external things or pleasures themselves. They are all fair and gracious enough; their place is to stand round the throne and offer their homage—rank behind rank in their multitudes—if so be we will accept it. But for us to go out of ourselves to run after *them*, to allow ourselves to be divided and rent in twain by *their* attraction, that is an inversion of the order of heaven; and in so doing does sin and all suffering enter in.

Of all pleasures the sexual tempts most strongly to this desertion of one's true self, and stands as the type of Maya and the world-illusion; yet the beauty of the loved one and the delight of corporeal union all turn to dust and ashes if bought at the price of disunion and disloyalty in the higher spheres—disloyalty even to the person whose mortal love is sought. The higher and more durable part of man, whirled along in the rapids and whirlpools of desire, experiences tortures the moment it comes to recognize that. It is something other than physical. Then comes the struggle to regain its lost Paradise, and the frightful effort of co-ordination between the two natures, by which the centre of consciousness is gradually transferred from the fugitive to the more permanent part, and the mortal and changeable is assigned its due place in the outer chambers and forecourts of the temple.

Pleasure should come as the natural (and indeed inevitable) accompaniment of life, believed in with a kind of free faith, but never sought as the object of life. It is in the inversion of this order that the uncleanness of the senses arises. Sex to-day throughout the domains of civilization is thoroughly unclean, in the gutter. Little boys bathing on the outskirts of our towns are hunted down by idiotic policemen, apparently infuriated by the sight of the naked body, even of childhood. Lately in one of our northern towns, the boys and men bathing in a public pool set apart by the corporation for the purpose, were—though forced to wear some kind of covering—kept till nine o'clock at night before they were allowed to go into the water—lest in the full daylight Mrs. Grundy should behold any portion of their bodies! And as for women and girls their disabilities in the matter are most serious.

Till this dirty and dismal sentiment with regard to the human body is removed there can be little hope of anything like a free and gracious public life. With the regeneration of our social ideas the whole conception of Sex as a thing covert and to be ashamed of, marketable and unclean, will have to be regenerated. That inestimable freedom and pride which is the basis of all true manhood and womanhood will have to enter into this most intimate relation to preserve it frank and pure—pure from the damnable commercialism which buys and sells all human things, and from the religious hypocrisy which covers and conceals; and a healthy delight in and cultivation of the body and all its natural functions and a determination to keep them pure and beautiful, open and sane and free, will have to become a recognized part of national life.

Possibly, and indeed probably, as the sentiment of common life and common interest grows, and the capacity for true companionship increases with the decrease of self-regarding anxiety, the importance of the mere sex-act will dwindle till it comes to be regarded as only one very specialized factor in the full total of human love. There is no doubt that with the full realization of affectional union the need of actual bodily congress loses some of its urgency; and it is not difficult to see in our present-day social life that the want of the former is (according to the law of transmutation) one marked cause of the violence and extravagance of the lower passions. But however things may change with the further evolution of man, there is no doubt that first of all the sex-relation must be divested of the sentiment of uncleanness which surrounds it, and rehabilitated again with a sense almost of religious consecration; and this means, as I have said, a free people, proud in the mastery and the divinity of their own lives, and in the beauty and openness of their own bodies.

Sex is the allegory of Love in the physical world. It is from this fact that it derives its immense power. The aim of Love is non-differentiation—absolute union of being; but absolute union can only be found at the centre of existence. Therefore whoever has truly found another has found not only that other, and with that other himself, but has found also a third—who dwells at the centre and holds the plastic material of the universe in the palm of his hand, and is a creator of sensible forms.

Similarly the aim of sex is union and non-differentiation—but on the physical plane,—and in the moment when this union is accomplished creation takes place, and the generation (in the plastic material of the sex-elements) of sensible forms.

In the animal and lower human world—and wherever the creature is incapable of realizing the perfect love (which is indeed able to transform it into a god)—Nature in the purely physical instincts does the next best thing, that is, she effects a corporeal union and so generates another creature who by the very process of his generation shall be one step nearer to the universal soul and the realization of the desired end. Nevertheless the moment the other love and all that goes with it is realized the natural sexual love has to fall into a secondary place—the lover must stand on his feet and not on his head—or else the most dire confusions ensue, and torments æonian.

Taking all together I think it may fairly be said that the prime object of Sex is *union*, the physical union as the allegory and expression of the real union, and that generation is a secondary object or result of this union. If we go to the lowest material expressions of Sex—as among the protozoic cells—we find that they, the cells, unite together, two into one; and that, as a result of the nutrition that ensues, this joint cell after a time (but not always) breaks up by fission into a number of progeny cells; or if on the other hand we go to the very highest expression of Sex, in the sentiment of Love, we find the latter takes the form chiefly and before all else of a desire for union, and only in lesser degree of a desire for race-propagation.

I mention this because it probably makes a good deal of difference in our estimate of Sex whether the one function or the other is considered primary. There is perhaps a slight tendency among medical and other authorities to overlook the question of the important physical actions and reactions, and even corporeal modifications, which may ensue upon sexual intercourse between two people, and to fix their attention too exclusively upon their child-bearing function; but in truth it is probable, I think, from various considerations, that the spermatozoa pass through the tissues and affect the general body of the female, as well as that the male absorbs minutest cells *from* the female; and that generally, even without the actual Sex-act, there is an interchange of vital and etherial elements—so that there is a kind of generation taking place *in each other*, as well as that more specialized generation which consists in the propagation of the race.

At the last and taking it as a whole one has the same difficulty in dealing with the subject of Love which meets one at every turn in modern life—the monstrous separation of one part of our nature from another—the way in which—no doubt in the necessary course of evolution—we have cut ourselves in twain as it were, and assigned "right" and "wrong," heaven and hell, spiritual and material, and other violent distinctions, to the separate portions. We have eaten of the Tree of Knowledge of good and evil with a vengeance! The Lord has indeed driven us out of Paradise into the domain of that "fabro vulcano" who with tremendous hammer-strokes must *hammer the knowledge of good and evil out of us again.* I feel that I owe an apology to the beautiful god for daring even for a moment to think of dissecting him soul from body, and for speaking as if these artificial distinctions were in any wise eternal. Will the man or woman, or race of men and women, never come, to whom love in its various manifestations shall be from the beginning a perfect whole, pure and natural, free and standing sanely on its feet?

APPENDIX

"I analyzed a flower, I pointed out to her the beauty of coloring, the gracefulness of shape, the tender shades, the difference between the parts composing the flowers. Gradually, I told her what these parts were called. I showed her the pollen, which clung like a beautiful golden powder to her little rosy fingers. I showed her through the microscope that this beautiful powder was composed of an infinite number of small grains. I made her examine the pistil more closely, and I showed her, at the end of the tube, the ovary, which I called a 'little house full of very tiny children.' I showed her the pollen glued to the pistil, and I told her, that when the pollen of one flower, carried away by the wind, or by the insects, fell on the pistil of another flower, the small grains died, and a tiny drop of moisture passed through the tube and entered into the little house where the very tiny children dwelt; that these tiny children were like small eggs, that in each small egg there was an almost invisible opening, through which a little of the small drop passed; that when this drop of pollen mixed with some other wonderful power in the ovary, that both joined together to give life, and the eggs developed and became grains or fruit. I have shown her flowers which had only a pistil and others which had only stamens. I said to her, smiling, that the pistils were like little mothers, and the stamens like little fathers of the fruit...... Thus I sowed in this innocent heart and searching mind the seeds of that delicate science, which degenerates into obscenity, if the mother, through false shame, leaves the instruction of her child to its schoolfellows. Let my little girl ask me, if she likes, the much dreaded question; I will only have to remind her of the botany lessons, simply adding, the same thing happens to human beings, with this difference, that what is done unconsciously by the plants, is done consciously by us; that in a properly arranged society one only unites one's self to the person one loves.'"—(Translated from "La Revendication des Droits Féminins," O Shafts, April 1894, p. 237.)

~FIN~

Printed in Great Britain
by Amazon

59554874R00132